TRAPPED BY EVIL AND DECEIT

The Story of Hansi and Joel Brand

Cherry
Orchard
Books

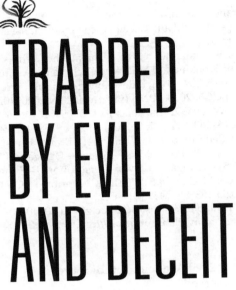

TRAPPED BY EVIL AND DECEIT

The Story of Hansi and Joel Brand

Library of Congress Cataloging-in-Publication Data

Names: Brand, Daniel, 1940–author.
Title: Trapped by evil and deceit : the story of Hansi and Joel Brand /
    Daniel Brand.
Other titles: Be-malkodet ha-resha', ha-adishut yeha-siluf. English
Description: Brookline, MA: Cherry Orchard Books, an imprint of Academic
    Studies Press, 2020. | Includes bibliographical references.
Identifiers: LCCN 2020040233 (print) | LCCN 2020040234 (ebook) |
    ISBN 9781644694992 (hardback) | ISBN 9781644695005 (paperback) |
    ISBN 9781644695012 (adobe pdf) | ISBN 9781644695029 (epub)
Subjects: LCSH: Brand, Joel, 1906-1964. | Brand, Hansi, 1912-2000. |
    World War, 1939-1945—Jews—Rescue—Hungary. | Holocaust, Jewish
    (1939-1945)—Hungary. | Jews—Persecutions—Hungary.
Classification: LCC D804.6 .B73613 2020 (print) | LCC D804.6 (ebook) |
    DDC 940.53/18350922439 [B]—dc23
LC record available at https://lccn.loc.gov/2020040233
LC ebook record available at https://lccn.loc.gov/2020040234

ISBN 9781644694992 (hardback)
ISBN 9781644695005 (paperback)
ISBN 9781644695012 (adobe pdf)
ISBN 9781644695029 (epub)

Book design by Tatiana Vernikov
Cover design by Ivan Grave

Published by Cherry Orchard Books,
    an imprint of Academic Studies Press
1577 Beacon Street
Brookline, MA 02446, USA
press@academicstudiespress.com
www.academicstudiespress.com

To my older brother Michael,
who was only six years old when the Holocaust
arrived in Budapest. He was my main source
of support and stability as we survived the long
and difficult war without our parents.

To my parents, Joel and Hansi,
who did everything they could to rescue oppressed and
persecuted people, risking their own lives.
They did so throughout the Holocaust, years before
it arrived at their doorstep in Hungary.

To everyone who joined the effort
to rescue complete strangers, risking their lives
and livelihoods when they could have otherwise
avoided danger. Especially to the few Jews among
those rescuers, of whom some remained anonymous
and others were defamed and deliberately wiped out
of history books.

Table of Contents

Acknowledgments

Many thanks to those who helped and encouraged me to write the original Hebrew version of this book, including many of my friends, colleagues, and my three sons: Joel, Ariel, and Michael. Above all, I owe a debt of gratitude to my loving wife, Fruma, who supported me throughout this project.

Special thanks to Dr. Shaul Chorev, who consistently and enthusiastically nudged me to write this book. Without him, this book would not have been written.

Dr. Nehama Baroukh skillfully and dutifully turned my research and notes into a readable manuscript, both in Hebrew and in English. Iris Lavi translated the original Hebrew book into English, while navigating some challenging texts from the 1940s—her work is the basis for this book. Roberta Revesz helped me bring the updated English manuscript to the point that I felt comfortable submitting it to the publication. Alessandra Anzani and her team at Academic Studies Press capably breezed through the publication process with ease and efficiency to allow this book to see the light of day. Thank you all!

PROLOGUE

I, Daniel Brand, was born in Budapest as the younger son of Hansi and Joel Brand and survived the Second World War and the Holocaust there. During the Holocaust I was too young to realize the full implications of the events around me. Due to my young age at the time and the many years that transpired since then, I have not relied on my memory from that time when writing this book. With regard to the events during the Holocaust, this book is entirely based on printed, recorded, or registered data that the general public may access and examine, just like I did.

I am not an historian but an engineer who specializes in the analysis of reliability of safety systems. This profession requires me to sift through technical material to identify missing, distorted, or misleading essential data that manufacturers may not be proud of. For the purpose of this historical analysis, I implemented the same techniques I use in my professional life. Specifically, I analyzed and verified the facts regarding the activities of Hansi and Joel during the Holocaust.

This work validates many statements Hansi and Joel made and wrote years ago on the basis of personal knowledge, at the time without verifying them with documents or other independent sources. The book does not attempt to tell the whole story of the Holocaust of Hungarian Jewry and the rescue attempts. Its purpose is to fill in some missing details and correct some distorted perceptions of events and personalities involved, especially those related to the rescue initiatives of Hansi and Joel Brand.

This book is based on analysis of eyewitness testimonies, documents from the relevant period, and the protocols of the Kasztner and Eichmann trials. Naturally, these references tend to include mistakes and contradictions, and hence the need to verify the data by comparing information from different independent

Joel Brand   Hansi Brand

sources. Thankfully, many of those involved in the events and the eyewitnesses who were present documented their memories, but many years after the actual events. These valuable resources have been carefully scrutinized and analyzed with the benefit of hindsight, taking into account the personal and political considerations of the witnesses at the time of the actual events as well as at the time of the later testimonies.

Even historical documents from the relevant period require a thorough examination. Such an examination often reveals that the data in the document is not only inaccurate but, in some cases, its real purpose is to mislead the reader.

History books may suffer from the same problem as their authors: historians who make a living from the book they write might, deliberately or inadvertently, align themselves with perspectives of organizations providing grants and other funding resources. Thus, publications of historians about the period and the events on which this book focuses also require a thorough examination. This is particularly evident in countries with nationalist or totalitarian regimes. Unfortunately, historical research in Israel, at least in its early years, suffered quite a bit from this phenomenon.[1] Bearing this

---

[1]   Ronen, 2011, p. 272; Beit-Zvi, 1977, p. 17.

in mind, publications of historians are mainly used as background data for the description of the period and as a source for general data and not as a primary source for describing the activities of Hansi and Joel. In fact, as far as the events in Hungary are concerned, there are significant gaps between events as documented in primary sources (eyewitnesses and historical documents from the period) and how these events are portrayed by some historians.

Michael (Miki) Brand

Yad Vashem is the official Israeli organization charged with commemorating the Holocaust. It has done a tremendous and admirable job ensuring that the six million who lost their life will never be forgotten. But at the same time, this institution is doing its best to conceal the fact that the Jewish and Zionist leadership in Palestine and the free world did not understand in real time the extent of the disaster that was occurring and did not devote enough attention and means to try to reduce its dimensions. While the leadership was busy with other issues, a small number of Jews, who understood what was happening, did their best to save their fellow Jews. The achievements, even if limited, of those few still embarrass the leadership since it may reveal the uncomfortable truth that the leadership could have done more. To prevent this inconvenience, Yad Vashem is doing its best to eliminate these Jewish rescuers of Jews from the pages of history.

In this book I did my best to document the rescue operations of Hansi and Joel Brand during the Holocaust, which Yad Vashem and some of its historians try to eliminate from history or to present in a distorted way.

1. Background

Only a very basic historical overview is provided here—just enough to clarify the background and the prevailing atmosphere in Hungary at the time. Comprehensive historical review of the factors that set the stage for the Holocaust in Hungary are available in many history books.[1]

Hungary

The Hungarian tribes arrived in Europe at the end of the ninth century and founded a kingdom in the area where modern-day Hungary is situated. Around the end of the first millennium, Hungary became catholic. The Mongols invaded it in 1241, and three hundred years later, in 1541, it was conquered by the Ottomans. The Ottomans ruled over Hungary for about 150 years, until at the end of the seventeenth century it was taken over by the Austrian House of Habsburg. Following the Austrian-Hungarian Compromise of February 8, 1867 Hungary received full internal autonomy and, in return, agreed that the empire should still be a single great state for purposes of war and foreign affairs. The framework of the Austro-Hungarian Empire existed from 1867 to 1918.

As part of the Austro-Hungarian Empire, Hungary fought in World War I alongside Austria and Germany and was the biggest loser in that war. As part of the peace treaties signed after the war in Versailles and Trianon,[2] Hungary's territory was reduced to one third of its prewar area, its population and economy shrunk

---

[1] See, for example, Braham, *The Politics of Genocide*, 1981 or 1994.

[2] Peace treaties relating to Hungary were signed after World War I in Trianon Palace and are included in the general peace treaties signed in Versailles.

accordingly, and its access to the sea, which had been available for about one thousand years, was lost. These treaties created a fertile breeding ground for collaboration with Nazi Germany that faced a similar fate, although the peace treaties damaged it to a far lesser extent than they damaged Hungary.

In 1919, after the war, a short-lived "Hungarian Soviet Republic" ruled over Hungary. This government was established by the Social Democratic party, but its de facto leaders were the Communists led by Béla Kun who were included in the government in the hope that they would bring Russia's Red Army to help the Hungarians in their struggle against the peace treaties. The Communist government imposed a regime of terror and oppression, which made the public hate it. Moreover, it failed to deliver the assistance they expected to receive from Russia in their struggle against the peace treaties enforced on Hungary.

The Communist regime in Hungary was overthrown by Hungarian nationalists headed by Admiral Miklós Horthy. Horthy appointed himself as Regent and actually controlled Hungary until the German occupation.

The war in Hungary began in 1938, when Hungary tried to reclaim at least some of the lost territories under the peace treaties. With the encouragement and diplomatic support of Germany and Italy, Hungary succeeded in occupying territories from Romania, Yugoslavia, and Slovakia. Yet, these territories were still considerably smaller than those it had until World War I. Regardless of World War II, which erupted in September 1939, Hungary continued annexing territories until 1941.

In June 1941 Hungary decided to join Germany in its war against the Soviet Union. In December that year Hungary also declared war on the United States, thereby becoming a full partner of Germany and Italy in the war. At the outset, it seemed that the German invasion of the Soviet Union was easy, as they had several impressive military victories in which Hungary participated. However, in the summer of 1942 the Hungarian army became entangled in battles near Stalingrad. Later, at the beginning of 1943, most of the Hungarian Second Army was decimated in the Battle of Voronezh.

The severe losses sustained by Hungary, especially in the Battle of Voronezh in which it lost more than a hundred thousand people, made Hungary reconsider the justification of joining forces with Germany. Hungary started to look for ways to leave its allies and join forces with the West. Careless diplomatic explorations and widespread presence of pro-Nazis in the government quickly exposed these plans. In retaliation, Germany conquered Hungary in one day, on March 19, 1944, without any real resistance.

The invaders replaced the government with an even more pro-Nazi coalition than the previous one, and they arrested anti-Nazi senior officials and intellectuals. For the average person, however, the occupation had little impact on day-to-day life. Regent Horthy remained the official ruler of Hungary and allegedly, its sovereignty remained intact. However, the German army, which was present in the country, was entirely independent and not subject in any way to the Hungarian authorities.

Following another unsuccessful Hungarian attempt to break the alliance with the Germans, extreme Hungarian fascists, the Arrow Cross Party (Hungarian: *Nyilaskeresztes Párt*), assisted by Germans, took over the state on October 15, 1944. At that time, the Regent Horthy was removed from power, and very quickly the state deteriorated into total chaos which continued until the Russian occupation at the beginning of 1945.

The Jews in Hungary

Jews have lived in the territory of modern-day Hungary from an early stage, at least from the Middle Ages and perhaps much earlier than that.[3] They lived there in relative peace, barring the occasional sufferings and persecutions Jews experienced in most of Europe.

The situation of the Jews in Hungary under the Ottoman rule was relatively good.[4] However, it deteriorated considerably following

---

[3]   This does not mean that the Jews who lived in Hungary in the modern age are the descendants of those Jews.

[4]   Wherever it conquered, the Ottoman regime was tolerant to the Jews more than the European catholic states.

the Austrian conquest. Their condition was improved again during the nineteenth century and especially following the foundation of independent Hungary in 1867 as part of the Austro-Hungarian Empire. Shortly after the foundation of the new Hungarian state, the emancipation law was enacted. This law cancelled most of the limitations imposed on the Jews by the catholic Austrian Empire and granted them full civil rights. Some years later, in 1895, Hungary acknowledged Judaism as one of its national religions, just like Catholic Christianity and Protestant Christianity.

The geographical change of Hungary's borders following World War I resulted in significant demographic change as well. Before World War I, Greater-Hungary had a large number of minorities, and in order to ensure a Hungarian majority in the country, the Hungarian authorities considered the Jews as Hungarians.[5] After World War I, when the territories housing foreign ethnic minorities were separated from Hungary, the country became more ethnically homogenous. The Jews, who until that time were considered Hungarians, became the main distinguishable minority. Their status quickly deteriorated and they became the scapegoat for all of Hungary's hardships. In particular, the Jews were blamed for Hungary's catastrophic economic condition after the defeat in the war. They were even blamed for the defeat itself and its diplomatic results, first and foremost losing territories, which for some Hungarians were considered (and are maybe still considered) "homeland territories."

The situation of the Hungarian Jewry was badly worsened also due to the communist leader of Jewish origin, Béla Kun, of the "Hungarian Soviet Republic" that ruled Hungary for several months during 1919. The Jewish image of this loathed government greatly contributed to increasing hatred against the Jews in Hungary after World War I.

The nationalist government that replaced the communist one, in retaliation to the "Red Terror" that was identified with the Jews, introduced anti-communist "White Terror," the main victims of

---

5   The affiliation was determined by the language of speech.

which were Jews. The White Terror subsided after a short period, but the anti-Semitic residues lingered and gradually worsened.

In 1920 the *Numerus clausus* (Latin: "closed number") law, the first law of its kind in the world after World War I, was enacted in Hungary to restrict the number of Jews in universities. In 1938, 1939, and 1941, three stricter laws were enacted. The law of May 1938, known as "the first anti-Jewish law," restricted the numbers of Jews who could be employed in white-collar professions to twenty percent, a rate which was larger than the rate of Jews in the population but smaller than the number of Jews who were employed in these professions at the time.

Hungary's renewed expansion that began in 1938 once again changed its demographic situation. Following the annexation of new territories, the Jewish population in Hungary increased considerably: the number of Jews in post-Trianon Treaty Hungary was less than half a million; following the annexations their number almost doubled to eight hundred thousand.[6] The Hungarian culture was foreign to a large portion of the annexed Jews, which exacerbated their negative perception among the local population.

In May 1939, a new law was enacted, which included a definition of who was a Jew and further restricted the professional options of Jews. Consquently, most Jews were expelled from public service. In August 1941, another law was enacted, which dealt with the very definition of "a Jew." It was designed to prevent mixed marriages and segregate the Jews from the rest of the population. Unlike the previous laws, which were initiated by the Hungarians, this law was similar in spirit to the Nuremberg Laws and clearly reflected Germany's influence.

Nowhere else in Europe, except for Germany, has there been an ongoing institutional incitement against the Jewish citizens of the country as it has been in Hungary. Hungary enacted laws that restricted the Jews' rights. The Jews as a group (the entire community and not individual people) were defined as people whose loyalty to a country was in doubt. They were fired from the civil service,

---

[6]   See Braham, 1994, p. 78.

expelled from the army, and forced to serve in "labor service" under disgraceful conditions. The right to own their businesses was denied and they were obliged to transfer the ownership to non-Jews. All of this occurred in independent Hungary prior to the German occupation.

At the end of the 1930s the Jewish population in Hungary experienced a considerable growth. As the Nazis seized power in Germany and annexed territories in Europe, many Jews from Germany, Austria, and Czechoslovakia escaped and took refuge in Hungary, which until 1944 was a relatively safe harbor for Jews. At the end of 1939, when Germany and Russia divided Poland between them, thousands of refugees escaped from Poland to Hungary, many Jews among them.

In addition to the refugees who flooded Hungary from its neighboring countries, the Jewish population in Hungary considerably increased as a result of the territories it annexed at the beginning of World War II. The annexed territories housed many Jews, mainly observant. Contrary to most of the Jewish population in post-World War I Hungary, the Jews in the annexed territories did not command the Hungarian language and were not rooted in the Hungarian culture. Fueled by anti-Semitic incitement on the part of the Hungarian fascists, these Jews were perceived by the public as aliens. Within a short time, the public wanted to dispose of them.

In the course of 1941, the Hungarian authorities formulated a plan to get rid of the Jews, particularly those they classified as "aliens."[7] The Hungarians used the term "alien" (Hungarian: *idegen*) very broadly to identify people with no Hungarian citizenship certificate. These were mainly refugees from surrounding countries already taken over by the Nazis, as well as the residents of the territories that Hungary annexed at the beginning of the war. In the summer of 1941, shortly after Hungary joined the war alongside Germany and Italy, the Hungarian government decided to deport tens of thousands of "alien" Jews from its sovereign territory to the German-Hungarian occupied areas north-east of the country.

---

[7]   For more on this topic, see Braham, 1994, pp. 205–214.

The police and the gendarmerie—and in some areas the Hungarian army—enthusiastically carried out the deportation with the help and encouragement of the local authorities. In July and August 1941, the Hungarians deported almost twenty thousand "aliens" to the mercy of the authorities in German-occupied Poland, including people with proven Hungarian citizenship.[8] The deportees suffered from persecution and abuse. By the end of August most of them were murdered in cold blood by the Germans, assisted by Ukrainians and other collaborators. This was one of the largest massacre operations of the beginning of the war. Report on this incident reached the free world from various sources, including the team who later established the "Budapest Relief and Rescue Committee."[9]

Several months later, in January 1942, another mass murder of Jews occurred, this time in Delvidek, in the area of Bačka (earlier annexed by the Hungarians from Yugoslavia). Unlike the murder of the "alien" Jews, which was committed by the Germans and their collaborators, this time the killers were Hungarian gendarmes and soldiers who followed the inhumane instructions of their Hungarian commanders in an alleged "combat mission," supposedly against Yugoslavian partisans that operated in that area.[10] About five thousand civilians, half of them Jews, were killed in that mass murder. The instigators were supposedly prosecuted in Hungary but in fact they were allowed to escape to Germany. After the German occupation they returned to Hungary and were promoted to key roles in the government.

Following the anti-Jewish legislation, Jews were gradually expelled from military service and tens of thousands were enlisted to special labor service battalions. The treatment of the enlisted was disgraceful and it deteriorated during the years of the war.

The labor service was introduced in Hungary in July 1939.[11] It was originally intended for civilians who were not suitable for

---

[8]   Braham, 1994, p. 210.

[9]   Ibid., p. 213.

[10]   For more details on the subject, see ibid., pp. 214–222.

[11]   Ibid., p. 301.

military service and instead, were required to perform civil duties or miscellaneous tasks needed by the army. "Unsuitable" people were people whose loyalty to the state was questionable.[12] Labor service was not intended specifically for Jews; Communists, for example, were also sent to labor service. But in practice, labor service was predominantly for Jews. At first the service conditions were similar to those of the soldiers in the regular army, but from 1940 to 1942 the enlisted were gradually denied their rights, and their weapons and uniforms were taken away. While enlisted men and their commanders were subject to Hungary's military justice law, the reality was different: many commanders took the law in their own hands, and in extreme cases instructed not to let Jews go back home alive.[13]

The catastrophe of the Hungarian Jews who have been enlisted to labor service has not yet been fully told and it merits separate research. Some of the draftees remained in Hungary and their conditions were relatively better, at least until the fascists' takeover in October 1944. The conditions of draftees who were sent to the Russian front or to the copper mines in Bor, Yugoslavia, were dire. When the Hungarian fascists (Arrow Cross people) took over, they murdered thousands of men in labor service and worked others to death.[14] In spite of the conditions, some of the labor service draftees were lucky: they were not with their families in the Hungarian periphery and were therefore not deported to the extermination camps.

Unlike the rest of the Hungarian population, following the German occupation, the Jews experienced a dramatic change: the Hungarians assigned the responsibility for the Jews exclusively to the German authorities, and at the same time they provided the Germans with all the manpower and logistical means needed for carrying out all phases of the extermination of the Jews short of the actual killing.

[12]   Ibid., p. 294.

[13]   Ibid., p. 358.

[14]   Ibid., p. 358.

Most of the Hungarian Jews who lived outside the capital were sent to extermination during May and June 1944. The Jews of the capital, subject to countless decrees imposed on them, survived until the fascist coup on October 15, 1944. At that time killing of Jews without any reason was encouraged by the new anti-Semitic government and many Jews were murdered on the streets, on the banks of the Danube, and by "death marches." The Russian occupation in early 1945 saved those who managed to survive to that date.

Almost two thirds of the Jewish population in Hungary were *neológ* (something like Conservatives or Reform) Jews, less than a third were Orthodox, and other streams constituted the remaining five percent.[15] This data does not include the Zionists whose weight in the population was negligible—in its peak, the Zionist Movement in Hungary included less than five thousand members.[16] The small Zionist Movement focused on collecting money for causes associated with Palestine. It was centered on the Palestine Office which was responsible for, and had the final say in, distributing immigration certificates to Palestine. While the main Jewish communities in Hungary had disagreements about almost everything, they shared common hostility towards the Zionists. The absolute majority of Hungarian Jews considered themselves Hungarians of Jewish Faith. The concepts of a separate nation and a Jewish national home was unthinkable for them. This was partially true for some of the Zionists as well. Many young Zionist intellectuals were primarily *Galut*[17] Zionists—they were not really interested in emigration.[18] Given the animosity, when the Zionists attempted to warn the general Jewish population about the impending disaster, they were suspected of spreading horror rumors to enhance immigration to Palestine.

---

[15]   Ibid., p. 87.

[16]   See Cohen, 1984, p. 28.

[17]   Hebrew: "exile" or "diaspora."

[18]   Braham, 1994, p. 91; See also Cohen, 1984, p. 52.

2. THE BRANDS

The Beginning of the Holocaust and the First Rescue Operation

Persecution of Jews in Europe was not a new phenomenon and the events in Germany between 1933 and 1939 with regard to the Jews including the pogrom of the *Kristallnacht* ("Crystal Night"), the night between November 9 and 10, 1938, were not something unknown before. After September 1, 1939, the beginning of World War II with the German and Russian invasion of Poland, the situation did not change dramatically. The condition of the Jews in the German occupied parts of Poland deteriorated significantly but this was not yet the Holocaust.

The turning point came with the German invasion of Russia, Operation Barbarossa that started on June 22, 1941. At this operation, for the first time in the war and in history, special extermination groups were attached to the invading German military units with the specific task of clearing the newly occupied territories from all Jews by systematically killing them. This was the beginning of the Holocaust.

The first to feel the difference were the Jews in the new territories occupied by Germans and soon after—the Jews of Hungary. On June 27 1941, five days after the beginning of Operation Barbarossa, Hungary declared war on Russia and joined the war alongside Germany.

In July 1941, shortly after joining the war alongside Germany, the Hungarian Government decided to implement a pre-planned program to evacuate Jews living in Hungary without Hungarian citizenship out of its sovereign territory into the newly German-occupied areas.

During July and August 1941, almost twenty thousand Jews were deported from Hungary and extradited to the Germans, most of them were killed by the Germans shortly afterwards together with the local Jews.

The Germans at that time were unaware of the need for secrecy with regard to their attempt to destroy the Jewish population of Europe, and so it happened that Hungarian soldiers, and a few Jews among them, witnessed the killings. These soldiers spread the news about the fate of the deportees all over Hungary and thus, the Hungarian Jews became the first Jewish community to have the ability to understand the fate awaiting the Jews in German-dominated areas.

Among the "alien" Jews deported from Hungary in the summer of 1941 was Hansi Brand's sister Karoline and her husband Lajos Stern, who was a citizen of Poland.

Hansi Brand decided that she had to bring her sister back at all costs and together with her husband Joel, with considerable effort and with a lot of money, they managed to do it.[1]

This is the first documented successful rescue operation involving border smuggling in Hungary. It had a tremendous effect on things to come. This rescue of the sister and the brother-in-law was a defining event in the history of the rescue efforts in Hungary. With it, the Brands became rescue operatives from the very beginning of the Holocaust.

The successful return of the sister and the brother-in-law from the deportation had many consequences. It allowed those who were willing to listen to understand that the real meaning of the term "deportation" was death. The reports of the rescued couple were the first available information about systematic killing of Jews by official state authorities, thus marking the beginning of the Holocaust.

Later we shall see how these reports have led to the early cessation of deportation and thus saved many lives.

---

[1]   Springman's testimony to Yad Vashem (Hungarian—p. 9, German—p. 7); Brand, 1957, pp. 13–14 (Weissberg, 1958, pp. 11–13); Braham, 1994, p. 213.

Joel

Joel was born in 1906 in the city of Năsăud, Romania (then Naszód, Hungary), and was named after his grandfather, Joel Ben Dov Brand, who died the same year in Jerusalem (during the period of Ottoman rule in Palestine). As was common at the time, he was also given a Hungarian name, Jenő, which was the closest Hungarian version to his Hebrew name, Joel (pronounced in English like Yoel). The registered surname was Brandt, probably a distortion by an overzealous nationalistic Hungarian official who decided that this was how the name Brand should be written in Hungarian.[2] Joel's family—in terms of the period—was financially well-off; Joel's grandfather was a wealthy man, who was raised and made his fortune in Mukachevo, Ukraine, which at the time was part of Hungary and was called Munkács. The grandfather came with his wife Haya Ethyl to Jerusalem in the second half of the nineteenth century, hoping that his sons would follow. It is unclear in what year exactly the grandfather arrived in Palestine, but according to the records of Chevra Kadisha,[3] it is known that his wife passed away in 1886. The grandfather built a house in Jerusalem containing seven apartments for his children and a synagogue.[4] None of his children followed him and the house remained as the community's property. The information regarding Joel's early years is based on some of his personal documents, the book he wrote[5] in the 1950s and the testimony he gave his British interrogators in 1944.[6] Both sources are lacking many details and include inaccuracies, mainly in terms of dates.

---

[2] His older sister Meta is registered as "Brand."

[3] Hebrew: "Holy Society," a Jewish organization that sees to the proper burial of deceased Jews according to Jewish tradition.

[4] The dedications to his memory are in a new synagogue, which replaced the one that was built with his money.

[5] The official author of the non-Hebrew version of the book is Alexander Weissberg. The reason for this, as explained in his second book (Hebrew only), was to overcome difficulties imposed by the Israeli censor.

[6] See Joel Brand files in the British Intelligence, 1944.

The synagogue Joel's
grandfather built
in Jerusalem
around 1900.

Joel's father was also born in Munkács, which remained part
of Hungary, and his registered given name was probably "Jechiel
Michael."[7] The name changed according to place and time: in
Hungary he was called Miksa and later on, in Germany, he was
Max. Joel's father had three daughters and one son. The son, Joel,
was the youngest. Not long after his birth the family moved to
Budapest, where his father founded the local telephone company.[8]
In 1910 or 1911, when Joel was about four years old, his family left
Budapest and moved to Erfurt, Germany. In Germany his father
used the name Max Brand, and in certain cases also Brandt. In Erfurt
he founded another telephone company named Die Thüringer
Telefongesellschaft mbH (Thuringia Telephone Company Ltd.). The
company was first mentioned in the address book of Erfurt in 1912,
and it continued to be active under the family management up until
the very eve of World War II.[9]

---

[7]   The birth certificate is partially illegible.

[8]   According to Hansi, in 1935, prior to their marriage, Joel was required to prove
       his entitlement to a resident status in Hungary. After some search, records
       (municipal or governmental) were found, confirming that his father had paid
       taxes in Budapest during a certain period, probably for the operations of this
       telephone company, which entitled Joel to a resident status in Hungary. Joel's
       status as a resident is confirmed in the British interrogation report.

[9]   The company did not appear by this name after 1916, probably since its name
       was updated.

The synagogue Joel's
grandfather built
in Jerusalem
around 1900,
and dedications
in his memory.

לזכרון עולם יהי לפני ד בחר הקדש
בירושלם תובבא
כי ביהכנס הזה נבנה מנדבת
הר' יואל בּר דוב ז'ל בּראנד
בעד דרך בית ישראל תו והסביכה
להתפלל בו נוסח ספרד דוקא
נפטר המנדב ר' יואל הנז
ביום ז שבט שנת תרסו תנצבה
צדקתו תעמוד לעד

בעזרת
אברון טוב בהיכל ה והאבן הזאת תהי לעדה ולראה השבית
כי הביהכנ הזה ועזהנ ותאיו
אשר הקדיש הנדיכר יואל בראנד ז'ל לזכרון
שמו לעולם מבונה בשם ביהכנבית ישראל ע'ש
ארמור הרב הצדיק הקדוש מוהר ישראל זצלה
ונמסר בכתב מאושר ע'י בכ הנריב הנז ז'ל לחסידי
קארלין תחת הנשיאות של אדמור הרהצ הקדוש
ראברהם אלימלך פערלאוו שליטא
מקארלין לחלוטין ולצמיתות עולמין לתורה ולתפלה
עפי נוסח ומנהגם אשר יסדו להם רבותיהם
הקדושים נע זיעא ורק על פיהם יתנהגו כל עניני
הביהכנ עד ביאת הגואל בב אמן

Joel at the age of ten
in a German school uniform during
World War I, 1916.

As a young boy in Germany, Joel joined a socialist Zionist youth movement. After a while, the movement split and Joel remained with the group that became Communist.[10] In 1920, when he was fourteen, his father passed away, leaving him, his mother Ida, and his sister Hanna at the house at the time. Joel's school report card from 1920 showed that he was a less-than-average student. As an immigrant who came from a different culture as a child, a real redhead, with a stormy temperament, whose nickname in the family was Fox, he probably struggled to adjust to the strict German discipline prevailing in schools, which were still conducted in keeping with the Kaiser's spirit.[11] The phone company remained in the possession of the family and Joel's brother-in-law, Alexander Salgo, the husband of Meta (or Meda), Joel's middle sister, took over its management.

---

[10]   According to the testimony to the British (Joel Brand Files in the British Intelligence, 1944).

[11]   His cousin, Andreas Biss, who wrote his book in 1966, did not like Joel all too much at that time and described him as "bright and intelligent" but having no inclination to studies. This description is probably close to reality (See Biss, 1975, p. 35).

When Joel turned seventeen, he decided he had enough of school and traveled to the United States. He arrived there on July 4, 1923 on the German ship Westphalia[12] with twenty-five dollars in his pocket. Joel's first stop in the new world was the home of his uncle Jacob Brand,[13] and possibly his cousin Bernhard Brand, who lived in New York. The young socialist stirred quite a commotion at his relatives' Republican conservative house. After a few months in New York his money ran out, as did his relatives' patience, and he started looking for a job. He took all kinds of odd jobs and moved from one place to another, including Philadelphia, New York, Atlanta, Detroit, Cincinnati, and San Francisco before moving back to New York. While on the West Coast, he found a job as a sailor (having no seamanship professional background or training), and this is how he had the opportunity to visit and sometimes stay for short periods of time in Hawaii, the Philippines, Japan, China, South America, and possibly other places.

It is unclear when or why Joel came back from the United States to Germany. In his book he mentioned that he returned to Germany in 1930, but the British interrogation report, which was based on his testimony, noted that he came back at the beginning of 1927. The truth is probably somewhere between these two dates.

Upon his return, Joel integrated into the family's telephone company as a technician and salesman, and traveled a lot across Germany and around Europe. He continued to be active on the left-wing side of the political spectrum, but there is no reliable documentation as to any specific role he took in any party. At that time, his brother-in-law, Alexander Salgo, who ran the family business after the father's demise, tried to train him as a technical expert for telephone systems (*Meister* or *Ingenieur* in German terminology),

---

12   The details are taken from Ellis Island's Internet website: https://heritage.statueofliberty.org/passenger.

13   Joel probably had four uncles. Besides the uncle in America, he had an uncle named Phillipp (Hungarian: Fülöp) who lived in Berlin at the beginning of the twentieth century, an uncle named Solomon, and one named Bernhard of whom I have no information.

but this process was never completed.[14] In March 1933,[15] just after the Reichstag fire, Joel was arrested for being involved in street fights between Nazi supporters and their opponents, who were mainly Communists. He was prosecuted for espionage and treason and was sentenced for two years imprisonment. In the summer of 1934, after about eighteen months in prison, he was released and deported[16] from Germany.

Joel left Germany and moved to Romania, his country of birth. He spent the short period in Romania close to his cousin Andreas Biss (nicknamed Bandi). Joel did not fit well in the small town in Romania, an environment whose culture and language he did not know. He quickly exploited the fact that he had an (expired) Hungarian passport to move to Hungary. While his command of the Hungarian language was extremely limited, he nevertheless found his place very quickly in the big city of Budapest. He maintained his radical socialist views also after moving to Hungary,[17] but he was not a communist. In Hansi's documented history and in the memoirs of his acquaintances, no trace can be found of any communist activity or of any contact that he may have had with any communists from the day he came to Hungary in 1934 until his death.

Joel's first stop in Hungary was the secretariat of Po'alei Zion movement (Workers of Zion, a Zionist social democratic party). He arrived there with another refugee named Ozer carrying a letter to the secretary of Po'alei Zion in Budapest. At the secretariat the two refugees met Moshe Israel,[18] and he entrusted them with a Zionist activist named Sámuel Springman. Springman included them in the Hachshara, an agricultural training program where Zionist youth learned technical skills necessary for their emigration to

---

[14]   The details have been conveyed by his niece, Mr. Salgo's daughter, Margit Fendrich-Salgo.

[15]   This date was taken from the British investigation report.

[16]   Hebrew: Brand, 1957, p. 8. (English: Weissberg, 1958, p. 5; The English translation here does not match the German source).

[17]   Révész, 2001, p. 73; Benshalom, 1977, p. 54.

[18]   Israel and Lazar, 1994, p. 94.

Palestine and subsequent life in *kibbutzim*.[19] The training center on Podmaniczky street is where Hansi and Joel met for the first time. Joel did not need the financial support of the movement as he had income from the family's telephone company, so the only thing that could have led him there was a genuine wish to immigrate to Palestine.

In Hungary Joel was considered a member of a movement called Ihud, which was identified with Mapai, Ben-Gurion's party, the leading party in Israel at the time. His socialist views did not stop him from becoming a member of Ihud and did not undermine his actions for refugees or for his private business. At the time socialism was part of the ideology of most of Halutz[20] youth movements and Mapai, too, considered itself socialistic. The only exception was HaShomer HaTza'ir (The Young Guard)—the Radical Socialists Zionists (RSZ) group, which was associated with Mapam (the United Workers Party) at the time. Mapam was truly communist, in addition to being Zionist, and maintained that ideology for many years after the war.[21] According to Hansi, who was not a big fan of Communism, she did not notice any Communistic activism or tendencies in Joel during their entire life.

Joel had a somewhat flamboyant image, which he made great efforts to maintain even when there was not a penny in his pocket or when his health was already very poor. He apparently went out of his way to ensure his friends and guests had a good time, but he was probably more conservative than he let on. He always made sure to stock sufficient amount of alcohol at home, but he never touched it when he was by himself. Even during the fifties, the austerity period in Israel, when real coffee was hard to get on the market and his financial situation was dire, he somehow managed to offer his guests quality coffee and drinks.

---

[19] Communal agricultural settlements in Israel.

[20] *Halutz* means a pioneer in Hebrew.

[21] The admiration of Mapam and the RSZ to the Soviet Union and Stalin continued in Israel until the dictator's death, as reflected in the eulogies of the movement's seniors published in its newspaper *Al HaMishmar*.

Hansi

The information about Hansi's family is extremely limited. Hansi (pronounced Hanzi in English) did not write memoirs and, unlike Joel, she was not interrogated by the British as the events unfolded. Most of the information about her was collected from Hebrew language publications documenting her activity in Ḥalutz youth movements from the end of the 1920s. In 1995, when she was about eighty-three years old, Yad Vashem researchers recorded an interview with her. Sadly, the recording in the Hungarian language is in poor technical quality. More importantly, the interviewers, Dr. Gabriel Bar-Shaked and Mr. Barak Ben Amos, were either poorly prepared or possibly prejudiced.[22]

Hansi was born in Budapest in 1912. She had two sisters — Karoline (Lenke) and Erzsébet (Bözsi) — and one brother Józsi (József?), all her senior. None of them or their offspring who are still alive could be found.[23] Her father, Dániel Hartmann,[24] came from Miskolc and his family might have arrived there from the area of Kosice, Slovakia[25] (Hungarian: Kassa). The family of her mother, Rozália Steiner, probably originated from the city of Vác, Hungary. Her father was a small textile merchant who managed to make a modest living until he lost all his savings investing in state bonds that lost their entire value following Hungary's defeat in World War I.

Hansi was raised in a traditional Jewish home that must have had certain affection to Zionism since they kept a Jewish National Fund donation box: the iconic Blue Box. However, they showed no tendency toward Zionist activism or toward immigrating

---

[22] After that interview, Barak Ben Amos wrote a book in which he claims that based "on test of logic," the rescue of Hansi's sister, which is a well-documented fact, could not have happened. The book, *Am I My Brother's Keeper*, is not on the market but available at Yad Vashem as confirmed by a letter from a member of their team, Yosi Gvir, from March 20, 2019.

[23] Some at least, including her mother, survived the Holocaust in Budapest.

[24] On her birth certificate, Hansi's father's name is listed as Dávid, but this is probably a mistake. On her marriage certificate, her father is listed as Dániel. This is probably the correct name.

[25] This area was part of Hungary until 1921.

Hansi's family (Hartmann), 1911. Right to left: mother Rozália, son Józsi (József?), father Dániel and daughters Lenke (Karoline) and Bözsi (Erzsébet). This photo was found in Hansi's old photo album and it was probably the only family photo that survived the war.

to Palestine. In interviews, she mentioned that her inclination to help others was well rooted at home as her parents assisted refugees during (or at the end of) World War I. She also mentioned some unpleasant anti-Semitic experiences in her youth that did not include any personal abuse or physical injury.

In the midst of her teens, Hansi's family became poor and she was forced to quit studying and start working. Together with her sister, she opened a small knitting workshop utilizing two knitting machines they received from one of their aunts. This tiny workshop, located in a small room, must have been pretty successful as it sustained her until she married, at which point it was enlarged and expanded.

In her youth Hansi joined a Zionist youth movement and was one of the first activists in the Ḥalutz youth movement in Hungary.[26] When she was sixteen (at around 1928), she joined the RSZ but

---

[26] For details regarding her activity as part of the youth movements and Zionist Hachshara in Hungary, see Israel and Lazar, 1994; Israel, 1999; Hansi's recorded memoires at Yad Vashem, 1995.

left it after a short time. It was an "elitist" movement that mainly appealed to educated, financially established college students rather than working-class girls. In addition, she loathed the exaggerated admiration, in her opinion, of everything Russian. In 1930, Hansi, alongside Yosef Rosenberg and others who left the RSZ, founded the Zionist social democrat youth movement Netzaḥ (Hebrew: "eternity," also an acronym for No'ar Tzofi Ḥalutzi, which means "pioneering youth"). In 1931 she took part in forming a federation of Zionist social democrat youth movements which later became HaNo'ar HaOved (The Working Youth, as opposed to the elitist RSZ). During 1931-1932 she travelled on behalf of these movements to Vienna to establish relationships with a similar Austrian Jewish Zionist movement called Blau Weiss (Blue White).

Between 1931 and 1934 Hansi continued to be active in the Ḥalutz youth movement while waiting for her immigration certificate to Palestine. She took part in organizing summer camps and trainings, and establishing branches in the Hungarian periphery. She also began initiating aid activities for underprivileged children.

Hansi sensed that people with less seniority than her were given immigration certificates to Palestine, while she was passed over. She believed that as a single woman, she was discriminated against. To circumvent the situation, she considered more than once finding a partner for fictitious marriage. In her recorded memories, she tells that in one of her visits to Vienna she met a suitable candidate who already had an immigration certificate. The candidate agreed to this proposal but her family refused to send the required documents from Budapest. The intended groom, who was basically on his way to Palestine, could no longer wait, and the fictitious marriage never materialized.

The Wedding, 1934–1935

Hansi and Joel first met at the end of summer or at the beginning of autumn 1934, and they married after one year, on October 30, 1935. They met at the Hachshara training in preparation for immigration to Palestine, when Hansi was summoned to serve as an interpreter for Joel. His command of the Hungarian language was minimal

The founders of Netzaḥ youth movement in Hungary, 1930. Hansi is standing
at the back in the middle, and to her right, is Efraim Broder "Móc"
(the "adopting" father of her children in Kibbutz Givat Haim in 1946).

Hansi (on the right) in a delegation
of HaNo'ar HaOved in Vienna, 1932.

Hansi in a mission to Vienna
with Simcha Weida, 1932.

while the other attendees could not speak much German or English. This is puzzling, considering the fact that Hansi quit school when she was fifteen. Nevertheless, she knew German better than most Palestine-bound attendees around her.

Much gossip occupies the pages of the literature about this marriage and there might be some truth to it. Hansi said several times that she loved Joel for his soul and humanity[27], and she loved Kasztner—with whom she spent time during the war under indescribable conditions of stress and anxiety—for his cleverness. Shortly after the war, Hansi cut all ties with Kasztner,[28] and her marriage continued in a stable and uninterrupted manner.

An insight to her attitude towards men and to men's attitude towards her may be found in her recorded memories in Yad Vashem in which she tells, much to the interviewers' surprise, that during her teens she used to sit alone in cafés and read newspapers without anyone bothering her—completely uncharacteristic for a European girl in the 1920's.

The only other person Hansi ever mentioned as having feelings for is Yosef Rosenberg, whom she adored and with whom she left the RSZ. She highly regarded him but in her statements about him there was no trace of a romantic relationship.[29] Yosef Rosenberg was a highly educated conservative Jew, student, Zionist, and intellectual, and in 1932 he illegally immigrated to Palestine.[30]

---

[27]   Hungarian: *a lelke miatt.*

[28]   In one of her recordings from 1998, she said that she considered to sue M. Lerner for his screen and TV play about the Kasztner affair for showing her in bed with Kasztner and for showing Joel drunk. According to her, none of this ever happened. The recording was made by a Revesz family member in the presence of Perez Revesz

[29]   Reading his arguments for leaving the RSZ (together with Hansi), which were written more than eighty years ago, one may share Hansi's appreciation for him (Israel and Lazar, 1994, p. 16).

[30]   According to Hansi, he disguised himself as a newspaper photographer who was sent to cover the first Maccabiah Games (Jewish Olympics in Palestine). She equipped him with a camera to have his cover complete. Rosenberg stayed in Palestine as a member of Kibbutz Giv'at Ḥaim (the united one, before the split). Rosenberg was killed in 1945 by the British, who tried to

When Hansi and Joel met, Joel had no local family and Hansi viewed that as an advantage. There is no explanation for this preference, but she said once that she preferred to marry a man rather than a family. How ironic it was, then, that after the wedding all of Joel's family escaped from Germany to Hungary, and during her life, she spent considerable resources on them. In fact her relations with them were far closer than with her own family.

There is no documentation about the conduct of daily life in their home before the German occupation but from memoirs of refugees who visited their home it is clear that they managed together well and cooperated in all their activities. About their relations in Israel one may learn from the book they wrote together (Brand, 1960) and from the firm support of Hansi to Joel when the authorities tried to prevent the appearance of his book among other means by preventing his livelihood. Joel's health deteriorated following the war and the reception he received from the representatives of the Jewish/Palestinian rescue delegation in Turkey. Hansi was the primary breadwinner. Nevertheless, she was always willing to leave everything, entrust her children with neighbors, and look after Joel anywhere he needed her, including abroad. In the book they wrote together, Hansi describes, among other things, how she thwarted an attempt by Israeli politicians to declare Joel mentally ill and to forcibly hospitalize him in an attempt to prevent publication of his book.[31]

The "Golden Age": The Calm before the Storm

There is no information in the literature about the Brands regarding the period between their marriage in the autumn of 1935 and the deportation of "alien" Jews in the summer of 1941.[32] Hansi was

break into the kibbutz during the siege. He was the first victim in that incident.

[31] *The Satan and the Soul* (Brand, 1960), pp. 179–180 (Heb).

[32] The deportation of "alien" Jews is a significant event in the development

Hansi and Joel shortly before their marriage, September 1935.

already financially independent from her parents as the small knitting workshop sustained her well. This shop sustained her until her marriage after which it was expanded and became very successful financially. In his book, Biss claimed that he helped the Brands to establish the workshop, but in reality, he may have helped them to expand it after their marriage since the workshop existed well before Hansi met Joel.[33]

The expanded knitting shop thrived and allowed the family to maintain a high standard of living. Joel's excellent sales skills brought plenty of business. He had a remarkable ability to connect

of the anti-Semitic policy of the Hungarian government (see more details below).

[33] It seems that Biss provided many with financial help, and according to Brand, 1960, p. 104, he helped Kasztner in financing the writing of his report.

with people, especially with the average person on the street. The relationships he built turned out to be especially important during the war. These contacts allowed him to obtain raw material which was in short supply due to the war and extract good prices for finished goods. His widespread contacts included people from all walks of life, including merchants, dealers, policemen, detectives and even smugglers. Biss said that Joel had contacts on the grey and black markets—he was probably right about that. During his obligatory military service Joel formed close relationships with non-Jewish Hungarian soldiers, most likely communists, who alongside him served as "elements whose loyalty to the state was questionable."[34] One of these friends, who became a civil servant in the postwar Hungarian government, arranged for Hansi a passport that allowed her to leave the country at the early stages of the Iron Curtain.[35]

Among the documents Joel had was a Hungarian certificate confirming his status as a "travelling businessman." This certificate helped him enjoy a relative freedom of movement in the first years of the war that began in Hungary in 1938, one year before the German invasion of Poland. Joel skillfully mixed salesmanship with other activities: buying hard-to-obtain goods, assisting the poor, and spending time in top restaurants and hotels. This combination of skills and diverse activities benefited and satisfied everyone involved—friends, refugees, and his wife.

The Brands continued their involvement in Zionist activities in Hungary, but their expectation to immigrate to Palestine fizzled. From 1936 to 1939 all of Joel's family gradually moved from Germany to Budapest. His niece, Margit (Salgo then and Fendrich after her marriage),[36] who was born in 1922, arrived first. The last family members came on the eve of the war. His mother Ida and

---

[34]   The official definition of the candidates for labor service that referred mainly to Jews but not only to them.

[35]   It seems that Hansi left Hungary in March or April 1946, shortly before her children.

[36]   She passed away in 2019.

his sisters, Meta (or Meda) Salgo and Hanna Brand, arrived in Budapest on the day World War II erupted, September 1, 1939, after a three-week journey by trains. Alexander Salgo, the husband of his sister Meta, died shortly after arriving in Budapest. As events unfolded, the whole clan was included on the manifest of the "train of the privileged," known also as the "Kasztner train," but none of them made it to Switzerland as did the other train passengers, nor were they released to the Allies like the other inmates of the concentration camp, Bergen Belsen, where they were kept when the Germans withdrew from the area. They remained in German custody until the very end of the war.

Whatever money Joel's relatives brought with them from Germany lasted a very limited time. The responsibility to support their extended family fell squarely on Joel and Hansi's shoulders. The expanded knitting workshop that operated at 70 Rózsa Street[37] was sufficient to provide for the entire family as at that time, the Brands were not too troubled with financial problems. The business thrived. Strictly from a financial perspective, this was the best period in Hansi's life. Later on, the workshop served as a working place for refugees and a meeting place for the leadership of the Jewish Pioneer Underground (JPU) in Budapest.[38] Hansi ran the business and Joel was the salesperson and probably the procurement manager. In particular, he was able to obtain wool, which was an expensive and rare commodity at the time. Wool linings for leather gloves became the main product of the workshop.

The knitting workshop founded and run by Hansi was registered early on in the name of one of the workers, a catholic Christian woman named Kövesdi Pálné.[39] This was necessary in order to circumvent the anti-Jewish laws of 1938–1939 that extremely limited the ability of Jews to own and operate businesses. This woman never abused

---

[37] The address is indicated in Joel Brand files in the British Intelligence, 1944.

[38] Cohen, 1984, p. 53.

[39] Hungarian: Kövesdi Pál's wife. This name is also mentioned in Brand, 1957 and Révész, 2001.

The happy father, winter 1940-1941.

her role and always looked the other way when it was obvious that refugees were given shelter and work at the shop.

Joel spared no expenses entertaining his friends, as well as people he met briefly on his many trips across Hungary as a salesman. This is how he formed bonds with many people, some of them dubious characters. These smugglers and other questionable characters helped him later on, when he needed to transport refugees and money across closed borders. A good description of Joel's operations during this period can be found in Anna Porter's book. Porter, who did not know Joel, borrowed her description from the book written by Biss who knew the Brands quite well at that time[40]:

> Brand worked for his wife's gloves-manufacturing business as a sales representative, calling on shops throughout Hungary, Slovakia and Romania. His job as a salesman provided him with an income and a chance to spend time in the coffeehouses, better restaurants, and old clubs where he had become a favored client.

[40]   Porter, 2008, p. 42.

The people he met in these places brought him useful contacts. Joel loved to play cards, had a knack for poker, and often won in a single night more than his salary for the week. Much to his wife's surprise he had turned out to be exceptionally good at sales. He could also procure things that had become difficult to buy. He could still find silk stockings and extra-fine flour for cakes; he could connect you to the right supplier for filter-tipped cigarettes, Parisian scented soap, and delicate lipstick colors.

During this period, not only had the business expanded, but so did the family. At the end of summer 1938 the couple had their first son, Michael (Miki), and two years later the second one, Daniel, was born.

Part I

TOWARDS

HOLOCAUST

3. EARLY RESCUE OPERATIONS

Evasion of Labor Service

As already mentioned, the war in Hungary began in 1938, when Hungary tried to reclaim some of the territories it had lost in the peace treaties that followed World War I. In 1939 Joel was drafted into the Hungarian army and served for several months in various locations in Hungary, including recently reclaimed territories. In his book he wrote that he participated in the campaign to free Transylvania.[1]

It is unclear how long Joel's service in the Hungarian army actually lasted. The last entry in his service book was from 1943, a considerable time after the Jews were expelled from the army and were assigned to separate labor service. It is obvious that the term of his service was not continuous but the details are still unclear. The letters "Zs" on the cover of his service book indicated that he was *Zsido* (Jewish), but the book itself indicated his military profession, *nehézpuskás*, namely a gunner or heavy rifleman. Such function clearly points to a regular military service as opposed to labor service. Joel's friends from that time were not necessarily Jews, a further indication that he indeed served in the general army and not in the labor service units.[2]

During 1940–1941, the Hungarian army's willingness to enlist Jews gradually decreased. At a certain point it was decided to expel all Jews from the regular army and transfer them to the labor

---

[1]   In 1940 Hungary annexed part of Transylvania from Romania.

[2]   At the beginning of the war Jews were integrated into regular units in which they were also probably armed. Later on, they were expelled from the army and were relieved of their weapons, uniform, and any other soldiers' rights.

Joel in uniform of the Hungarian army
(1939-1940)

service units. Joel, too, was expelled from his army unit and was required to report to labor service, but according to all sources, he never reported to his assigned unit. Joel was released using a successful combination of bribery, contacts, effective exploitation of the Hungarian law, and a false representation of diabetes by loading up his blood sugar level. Sadly, diabetes actually ran in Joel's family, so the sugar load turned into a real condition from which he never recovered. Technically, the disease itself would not preclude someone from reporting to labor duty. When the Hungarian authorities went after Joel, Hansi stepped in and stated that she did not see fit to forward the order to Joel who, she claimed, was in severe condition in a hospital. When the Hungarians tried to blame her for Joel's failure to report to duty, she claimed to her defense that she was not aware of any law that required her to serve as the army's mailwoman.

Evasion of labor service was the first real step Joel and Hansi took on the road of dangerous actions and crucial decisions, each of which could have led to a catastrophe. Evasion of mandatory service was also the transition point from being law abiding citizens to taking matters into their own hands, assuming full responsibility for the results. This would have been inconceivable for the majority of Hungarian Jews who valued their Hungarian identity, not

The cover of Joel's military service book. The "Zs" mark means *Zsidó*— Jew in Hungarian.

Joel's military service book documenting his enlistment in 1939 and his last assignment in 1943. The book identifies sizes of uniform, military profession (literal translation: "heavy rifleman," which could mean a gunner), etc. This is evidence that Joel served in a regular military unit and not in a dedicated labor service unit.

to mention that following rules and regulations "to the T" was (and still is) common to the Jews in the region.[3] For Joel, this was a relatively easy transition, due both to his past in the German prison and his business "flexibility" that included ties to the black market. Once the first illegal step was made, the following steps became easier.

Like everyone else, Joel had no idea of the implications of being enlisted to labor service. Other than maybe for diehard Hungarian patriots, regular army service was not exactly the dream of anyone aware of the fate of the soldiers in World War I. Those intended for labor service were unflatteringly labeled "elements whose loyalty to the state was questionable," but this title provided no evidence that their fate would be any worse than the future of those sent to the front. So, it was not a choice of convenience or laziness. Joel was willing to fight for his adopted country, as a citizen with equal rights, even though he was well aware of its fascist government and its alliance with Nazi Germany. But he was not willing to serve as a C-class citizen.[4]

Evasion of labor service was not the general trend among the Hungarian Jews. Most of them, as law-abiding citizens who valued their Hungarian citizenship, did not even consider such behavior and thus the number of evaders was not significant.

The Rescue of "Alien" Jews from Deportation

At the end of the 1930s the Jewish population in Hungary experienced a considerable growth. As the Nazis seized power in Germany and annexed territories in Europe, many Jews from Germany, Austria, and Czechoslovakia escaped and took refuge in Hungary, which until 1944 was a relatively safe harbor for Jews. At the end of 1939, when Germany and Russia divided Poland between them, thousands of refugees escaped from Poland to Hungary, many

---

3   At least ostensibly.

4   The details about Joel's military service are taken from his book and from Hansi's testimony to Yad Vashem.

Jews among them. The Polish were warmly welcomed in Hungary, thanks to the good historical relations between the two countries, but the same hospitality was not extended to the Jews.

In his documented testimony in Yad Vashem,[5] Sámuel (Samu) Springman (who, as mentioned previously, introduced Joel to the Zionist agriculture training program) said that back in February 1941, six months before the actual deportation, he heard for the first time of the intention to deport a hundred thousand "alien" Jews from Hungary. In his testimony at the Eichmann trial,[6] Rabbi Pinchas (Philip) Freudiger, the former leader of the Orthodox Jewish community of Budapest, stated that at least a hundred thousand people were intended for deportation.[7] According to Randolph Braham,[8] the original intention of the Hungarian fascists and anti-Semites was to deport as many Jews as possible within the shortest possible time. Instead of a total number of planned deportees, Braham provides Máramaros County as an example: the county claimed to have found in its territory forty-five thousand alien Jews "who or whose ancestors infiltrated the country" and therefore had to be deported. A few months after the deportation was halted, Hungarian fascists tried to renew it. It is believed that they wanted to deport three hundred thousand Jews at that point but "settled" for one hundred thousand.[9] The number of Jews intended for deportation was much greater than all of the Jewish refugees (from Poland and elsewhere) who were situated then within the boundaries of the Hungarian government. Braham explains that the Hungarian fascists planned to reach these numbers by extending the term "alien" to all Jews, with or without Hungarian citizenship.

---

5   And to A. Cohen at GFH.

6   Adolf Eichmann (1906–1962) was a German/Austrian Nazi, Lieutenent Colonel in the SS. He was one of the major architects of the Holocaust, and was prosecuted and executed in Israel in the early 1960s.

7   See: his testimony in Hearing No. 51 of the trial, p. 773 of the minutes.

8   Braham, 1994, p. 208.

9   Ibid., p. 288.

Springman testified that he had told representatives of the Jewish leadership about the planned deportations. These representatives tried to confirm it with the authorized government officials in Hungary, but received absolute denial in response. They settled for that and abandoned the entire issue. Springman felt that the information was reliable and that the first victims were intended to be the thousands of Jewish refugees from Poland. In his opinion, had the leadership treated this issue more seriously from the beginning, the deportation may have been prevented.[10]

At the beginning of July 1941, a relative of Springman was arrested for committing a minor offense. With legal assistance, he was expected to be released as a result of routine legal proceedings. Surprisingly, the release was cancelled at the last minute. Springman's inquiries revealed that the release was cancelled since his relative was a Polish citizen (Jewish of course). He associated the arrest with the intention to deport 100,000 "Polish" Jews. From that moment, Springman attempted to warn anyone he could, including Joel and Hansi. Springman himself hid in the house of a Polish diplomat and placed his relatives in similar locations where they could not be found.

Thanks to Springman's explicit warning, in the summer of 1941, Joel and Hansi were already aware of the expected deportation. Hansi's eldest sister, Lenke (Karoline), was married to a Polish Jew named Lajos Stern. Hansi recommended to her sister not to appear before the authorities should she be asked to do so. Hansi also made her apartment available to her sister and her husband. This way, they would not be found at home and would not even receive the order in case it was sent to them. Hansi took her two sons and moved to a hotel, as she often did when precarious situations like this presented themselves.[11] Despite the explicit warning, Hansi's

---

10   See: Springman's testimonies at GFH archives (Ghetto Fighters' House, in Hebrew: Beit Loḥamei HaGeta'ot, a kibbutz founded by Holocaust survivors, among them fighters of the ghetto undergrounds and partisan units. The museum and the archives is named after Itzhak Katzenelson, a Jewish poet who died at Auschwitz).

11   It was usually the little Majestic on Karthauzi Street.

sister and her husband decided to remain law abiding citizens, believing that nothing would happen to them if they reported as required. Without consulting with Hansi and Joel they reported, as required, at the yard of the synagogue on Páva Street, which nowadays serves as a Jewish museum. The moment they set foot there, they realized their mistake and made efforts to alert Hansi to their situation. Their rescue turned out to be an extremely difficult mission.

When Hansi found out that her sister had been arrested at the deportation camp, she frantically started to look for help.[12] She contacted anyone who might be able to assist, especially attorneys and other people with contacts at the police department, but to no avail. Finally, Joel found in one of the cafés he had frequented a police agent named Jozsi Krem, who was known for his constant lack of cash. The man agreed to look for the deported sister and her husband for the huge amount of 10,000 pengő.[13] He also demanded 500 pengő in advance to repair his car and buy fuel, but Joel refused to pay anything in advance, which derailed the deal. When Hansi heard the story, she found Krem, gave him her sister's wedding picture and the requested advance payment in exchange for a promise to help. At that time the exchange rate of pengő was about one-fifth of the American dollar: the money paid in advance amounted to about 100 US dollars and the price for the rescue itself was about 2,000 US dollars of 1941. Given inflation, a 1941 US dollar is equivalent to something between 17 to 65 US dollars in 2018. Hence, in 2018's terms, the advance amounted to about 3,500 US dollars, and the sister's rescue to approximately 70,000 US dollars.[14] Hefty amounts indeed.

---

[12]   This part is detailed in Brand 1957 and in Hansi's testimony to Yad Vashem.

[13]   The currency pengő was a legal tender in Hungary from the end of World War I until the end of World War II.

[14]   According the various methods of calculation, one USD of 1941 is equivalent to somewhere between 17 and 65 US dollars of 2018. The 35 dollar-rate is about the average and was chosen for convenience. For the calculation, see: https://www.measuringworth.com/calculators/uscompare/relativevalue.php.

Investing such amount of money for saving the life of a sister may seem reasonable to the reader today, but in the summer of 1941, things looked much different. No one could think about "saving" or "rescuing" anyone from deportation. It was just a matter of bringing them back. Eli Wiesel describes the atmosphere that prevailed at the time in the following words: "A few days after they (the deportees of 1941) left, it was rumored that they were in Galicia, working, and even that they were content with their fate."[15] The term "Holocaust" had not yet been invented and no one could imagine at that time that deportation might mean the death and mass murder of men, women, the elderly, children, and babies. This huge financial investment indicates that Hansi had sharp senses and an exceptional ability to understand reality well before others. At this early phase of the war, she must have felt that this deportation was far more than just a relocation, otherwise, her determination and efforts to bring back her sister could not have been explained.

In her testimonies to Yad Vashem, Hansi mentioned that she consulted with a few relatives and close friends, all of whom considered the money she paid as wasted. Despite these reservations, Hansi decided that the amount, and especially the upfront money, was reasonable for her peace of mind and that she had indeed done everything she could for her sister. Krem came back a few days later with a group of Jews whom he squeezed into his car, but without Hansi's relatives whom he could not find. This must have been a profitable endeavor for Krem, since each and every one of those survivors was happy to pay him for their rescue. However, after a few trips he decided that this was becoming too risky and refused to make additional attempts to locate Hansi's sister without an accurate address. A short time thereafter, a Hungarian soldier knocked on Joel and Hansi's door with a note from the deported sister. He asked for 300 pengő[16] (about 2,000 US dollars in 2018

---

[15]   Night, p. 6.

[16]   The amount Peretz Révész was required to pay the smuggler who brought him and his wife from Slovakia to Hungary a few months later amounted to 500 pengő, of which Révész said in his book: "500 pengő was certainly a large amount" (Révész, 2001, p. 67).

terms), which Hansi was happy to pay. The note contained the address and an urgent plea for help.[17] Hansi immediately alerted Krem, and after a short delay for repairing his car, financed by Hansi, he went on his way. This time he came back with the sister and her husband.

The return of the deported sister was supposed to be the end of this story, but as Joel wrote in his book, it was only the beginning. The deportees returned by Jozsi Krem conveyed their experience to their relatives and the word spread. Many came to Joel and Hansi with a request to rescue their relatives too, but there are no reports about any additional successes. The only other rescue operation mentioned in the literature was an attempt by the Baroness Edith Weiss to save some people from deportation.[18] It seemed that she tried to save random people on her personal initiative, but the degree of her success was unclear. Other rescue operations from the deportation of "alien" Jews may have been attempted, but there are no reliable references to this, certainly not to any success story.

The rescue was a turning point for Joel and Hansi. Following the successful rescue, they turned their complete attention to helping refugees and Jews at risk. At the outset they did it alone. Later on, others joined them, at first Sámuel Springman, a veteran Zionist, and after a month or two, Israel Kasztner. This group became the core of what will later be known as the "Budapest Relief and Rescue Committee." Initially, aid was given to refugees who found their way to Joel and Hansi's house on their own. As the operation expanded, Joel and Hansi, as well as their friends and refugees who previously arrived in Budapest, helped to smuggle and harbor refugees from occupied countries bordering with Hungary.

---

[17]   According to Hansi's recorded memories, the note said Zablatov, probably meaning Zabolotiv, Ukraine, about 150 kilometers from Kamianets-Podilskyi, Khmelnytskyi province, where most of the Hungary deportees were murdered in 1941.

[18]   This woman did a lot for Jews in distress but she is hardly known or mentioned in Israel.

4. The Refugees

The Refugees who Arrived in Hungary

During the first years of the war up to the German occupation, the Jews of Hungary continued to live in relative peace despite the internal and external challenges. Until Germany's invasion in March 1944 they were under no immediate, direct threat and they needed no rescuing.[1] With two exceptions—the aforementioned deportation of "alien" Jews in the summer of 1941 and the murder in Delvidek (or Bačka, Yugoslavia) at the beginning of 1942—there were no organized attacks on Jews in Hungary.

Upon the Nazis' rise to power, before and during World War II, thousands of Jews tried to escape and a deluge of refugees arrived in Hungary. The first ones to arrive were the Germans, then the Austrians and Czechs, and at the beginning of the war the Yugoslavians,[2] Polish, and Slovaks. Joel arrived in Hungary from Germany at the second half of 1934 and is mentioned in the literature as one of the first two Zionist refugees who arrived from Germany to Hungary on their way to Palestine. The Hungarian authorities did not welcome refugees, especially Jews. Nevertheless, many of them were able to stay in the country and were not deported even after their capture, at least until the German occupation.[3]

---

[1] In fact, there was danger but the public and its leaders were not aware of the warning signs (see below).

[2] According to Cohen, 1984, p. 51, it was only in spring 1942 that non-personal aid was provided to refugees, but according to Hansi's interview to Yad Vashem, the Yugoslavians arrived before the Slovaks, probably back in 1941, and the Slovak refugees had probably received Joel and Hansi's address from them.

[3] David Huban (Huban, 2004) was one of these refugees, as well as a refugee

Until the beginning of the war, most refugees were Jewish. The occupation of Poland by Germany and Russia resulted in a large wave of non-Jewish Polish refugees, in addition to the Jewish ones. Hungary accepted the Polish refugees with open arms due to the good relations that had always prevailed between the two countries. The Jewish refugees benefitted indirectly. The Hungarians' attitude toward the Jewish refugees, and toward Jews in general, was less favorable than their attitude toward others. This situation improved slightly after the defeats of Germany and Hungary in Stalingrad at the end of 1942 and in Voronezh at the beginning of 1943.

Up until the German occupation, the rescue operations in Hungary focused on assisting foreign Jews who arrived and stayed in Hungary illegally. The official Jewish institutions in Hungary did a lot to help the local Jewish population which endured financial hardship due to the anti-Jewish legislation, but they refrained from helping the illegal foreigners, even if they were Jewish. They helped the poor with food and clothes but only if they were legal residents. Not to be underestimated, the Jewish community spent considerable resources to help those in need while making an effort to abide by the law. Several sources claim that the Orthodox Jews were the most willing to help illegal refugees, in addition to the few Zionist activists associated with the Brands.

The Hungarian Jews and the Refugees

The attitude of the official Zionist institutions to the refugees was similar to the other community institutions, mainly *neológ* (Reform or Conservative) and anti-Zionist Orthodox institutions. Moshe Krausz, Head of the Palestine Office in Budapest, official representative of the Jewish Agency and in charge of the distribution of immigration certificates, refrained from any contact with Jewish

from Poland named Zehava Roth. Roth escaped from Poland as a child, was caught near the border, and stayed in Hungary, in her opinion, thanks to the intervention of Baroness Edith Weiss. She told her story in a lecture she delivered to soldiers in 2015. At the time she lived in kibbutz Nir Galim.

Zionist Pioneers, referred to as *halutzim*, who were mostly illegal refugees. He adhered to the Hungarian law and refrained from any illegal action that might have endangered him or undermined his status. He did a lot to help local Jews and refugees but only within the frame of the law. Rafi Benshalom,[4] representative of the communist-leaning RSZ (the Radical Socialist Zionist) on the leadership of the Jewish Pioneer Underground (JPU) that operated in Hungary since 1942 until the end of the war, said: "Krausz became an opponent. His conduct was totally hostile towards the *halutzim*."[5] This is a pretty serious accusation from a member of RSZ, a movement that was Krausz's partner in leading the Palestine Office. Peretz Révész, representative of the Social Democrat Zionists (SDZ) on the leadership of the JPU in Hungary, had a similarly negative opinion of Krausz. He described in great length and detail how Krausz distributed the immigration certificates intended for the Zionist *halutzim* to his orthodox friends, most of whom were not Zionists at all.[6]

Actually, Krausz's behavior was not significantly different from the behavior of other senior officials in the Zionist establishment in Hungary. Révész, who was a refugee from Slovakia, described his failed attempt to meet the secretary of the Zionist Federation in Hungary, who, like most of the Jews of Hungary, avoided any contact with refugees and refrained from helping them.[7] It is interesting to note that Krausz had critics even from within his own movement, Mizrahi (Jewish religious Zionist political party).

---

[4]   Benshalom arrived in Hungary only in January 1944 and the RSZ's involvement in rescue activities until that time was minimal.

[5]   Benshalom, 1977, p. 100. There is a significant amount of ungratefulness in this accusation. Benashlom himself and many of his friends spent much of the occupation period in a "protected house" (the "Glass House" under Swiss protection) that Kraus made available for them.

[6]   Révész, 2001, pp. 109–111. Révész himself was active in Hungary since the spring of 1942.

[7]   Révész did not indicate the name in his book, but Ayala Nedivi (2009) indicated in her Internet book that the secretary, Dr. Bock, refused to accept him threatening to call the police (in the printed edition: "Dr. Boch").

Some Mizraḥi Zionists blamed him for discriminating against them in distributing immigration certificates and in prioritizing the orthodox Jews who were not entitled to the certifications (such as the Rebbe of Belz).[8] The attitude of the general Jewish population to the refugees was no better than that of their leaders. Zvi Goldfarb, a member of the Socialist Zionists (SZ) and one of the leaders of the JPU in Hungary, tells in his memoirs about the attitude of the local population to illegal Jewish refugees:

> One day we both entered a Jewish apartment. I pretended to be a refugee from Carpathian Rus[9] [Transcarpathia] who spoke a bit of German and a bit of Yiddish. The homeowner knew some Yiddish, but starting to speak Yiddish turned out to be a mistake. Once the man heard my Yiddish, he immediately recognized that I was not from Carpathian Rus and suddenly told the both of us, me and Eli Cohen: "Get out of here at once, or I'll call the police!"[10]

Goldfarb further tells about his work at a Jewish hospital in Budapest:

> For two weeks we worked there in gardening, but when they found out that we were refugees from Poland and not from Carpathian Rus—they dismissed us.[11]

Researcher Asher Cohen sums up the Jewish population's attitude to the refugees in Hungary as follows:

> Most testimonies bitterly point at a cold attitude and lack of sympathy on the part of the local population; in any event, this was the refugees' feeling. Relatives were usually willing to provide one-off support but refused to host the refugees in their homes.[12]

---

[8]   Siegfried Rott's letter from November 1943 in GFH.

[9]   Nowadays, Zakarpattia region, Ukraine. Hungary lost this area after World War I and reoccupied it at the beginning of World War II.

[10]   Goldfarb, 1980, p. 34.

[11]   Ibid.

[12]   Cohen, 1984, p. 42.

Not all the Hungarian Jews treated the refugees as harshly as Goldfarb described, but most of them feared any contact with them and refrained from housing their refugee relatives for more than one or two nights. Révész also mentioned in his book the reservations of the Jewish population in Hungary to have any contact with refugees, even refugees who were relatives. Similar detailed description of this behavior was included in most of the memoires of refugees who went through Hungary.[13] Hungary was at that time a police state and the risk of getting caught was great, as well as the potential punishment. Entire families were sent to detention camps for providing any kind of help to refugees.[14] In this environment, activists without Hungarian citizenship who provided aid to refugees faced even greater risk, namely being extradited to the Germans.

The Brands and the Refugees

Ignoring the immense risk, Joel and Hansi began helping refugees in a most unusual and exceptional way by the end of the 1930s. Systematic documentation listing all these refugees probably does not exist as Joel and Hansi were not the kind of people who kept such records and they certainly could not have remembered everyone who used their help. Hints to the scope of their activities are available in the literature. Asher Cohen writes:

> Out of plain generosity, or due to a sense of solidarity common to refugees, Joel Brand and his wife helped even earlier friends that escaped from Austria and Germany. The incident in 1941 was probably the Brands' first contact with planned smuggling of migrants. In fact, it had no connection with Zionist activism but rather had a clear personal and family nature.[15]

---

13   See Révész, 2001, p. 67; for summary see: Cohen, 1984, p. 42.

14   Cohen, 1984. p. 43.

15   Ibid., p. 51.

Cohen added that Joel (in fact, both Joel and Hansi) helped the refugees in those early stages when Joel "was already financially well off and moved on from his Zionist activism."[16] It transpired from the text that the Brands began helping refugees before the deportation of the Alien Jews in the summer of 1941 and that assistance was provided regardless of any political affiliation, Zionist or otherwise. At about the same time that Cohen's book was published, Hungarian scholar Mária Schmidt also published research indicating that Joel and Hansi were the first to have helped foreign refugees in Hungary and that this began as early as February 1942.[17]

There is no information about the scope of aid the Brands provided to refugees prior to the deportation period in the summer of 1941. The demand for assistance increased following this event, not only because the word spread out about their efforts,[18] but also since deportations began in Slovakia shortly after that time. Presumably, the additional survivors brought by Jozsi Krem during his endeavors to find Hansi's sister were among the people spreading the word. One way or another, in the spring of 1942 the Brands' house was well known as an aid center and many refugees found their way there.

Assembly of Jews into concentration camps began in Slovakia at the end of 1941 and their deportation to extermination camps started at the beginning of 1942.[19] At that time, the first refugees from Slovakia arrived in Hungary, specifically to the Brands' house. It would seem that they had previously heard of the successful rescue.

Peretz Révész said in his book that an acquaintance named Shimon Izraeli, a member of the SZ, directed him to Joel and Hansi for assistance after he was turned away by Zionist and Jewish institutions as well as his own relatives. This was in the spring (April–May) of 1942. Révész emphasized that the Brands welcomed

---

[16]   Ibid.

[17]   Schmidt, 1985.

[18]   See for instance: Israel and Lazar, 1994, p. 149.

[19]   Hadari, 1992, p. 119.

him warmly and provided him with financial and other assistance. In particular he noted that he was not required to present any documents or certificates and that he was not asked for his political affiliation.[20] The Jewish population in Palestine and in Hungary at that time was politically divided. Each faction looked after its own people. No assistance was provided without the "correct" political connections. In stark contrast, the Brands never inquired about the political affiliation of refugee seekers, they did not ask for identification of any kind, and they provided help regardless of any political, Zionist, or party-related considerations.

At the end of April or beginning of May 1942, Hanna Bin Nun, who had escaped from Poland through Slovakia, arrived at the Brands' house. She too was referred to Joel and Hansi by Shimon Izraeli. She was not a member of their Mapai youth movement (after the war she joined kibbutz Dafna of the Social Zionists— SZ). She came from Poland, had no knowledge of the Hungarian language, and probably did not know much German either. She had no blood connection to Joel and Hansi and there is no evidence that they knew her beforehand. Nevertheless, she was sheltered in the Brands' house for two weeks. In her book, Hanna Bin Nun did not mention any party-related connection or documentation. She only expressed appreciation for the kindness she met at the Brands' house.[21]

The lack of documentation may have resulted in some fraudulent representation. In her recorded testimonies, Hansi mentioned one extraordinary case of a Jewish refugee from Germany who was accepted to work in her house as a nanny. Hansi was uncomfortable as she was afraid that the person was an informer.[22] The solution was relatively easy: the children did not get along with her and she did not get along with the children, so she left with no incidents.[23]

---

[20]   Révész, 2001, p. 73.

[21]   Bin Nun, 1997, p. 165.

[22]   In the first half of CD 3 in Hansi's recorded memories in Yad Vashem.

[23]   The Hungarians had interest of the happenings in the Brands' house since they suspected that Joel engaged in illegal activity and he was once

Regarding Joel and Hansi's aid to refugees, Josef Kornianski wrote as follows:

> The Social Democrat Zionists (SDZ) were enlisted to Relief and Rescue when other parties were still afraid of these illegal steps. Joel Brand was among the first to have looked after the Slovakian *halutzim* who came to Hungary although he knew that this put him in danger.[24]

Jósef Baumer,[25] Radical Socialists Zionists (RSZ) member, also mentioned the Brands' care for the refugees. In his testimony to Asher Cohen dated November 1, 1978 he says:

> As to the personalities of the Brands and Springman, they were warm people who were always willing to help the refugees. I myself, when I had nowhere to house a refugee, would approach Joel or Hansi and they would always help, without asking any question as to which movement the refugee belonged.[26]

This statement by Baumer intended to distinguish between the attitude of the Brands and Springman, and the attitude of Moshe Krausz, who was Baumer's political ally at the time. The Brands and Springman were mentioned in the general context of assistance to refugees. But regarding the dangerous activity of harboring refugees, only the Brands were mentioned. Baumer emphasized

---

warned about it at the police. From Hansi's recorded memories in Yad Vashem.

[24]   Kornianski, 1979, p. 171. Josef Kornianski was a refugee from Poland and a leading figure of the SZ in Hungary in 1943. After immigrating to Israel, he lived in kibbutz Dafna in the Galilee and was a member of the SZ party all his life. According to various sources, he was very perceptive and was among the first to identify that the anti-Jewish activity in Germany was not a wave of pogroms but rather a planned policy aimed at extermination.

[25]   Peretz Révész says that for a certain period Baumer was Joel's assistant in *tiyul* issues but they did not get along as Joel failed to keep organized books (Peretz assumed this task) and due to Baumer's political extremism (Révész, 2001, p. 115).

[26]   P. 3 in Baumer's testimony on the online archive of GFH (Ghetto Fighters' House), https://www.gfh.org.il/eng/Archive.

that assistance was given "without asking any question as to which movement the refugee belonged to," highlighting a conduct that was unusual at the time. The default preference of the various movements to look after their own members went on until the end of the war, even after the establishment of some sort of unified leadership. Baumer's testimony is particularly interesting since he was an RSZ man. Members of this Communist-leaning movement were especially suspicious and skeptical of the Relief and Rescue Committee in which Joel and Hansi were active.[27]

The Smuggling Operation (*Tiyul*)

One of the key lessons from Hansi's sister's rescue was the need to plan and set up a cross-border smuggling operation for future rescue activities. This was an innovative, unique, and daring approach to transfer not only people, but also information and money. This smuggling operation, started by Joel and Hansi in cooperation with the refugees who had already arrived in Hungary, was inconspicuously titled *tiyul*, which means "trip" in Hebrew.

In his book, Kornianski mentions other SDZ activists, including Kasztner, Hillel Danzig, and Springman, but when it comes to assisting refugees, he singles out Joel Brand. Of the scope of Joel and Hansi's assistance to refugees he writes as follows:

> Among the activists organizing the *tiyul* [smuggling] was Joel Brand who dedicated himself entirely to this endeavor and demonstrated a deeply humane attitude. His home became the central place for everything related to rescue operations, thereby risking his family. He and his wife Hansi were relentless. I remember that one day they allowed into their home fifteen members of HaNo'ar HaZioni [the Zionist Youth] from Poland who arrived through Slovakia. People would also frequent his

[27] Benshalom was the leader of the RSZ pioneers after Baumer left for Palestine. See his comment about behavioral norms of the Committee members and SDZ people (Benshalom, 1977, p. 36).

business on *tiyul* matters. Unfortunately, some exploited their kindness to extort money.[28]

Joel's business travels as a salesperson and buyer for the knitting workshop brought him in contact with some dubious characters who introduced him to smugglers. These people included Germans,[29] mainly Wilhelm Franz Canaris's counter-espionage agents (Abwehr).[30] The fact that Joel grew up in Germany made it easy for him to befriend these people. Not only did they provide considerable help with the smugglings, obviously for a hefty commission, but they were also instrumental at later stages, in particular towards Germany's invasion and in the first days following it.

In the spring of 1942, the refugee *halutzim* who had already arrived in Hungary initiated rescue operations to bring their friends from their countries of origin, Slovakia and Poland. The Brands had no relatives or acquaintances in these countries. Nevertheless, they were approached by these *halutzim* with a request to locate smugglers who would help their friends cross the border. Joel's background, contacts, skills, and successful experience rescuing his brother-in-law from the deportation of "alien" Jews turned out to be a perfect match for the task. Just as he found the right man to rescue his relatives from the deportation, he managed to find suitable local smugglers. The smugglers must have been wisely selected or otherwise vetted since neither Joel nor Hansi were arrested for organizing this operation. Nor were they arrested for the ongoing contact they maintained with the smugglers, some of whom visited

---

[28]   Kornianski, pp. 186–187.

[29]   Biss, p. 22.

[30]   Canaris was a German admiral and chief of the Abwehr, the German military intelligence service, from 1935 to 1944. Initially a supporter of Adolf Hitler, by 1939 he had turned against the Nazis as he felt Germany would lose another major war. During World War II he was among the military officers involved in the clandestine opposition to Nazi Germany leadership. He was executed for high treason as the Nazi regime was collapsing.

their house.[31] In fact, *tiyul* operated discreetly and efficiently for about two years, until the German occupation. After the occupation, the smuggling activity continued by the Jewish pioneers, but in the opposite direction—out of Hungary.

According to Révész, the smuggling operation was running smoothly by the end of May 1942.[32] The smuggling operations were expanded in 1943, thanks to financial aid that started arriving from overseas, specifically for this purpose.

Yitzhak (Fishman) Bin Nun writes in his memoires:

> We benefited from the help of our devoted friends at the Hungarian movement, in particular I wish to note Sámuel Springman, and Hansi and Joel Brand, whose help reached all the way to Będzin, Poland. They dedicated nights and days to the rescue and help of our refugee friends.[33]

Gila Knafheiss's testimony, which is saved at the Ghetto Fighters' House (GFH), also attests to Joel's involvement:

> I was able to obtain forged documents in Srodula and travelled with a few more friends to the Polish-Czechoslovak border, where a contact person awaited us and helped us cross the border. From there we traveled to Hungary. On Yom Kippur [of 1943] I arrived with some friends at the house of the Zionist movement leader—Joel Brand. Over time we were joined by newly arrived partisans from Będzin, Sosnowiec, Katowice, who fought against the Germans.

The *tiyul* established by Joel and his friends operated quite successfully for two years under the nose of the Hungarians and Germans. It was not the only smuggling operation. A similar smuggling network operated on behalf of the representatives of the Jewish Agency in Istanbul, as described in Tuvia Friling's

---

31   Révész, 2001, p. 116.

32   Ibid., p. 75.

33   Israel and Lazar, 1999.

book.[34] The network operators were Teddy Kollek and Ehud Avriel,[35] who established a system of messengers to transfer information, instructions, radio equipment, and money into the occupied territories.[36]

According to Friling, a large number of the messengers they employed, whom the operators believed to be loyal, were in fact double and triple agents operated by Germany's military counter-espionage service (Abwehr) and by the Gestapo itself.[37] The network that Kollek and Avriel believed was serving them served, first and foremost, the Nazis. As a result, many of the actions the Rescue Committee of the Jewish Agency in Istanbul tried to initiate were entirely transparent to the Nazis. This included a considerable part of the botched paratroopers' operation to be discussed later in this book.[38] To be clear, some of these double agents who served Teddy Kollek also served the Relief and Rescue Committee and the JPU in Budapest. But there was a crucial difference: the activists in Hungary were aware that these people also worked for the Germans. Unlike Kollek and the Istanbul delegation who tried to use these agents for military operations, the activists in Hungary strictly used them for

---

[34]   Friling, 1998.

[35]   Teddy Kollek and Ehud Avriel were at the time members of the Jewish Agency rescue committee in Istanbul and later become senior civil servants in the State of Israel.

[36]   The radio equipment was for military purposes and not for saving Jews.

[37]   The German word "Gestapo" was an abbreviation of "Geheime Staatspolizei" (Secret State Police). Normally, the Gestapo was part of the German SS, which, in its turn, was an abbreviation of Schutzstaffel (German: Protection Squadron), a major paramilitary organization under Adolf Hitler and the German Nazi Party (NSDAP), headed by Heinrich Himmler. The SS was foremost an agency of security, surveillance, and terror within Germany and German-occupied Europe and was most responsible for the genocidal killing of an estimated 5.5 to 6 million Jews and millions of other victims.

Besides the Gestapo, the SS also included as its major subdivisions the Sicherheitsdienst (SD, Security Service) and Waffen-SS (Armed SS, politically devoted military units). The Gestapo system was later adopted by pro-Nazi states in Europe, for instance, there was a Hungarian Gestapo.

[38]   Friling, 1998, pp. 418, 452, and 456.

humanitarian aid. Therefore, there were no significant failures in Hungary and no damage resulted from unreliable agents.

Mária Schmidt noted that Joel's smuggling activities did bother the Hungarian police, but they thought that he was employed by the Germans and thus left him alone.[39]

---

[39]   Schmidt, 1985.

5. The Budapest Relief and Rescue Committee

The "Budapest Relief and Rescue Committee" (in short "the Committee" or "the Rescue Committee") was established in order to help refugees from German occupied territories who stayed in Hungary illegally. As time went on, the Committee expanded its activities and established contacts with remaining Jewish communities within the German-occupied territories. These contacts were used to collect information about the condition of the Jews in those places and to forward it to Jewish organizations in the free world. They were also used for forwarding financial support to those communities from foreign sources, as well as for assisting young *halutzim* (pioneers) to infiltrate Hungary.[1] This committee was probably the only Jewish entity established outside the German-dominated territories with the aim of illegally assisting foreign and unacquainted Jews. The group's activities were clearly illegal and some of its activities put the lives of those involved in real danger.[2]

The Committee started its activity at the beginning of 1942[3] as a private initiative of Hansi, Joel, and Springman in response to the growing need to help refugees who arrived to Hungary at an increasing rate. Within a short time, the founders concluded that they needed a representative figure with political experience in order to harness the Jewish public in Hungary and its leadership to support their activities politically and financially. For this purpose, Springman invited Kasztner to join the team, and thus

---

[1]   Révész, 2001, pp. 116, 119.

[2]   Cohen, 1984, p. 43; Biss, 1973, p. 42.

[3]   According to Maria Shmidt (1985) it started in February 1942.

Kasztner became the prime speaker of the Comittee.[4] Kasztner, who introduced himself as the director of the Rescue Committee, was not involved in actual rescue activities. He was not mentioned as a prominent rescue activist during 1943 in the book of Ze'ev Hadari (Wenja Pomeranz), a member of the Jewish Agency's delegation to Istanbul: "The rescue actions were handled mostly by Joel Brand, Peretz Révész from 'HaMaccabi HaTza'ir,' Yoshko Baumer from the RSZ, Yitzhak Knoll—a refugee from Poland and member of the RSZ, and Shaya Ratschprechter."[5] Kasztner dealt only with finance and politics. As such, he was also less exposed to the risks involved in rescue activities.

Towards the end of 1942, the Jewish community in Palestine established a rescue committee to help the European Jews. This committee sent a delegation to neutral Istanbul, from where it was easier to contact Jews in the German occupied areas in Europe.[6] The Istanbul delegation was supposed to form contacts with Jewish communities in the occupied countries and help them. This delegation sent letters to known Zionist activists in Europe whose addresses were known. The letters were vaguely worded on behalf of an unknown Jew in Istanbul to overcome the problems of censorship. Most of the recipients to whom the letters were sent were no longer alive or deported from their homes and moved to ghettos. One of the few who received a letter and responded to it was Springman. Responding to such a letter was no simple matter. One can try to explain to security officials the reasons for sending a letter to a relative or to a close friend in a foreign country during war, but it is very difficult to explain such a letter to an unknown person abroad. The writer of such a letter would have found it difficult to prove that he was not involved in an espionage attempt. Obviously, by responding to the letter, Springman took a huge risk.

[4]   Springman testimony to A. Cohen, GFH, p. 5.

[5]   Hadari, p. 177.

[6]   The Jewish community in British-controlled Palestine was mainly Zionist and self-governed by the Jewish Agency. The delegation in Istanbul was led by the Jewish Agency, but included representatives from all other Jewish factions in Palestine.

The Jewish Agency's delegation in Istanbul had financial resources for helping and rescuing young Jewish *halutzim*, but they were supposed to allocate funds only to recognized public entities, and thus, some formalization of the Budapest Rescue Committee was required. At the beginning of 1943, in response to the demand from Istanbul, Kastzner informed the Istanbul delegation that he had established a rescue committee which in reality had already existed for nearly a year. The Budapest Rescue Committee had never been an official organization representing any authorized entity on behalf of the Hungarian Jews. Its status was achieved first and foremost by virtue of its activity. The funds it received from overseas sources after it was formalized contributed to its stature.[7] The resources received from Istanbul enabled the Budapest Rescue Committee to expand the aid provided to refugees and the smuggling activities.

It is not evident why the Jewish Agency needed to rely on the services of an unofficial entity such as the Relief and Rescue Committee in Budapest. After all, the Jewish Agency had its own official representation in Budapest, the Palestine Office, headed by Moshe Krausz. The Office was situated in relative safety under the protection of the Swiss Consulate which also represented Britain's interests and, therefore, Palestine's interests. There is no formal explanation why this office was not used as a rescue and aid center for the refugees.

The exact date the Rescue Committee was established is unknown, and so is its exact members list. The list of names mentioned in Kasztner's report is probably inaccurate.[8] At the beginning of his report Kasztner did not mention Joel among the Rescue Committee members, but only as being active in organizing smuggling: "The organization of rescues of Jews from Poland to Hungary— . . . *tiyul*—was assumed by Joel Brand."[9] Only later in his report, Kasztner indicated that Joel had been a member of

---

[7]   Cohen, 1984, pp. 51–53.

[8]   See, for example, ibid., p. 56.

[9]   Kasztner's report, 1946, p. 7.

the Rescue Committee. The Hungarian researcher Mária Schmidt listed both Joel and Hansi as members of the Rescue Committee, together with a comment that they were included on the committee since "they were the first ones to have helped refugees."[10] These assertions are also only partially true: Joel and Hansi were indeed the first ones to have helped refugees in Hungary,[11] but Hansi had never been an official member of the Rescue Committee. She was very active, in fact, but on an entirely voluntary basis and without any official title or status.

Until the occupation, the Budapest Rescue Committee and the Brands in particular, were the only local Jewish entity who not only helped refugees who arrived on their own, but also engaged in actual rescue activities. Rescue activities involved smuggling Jews from German-occupied territories—where they were constantly at risk of deportation and murder—to Hungary, which was a relatively safe place until March 1944. This was the first and possibly only framework established in Hungary to help refugees, other than the refugees themselves.

Since the Rescue Committee was not an official entity and it did not represent any legal institution, the question of who exactly was a member is of no importance. The newly formalized Rescue Committee was headed by the President of the Zionist Federation in Hungary, Engineer Ottó Komoly, and Kasztner was its spokesman and senior political representative. The core figures of the committee were Joel Brand, Springman, and Kasztner. Other important members were Offenbach, Szilágyi, and Biss. The last three are less known since they did not immigrate to Israel after the Holocaust. Some other names are sometimes mentioned as members but their impact was less significant.

---

10 Schmidt, 1985. Schmidt mentioned other members of the Committee together with their titles and the names of the entities they represented.

11 It seems that Sámuel Springman preceded them and helped "illegal aliens," but his activity was always concealed and his direct contact with the refugees was limited. Even if Springman did not precede the Brands, there is no doubt that he cooperated with them right from the outset.

The Members of the Committee

The Brands, together with Springman, were the initiators of the relief activities for refugees in Hungary, but Hansi has never been an official member of the committee. Joel was a member with a well-defined task: "The organization of rescuing Jews from Poland to Hungary—this operation was called in our code *tiyul*—was assumed by Joel Brand."[12] In fact, he was the only one on the committee whose defined role, as well as his real activity, was rescuing.

Ottó Komoly

Ottó Komoly was born in 1892 as Ottó (Nathan) Kohn into a middle-class family in Budapest. His father participated in the First Zionist World Congress in Basel in 1897, and Ottó followed him by becoming a Zionist. He was an engineer by profession and was respected by all those who knew him and therefore he was asked to become the head of the Budapest rescue committee. Komoly served in the Austro-Hungarian army during World War I and earned a medal for his bravery. He was a reserve captain and therefore he was exempt from discriminatory anti-Jewish laws. Komoly became deputy chairman of the Hungarian Zionist Association in 1940, and in 1941 was chairman of the organization. On the first of January 1945, just before the liberation, Komoly was abducted by members of the Arrow Cross Party and most probably shot in the Danube on the same day.

Ottó Komoly was brought to the committee by Kasztner to elevate its status and gain prestige both in Hungary as well as in the delegation in Istanbul. His name and position as the chairman of the Hungarian Zionist Association gave the committee its status that enabled the Istanbul delegation to send them money. Komoly's direct involvement in illegal aid activities to refugees was limited, but his general contribution to the Committee was of utmost importance. Thanks to his personal stature, he managed the dialog with official political entities in Hungary, with the help and participation of Kasztner. Before the occupation, Komoly had an

---

[12]   Kasztner's report, 1946, p. 7.

Ottó Komoly in uniform of the Austro-Hungarian army. He later became the head of the Budapest rescue committee, the chairman of the Hungarian Zionist Association, and the founder of "Department A" of the International Red Cross.

important contribution to mitigating the Hungarian government's hostility toward Jewish refugees and Zionist activity. Komoly also mediated in the constant disputes between Kasztner and Krausz. He tried to stay within the boundaries of the law in an attempt to solicit sympathy and help from moderate political entities in Hungary. In addition, like the majority of Hungarian Jews, illegal activity was entirely unthinkable for him. Nevertheless, Komoly did not refrain from having his name associated with the Rescue Committee whose activity was clearly illegal.[13] One of his most important contributions was founding "Department A" of the International Red Cross. Officially, this office was tasked with immigration of children. In practice, "Department A," alongside other international organizations and embassies of neutral countries, provided cover and protection to orphanages established in Hungary by various

[13] Many Jewish leaders in Hungary were careful not to associate themselves with any activity that could have been interpreted as illegal. For example, Kasztner invited his father-in-law and Ernő Márton to the Committee meetings from time to time but they "refused to get their feet wet" (Brand, 1960, p. 42). Moreover, József Fischer (Kasztner's father-in-law) avoided signing a report to Istanbul that summarized the situation in Budapest before Germany's invasion (Brand, 1957, p. 56).

Jewish organizations. Later on, this network helped all of the Jews of Budapest, for example by providing food to the people of the ghetto. Another important contribution of Komoly was the prevention of the evacuation of the Jews from Budapest into camps that did not really exist in order "to protect them" as planned by the Hungarian authorities during the summer of 1944. When Hansi, in time, looked for a suitable man to continue the discussions and negotiations with Eichmann, following Joel's mission to Istanbul, she disqualified Komoly, since she thought that he could not lie and pretend as was needed in order to negotiate with cold-blooded murderers like Eichmann.[14]

Israel (Rezső) Kasztner

Israel (Rezső) Kasztner was born in 1906 in Cluj, Hungary at the time (Romania nowadays). From a young age, he was involved in politics and gained a lot of experience. A lawyer by education and a Journalist, he served as a political correspondent in Bucharest for the Hungarian newspaper *Új Kelet* (New East) that was published in his hometown Cluj. He was also a director in the Jewish Agency's Palestine Office there and a leader of the Zionist youth movement in Transylvania. He was an activist in the Zionist labor movement, and in addition he served as secretary of the Jewish faction in the Romanian parliament (his role in the efforts to save Jews in Hungary will be discussed later on).

Kasztner was targeted for assassination during in the night between March 3 and 4, 1957, and died of his wounds on March 15 in Tel Aviv.

Sámuel (Samu) Springman

Sámuel (Samu) Springman was born in Poland in June 15, 1905, and as a young boy moved to Budapest with his Family.

Springman was the most senior Zionist activist representing the SDZ in Budapest and one of the more important albeit lesser known

---

[14]   See the recorded interview of Yad Vashem researchers with her. Komoly's problem was not a lack of courage, but his inability to lie, pretend, and stoop so low as required in order to deal with people of Eichmann's type.

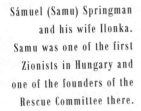

Sámuel (Samu) Springman and his wife Ilonka. Samu was one of the first Zionists in Hungary and one of the founders of the Rescue Committee there.

contributors to the establishment of the Rescue Committee and to the aid provided to refugees in Hungary. He was the one who integrated Joel into Zionist activism in Budapest back in 1934 and the one who brought Kasztner to the Rescue Committee. Springman was a fairly well-known figure, both in and out of Hungary. When representatives of the Jewish Agency began looking for contact people in Europe, Springman was one of the few who received their letter and dared to respond. This was an illegal and risky action since the Istanbul rescue committee represented Palestine, thus operated on behalf of the British enemy. This is how the initial contact was established between the rescue activists in Budapest and the outside world. Springman, a prudent and careful man, was strict about confidentiality, a trait that did not appeal to some of the *halutzim* representatives. He refrained, quite justly, from exposing communication channels and the identity of messengers who carried information and money. At the beginning of 1944, due to their poor health, Springman and his wife left Hungary and traveled to Palestine via Turkey. According to him, prior to leaving he delegated his responsibilities to Kasztner,[15] but in fact,

[15] Springman was concerned about Joel's excessive openness. In his opinion, Joel failed to keep an adequate level of confidentiality. Springman said so explicitly in an interview he had with Asher Cohen (The University of Haifa, The Historical Documentation Center).

he delegated some of the tasks to Joel.[16] On his way to Palestine he was arrested by the British and sent to Egypt where he met Joel, who was sent there later. He died in Tel Aviv on November 7, 1988.

Ernő (Zvi) Szilágyi

Ernő (Zvi) Szilágyi was born in the city of Kaposvár in Hungary in 1898. He was one of the prominent figures in his movement, the communist-leaning Radical Socialist Zionists (RSZ). He was a scholar and a graduate of several universities and an active Zionist: from 1937 to 1940 he was the head of the Keren Kayemet LeIsrael[17] in Budapest; in 1939 he represented his movement in the Palestinian Office in Budapest; from 1943 he took part in the activities of the Relief and Rescue Committee and represented his movement there together with Jósef (Yoshko) Baumer who represented the movement's refugees there; and he was the vice-president of the Zionist Organization in Hungary. Szilágyi also took part in the debates about the rescue of Jews held by Joel Brand and Israel Kasztner and took part in the selection of passengers who left Hungary on June 30, 1944 on the Relief and Rescue Committee train. Szilágyi was involved in the attempt to rescue Jews in Szeged by applying to the SS officer.[18] As a result, some of the Jews who were taken to the Strasshof labor camp instead of being sent to Auschwitz extermination camp were from Szeged. Szilágyi himself left Hungary on the Relief and Rescue Committee train.

Szilágyi gained much respect within his movement but he was an ideologist rather than action-oriented and practical person. He formed the strange coalition of the RSZ with *Mizrahi* (Jewish religious Zionist political party) at the Palestinian Office as he was not too bothered by the discrimination against the Zionist *halutzim* (pioneers) in terms of distribution of immigration certificates. Szilágyi relinquished his own immigration certificate more than

---

[16]   Acording to Biss, "Brand proved that he was remarkable successor to Springman" (Biss, 1973, p. 42).

[17]   The Israel National Fund.

[18]   On the SS and its structure, see note 117.

once and opted to stay in socialist Hungary after the war rather than immigrate to capitalistic Israel.[19] The limited interest Szilágyi demonstrated in the immigration certificates possibly explains his good working relationships with the Head of the Palestine Office, Krausz. According to other members of the movement, Krausz, a Mizraḥi representative, was clearly hostile towards the *ḥalutzim*.[20]

After the war he returned to Hungary but did not take part in Zionist activities. He worked as a bookkeeper in one of the institutions of high education and in 1958 he retired. In 1970 Szilágyi intended to immigrate to Israel where a suitable apartment was readied for him in kibbutz Ein Dor with the help of Arie Ya'ari. However, in the end he changed his mind. He died in Hungary in 1973.[21]

Sándor (Shalom) Offenbach

Sándor (Shalom) Offenbach was born in Łódź (Poland) in 1899 and moved to Budapest in 1920 where he became active in the textile industry. Being an active Zionist, he was elected as the treasurer of the Relief and Rescue Committee, following Shmuel Springman's immigration to Palestine on January 18, 1944. He was very successful in that role. He was considered an expert in raising money and earned the appreciation of everyone who came in contact with him. On May 27, 1944 he was captured by the Hungarian counter-espionage, together with Hansi Brand and Israel Kasztner, but they were all released a short while thereafter. Offenbach was among the staff that compiled the list of Jews who were to board the train from Hungary to Switzerland organized by the Relief and Rescue Committee.[22] When "Department A," headed by Ottó Komoly, was established in the offices of the International Red Cross at 4 Mérleg Street, Offenbach was in charge, among others, of obtaining funds

---

19   Szilágyi was the only member of the Rescue Committee who included himself among the train's passengers (see below).

20   Benshalom, p. 100.

21   David Gur (Grósz Endre), *Brothers for Resistance and Rescue.*

22   See later on, the chapter about "the train of the privileged."

for setting up and equipping children's homes. As the recipient of funds transferred from Istanbul and Switzerland, he allocated them to the Zionist youth movements for their rescue operations. After the liberation he continued his work in the textile business in Hungary until it was nationalized by the communist government there. He moved to Vienna in 1950 and to Germany in 1957, where he passed away later on.

André Biss

André (Andreas) Biss was born in Budapest on May 31, 1904, to Jewish parents but was brought up as a protestant by his father's second wife.[23] He was Joel Brand's cousin (Joel's mother and Biss's birth mother were sisters). When Joel was deported from Germany in 1934, his first stop was Biss's house. It seemed that Joel's aunt (Biss's mother) was the one who referred him to Biss. Biss, who did not know Joel prior to that, accepted him with open arms and helped him settle down in Romania until he left for Hungary.

Biss was not a member of the Rescue Committee until Germany's invasion of Hungary. After the invasion, he became an important operative engaged in rescue activities, financing operations, and negotiations with the Nazis. Thanks to his "German" mother and his protestant upbringing, he had good Aryan official papers that enabled him relative freedom. Upon the German invasion a newspaper article appeared attacking the Jewish clientele of the Hotel Majestic. Biss read this article, knowing that Hansi and her children stayed there, and with his highly developed political sense, he hurried there and persuaded Hansi to take her children and leave with him at once.[24] The same day at midnight, the SS surrounded the Majestic and rounded up all the Jewish residents. The Jews were sent to the gas chambers, and the hotel became the headquarters of the SS security service.[25]

---

[23]   Biss, 1975, back cover.

[24]   By this action Biss saved the author's life.

[25]   Weissberg (Brand), 1957, p. 69.

On the invasion day he made his office—which was his residence as well—available to the members of the Rescue Committee, at no charge. They stayed there during most of the occupation. Biss must had been involved with the Committee's activities at an early stage, but until the invasion he probably took a more passive role and possibly supported it financially. In his book, he identified his main political/rescue activism in his negotiations with Otto Klages, head of the SD (*Sicherheitsdienst*, Security Service) in Hungary who had the same rank as Eichmann's and reported directly to Himmler.[26] Peretz Révész painted Biss in a favorable light, indicating that he had not gained the appreciation he deserved. But Révész also mentioned that Biss had the tendency to embellish his own contributions, sometimes attributing to himself successes for which he had no part whatsoever.[27]

After the war Biss left Hungary and moved to Switzerland.

[26]   Biss, 1973.

[27]   Révész, 2001, p. 149.

6. The Gap between Data and Knowledge

Warning Signs of the Holocaust in Hungary

Neither the public nor its leadership were aware of the risk of extermination hovering above the Hungarian Jews since Hungary joined the war alongside Germany.

There were early signs that could have alerted the local Jewish population in Hungary to the future awaiting them. Nevertheless, Hungarian anti-Semitism, which was reflected in the deportation of "alien" Jews in 1941, in the massacre in Delvidek in January 1942, and in various anti-Jewish laws, had not been fully comprehended and its implications ignored. The writing was on the wall, but it was difficult to accept it. Even Kasztner, an experienced politician, who knew in real time and in great detail what was happening in the German occupied territories, including the progress of the extermination process, expressed his confidence that the Hungarian Jews would be rescued in a letter to the delegation of the Jewish Agency in Istanbul on July 18, 1943.[1]

In 1920 the *Numerus Clausus* law restricted the number of Jews in universities in Hungary. In May 1938, 1939, and 1941 three stricter laws were enacted: The law of May 1938 restricted the number of Jews who could be employed in white-collar professions to twenty percent, The law of May 1939 further restricted the professional options of Jews, and the law of 1941

---

[1]   Strochlitz Institute for Holocaust Research at the University of Haifa and The Ghetto Fighters' House, *Archive of the Communication Bureau in Istanbul, Catalogue A: Guide to Hungary Files 1942–1944*, edited by Frida Lester, experimental catalogue, November 1957. The document itself has disappeared and is not included in later versions of the catalogue.

that prevented mixed marriages and segregated the Jews from the rest of the population.

In the summer of 1941, in parallel to the legislation of the third anti-Jewish law, the deportation of "alien" Jews took place. Nearly twenty thousand Jews were deported from Hungary and extradited to the Germans who actually did not want them at the time. At the end of August 1941, sixteen to eighteen thousand of the deportees were murdered by the Germans and their collaborators. The deportation of "alien" Jews was the most severe anti-Semitic step taken by the Hungarian government before Hungary was occupied by Germany. This might have been the cruelest anti-Semitic step taken by any sovereign government since the Middle Ages, except during Germany's Nazi regime.

All the facts related to the abovementioned events were known to the leadership of the Hungarian Jewry but this was not enough to alert them to the imminent risk.

The difficulty in understanding this reality was probably exacerbated by what seemed to be a slack in the Hungarian government's anti-Semitic fervor during 1943. However, the anti-Semitic fervor of the Hungarian population and government did not subside over time. It is their alignment with Germany that changed. The defeats of the German and Hungarian armies during 1942–1943 made it clear to the Hungarian government that Germany's victory in the war was not guaranteed and that it should look after its own interests. The authorities relaxed their attitude to the Jews, especially after the Stalingrad defeat at the end of 1942 and the obliteration of the Second Hungarian Army in the battle of Voronezh at the beginning of 1943. As a result, the conditions of the Jews slightly improved, but this status quo only remained in effect until March 1944, the time of Germany's invasion of Hungary.

What Did the Hungarian Jews Know?

It was difficult to grasp the occurrence of the Holocaust in real time. Those who were not there will never be able to fully understand and explain the behavior of those who lived, took action, or were involved in any way with those events.[2] The unprecedented scope of the Holocaust and its inconceivable cruelty had made it challenging for most of the people at that time to believe the highly unreasonable information provided to them. The fact that the Holocaust was prompted and perpetrated by the representatives of a country perceived as progressive and enlightened made it all the more problematic to accept the real state of things. Understanding this difficulty is key in comprehending the events and the actions taken at that time.

There is no doubt that the intended victims of the Holocaust were in a most precarious situation. The information they had was limited and perceived as unreliable and more importantly, unreasonable. Since most of them had no practical way to cope with the reality around them, the easy, available, and convenient solution was to repress and ignore the information. The leaders of the local Jewish communities did not make matters easier since they, like the general public, did not believe the information. When the situation worsened and people became disillusioned, the leaders could only recommend the public to be obedient and calm since they had no real solution to offer.

In her recorded interview with Yad Vashem, Hansi said that she had previously heard (probably from refugees from Yugoslavia, where specific anti-Semitic actions began back in 1941) about persecution and deportations. But only after she heard from her sister and brother-in-law about their experience, did she realize that the persecution and deportations were intended to systematically murder Jews. Similar conclusions were reached by some of the refugees, such as Josef Kornianski from Poland and some activists of the youth movements, such as Eli Shayo from Slovakia.[3] This realization is what triggered Joel and Hansi to take action to save Jews and help them survive, even at great personal risk.

---

[2]   Yehiel De-Nur ("Ka-Tsetnik 135633," born as Yehiel Feiner) in his testimony in the Eichmann's trail coined the expression "different planet" to describe the Holocaust persecutions.

[3]   Révész, 2001, p. 45.

During the first years of the war, until the German occupation, the Jews in Hungary continued to live in relative peace despite the war going on. Thousands of refugees arrived at that time in Hungary from the neighboring occupied states. In addition, hundreds of survivors from the deportation of "alien" Jews succeeded to come back with considerable information. The stories of the refugees from Germany, Austria, Czechoslovakia, and later from Poland, Yugoslavia, and Slovakia, were available to the Jewish public and its leadership in Hungary. Even prior to that, the stories of the Hungarian soldiers, and in particular the stories of the few Jewish soldiers among them, were available. These were not one or two survivors, but rather thousands spread all across Hungary. At that time, it was also possible to receive radio broadcasts from foreign networks and to obtain information from neutral countries. The Jewish leadership in Hungary and especially the ultra-Orthodox and Zionist groups maintained ongoing contact with the Bratislava Working Group[4] and knew of the attempts to stop the deportations there. They also had details of the "Europa Plan" (halting the extermination in exchange for two million dollars). In other words, they were not short on information about what was going on.

Despite the abundance of information, the leadership and the general Jewish public failed to grasp the severity of the situation. It was not a matter of knowing. It was a matter of "burying one's head in the sand." Most people opted to ignore the reality of the situation, as did the majority of the leadership. The secular Jewish leadership did not pay enough consideration to the fact that, since the end of World War I, the Hungarian government and the Hungarian population at large, started distinguishing "Jews" from "Hungarians." The secular (or neológ, Reform/Conservative) leadership considered itself first and foremost "Hungarian" and believed naively, and somewhat blindly, that the Hungarian government would treat it the same way. Some of the secular Jewish leaders even justified the first anti-

---

4   A group of Jewish activists in Bratislava (Slovakia) who tried to save the local Jews by bribing the Germans. Their attempt seemed successful at the time.

Jewish law explaining that it was not discriminating against the Jews but rather preventing over-representation (beyond their rate in the population) in universities and certain economic areas. The religious population with its particularly strong leadership also assumed the Hungarian national identity. Judaism, for them, was a religion with no national association. The religious stream could not foresee the danger due to their blind "in God we trust" attitude. The various Jewish factions, from secular to Orthodox, unanimously rejected the warnings that mainly originated from Zionist sources. They viewed the information about the extermination as exaggerated "Zionist propaganda" and, despite all the information about the authorities' strict attitude toward the Jews, they maintained their position that "this cannot happen here."

Kasztner's report also shows that at the end of 1941, the Jewish Hungarian leadership had reliable information regarding the systematic extermination of Jews in the occupied territories. In the report that Kasztner claimed to have delivered to Jewish public figures at the end of December 1941, he said:

> At that time, it was already clearly possible to follow the dangerous developments and systematic exterminations of Jews from Budapest. In the summer of 1941 information reached Budapest about mass murders in the Ukraine, in the Baltic States, in Bessarabia and in Bukovina. Hungarian messengers brought the first news about trucks equipped with gas chambers.[5] The extermination of the 22,000 Hungarian Jews who were deported to Poland was then already known, including all of its cruel details. Dr. Kasztner delivered a comprehensive report about all of these terrible events and said that we should take into account a loss of more than one million Jews.

According to Kasztner, the participants of the meeting treated the report with skepticism.[6]

---

[5]　According to Yad Vashem's publication, https://www.yadvashem.org/odot_pdf/Microsoft%20Word%20-%201731.pdf, the use of gas vans started in November 1941. Note that Kasztner already knew about it before the end of the year.

[6]　Kasztner's report, 1946, p. 4.

This report by Kasztner was written in Switzerland in 1946. Another earlier report, from the beginning of 1942, also confirmed that information about systematic extermination of Jews in German-occupied territories was indeed available. Bernard Jacobson, the JDC (the American Jewish Joint Distribution Committee or "The Joint," a worldwide relief organization) representative in Budapest who left Hungary after it had declared war on the United States in December 1941, said similar things although he was more conservative regarding the numbers he provided. According to him, by the time he left Hungary, the number of Jewish victims who were killed by the Gestapo in the Ukraine had already reached two hundred and fifty thousand. His estimates were published in Palestine in March 1942. Other publications from that time reported murders of thousands of Jews within a matter of days, creating a continuous Jewish-free territory.[7]

In light of these details, it is abundantly clear that the information about what was happening to the Jews in the German occupied territories was known to the leadership of all the Jewish factions in Budapest. The fact that no actions were taken did not derive from a shortage of information. Not only did the leadership know, but so did the general public—and still they refused to believe. There are ample examples of the population's mistrust of information about the extermination.

In his book *Night*, Elie Wiesel described very well the ability of the Hungarian Jews to be oblivious to the reality. "The deportees were quickly forgotten," referring to deportations of the "Alien" Jews in 1941. He further wrote about the attitude to the survivors' stories as: "people not only refused to believe his tales, they refused to listen."[8] And yet, only a few pages after these descriptions, Wiesel described his own arrival in Auschwitz: "We didn't know. Nobody had told us." This perception was not unique to Elie Wiesel: it reflected

---

[7]   Porat, 1986, pp. 46–47.

[8]   Wiesel, 2006, p. 7.

to a great extent the inability of the majority of the Jewish population in Hungary to grasp the reality and internalize the available details.[9]

Even as late as 1944, people could not accept the reality. Laszlo Devecseri, the husband of Joel's niece, who was in ongoing contact with Joel and Hansi which presumably should have exposed him to the facts, wrote in his memoirs:

> On February 23, 1944 a man rang the bell to our flat at 179 Vilma királynő Street in Budapest. He presented his papers. He was an engineer, a refugee from Poland. He told us what they were doing there to the Jews. After I listened to him, I told him: "My dear friend, you shouldn't have told me these horror stories. No one can believe that they happened. I will help you anyway as much as I can." I did not believe his story.[10]

In his book Peretz Révész described the attempt to inform the members of one of the labor service units in Hungary of the content of the Auschwitz Protocols:

> A typical reaction to this kind of information was found in the words of Dr. Nátán Sándor, the future Head of the Palestine Office in Hungary: "A Zionist friend, Dr. Lajos Goteszman, who was from the Betar Movement[11] in Košice, slipped into my hands a long, detailed report that spread over several pages, which was the first authentic document about extermination of Jews in Auschwitz and Birkenau. There was also an attached announcement the essence of which was: 'Read and know what is happening to your family', and it called on the Jews, and especially people of the 'labor service units' to exercise armed resistance. This was at the end of June [1944]. After I read it, I didn't sleep for two nights. . . . I could not keep this information

---

[9] According to Ronen, 2011, p. 397, Efra Teichman (Agmon), a member of the RSZ at the JPU, found out about the extermination for the first time only in January 1944. Teichman claimed that he knew nothing until then, although he had an uncle who survived the Kamianets-Podilskyi massacre.

[10] Laszlo Devecseri's memoires were never published, but there is a copy of his original dairy in Hungarian in Strochlitz Institute for Holocaust Research at the University of Haifa.

[11] A Jewish Zionist political party that opposed the socialist Zionist majority.

to myself. I consulted with Zionist friends [within the 'labor service unit'] and it was decided that I was to read the document before the entire unit. The reaction was terrible. . . . [I was called] 'Defeatist! Traitor! Vile!' They threatened to extradite me. This was no laughing matter. If it were not for some Zionist friends, I would have been beaten to death. One of the guys lashed at me with a big iron rod and my friends took it out of his hands. The entire unit was convinced that I was a provocateur and this is how they treated me."[12]

A similar story is relayed by Asher Cohen in his book as told by Hanna Ganz.[13]

These are just a few examples out of the many available testimonies. It is unquestionable that the Jewish leadership in Hungary as well as the Jewish public had information about the exterminations. However, as in other places, including Palestine and the rest of the free world, there was an unwillingness to accept the harsh reality and understand the implications of the information. A denial, if you will, as the reality was too horrific.

12   Révész, 2001, p. 166.

13   Cohen, 1984, p. 107.

Part II

HOLOCAUST

7. THE OCCUPATION

The occupation of Hungary by the Germans was a peculiar process. The Hungarian army fought on the east front against the Russians under German command, and at the same time, on Sunday, March 19, 1944, the German army entered Hungary and took over the country within a few hours without any significant resistance. The Germans occupied Hungary because they feared the Hungarians would desert their alliance and join the Allied forces. It was highly doubtful that the Hungarians wanted to fight against Germany. They estimated that joining the Allies would prevent Russia from occupying their country, which they feared much more than they feared its occupation by the Germans.

There was no attempt to keep the anticipated invasion secret. Yet, it surprised all the Hungarians, including the Jews. For Hungarian non-Jews, nearly nothing changed following the invasion: the government was replaced and ministers were substituted by others with views better aligned with the Nazis. For the Jews, however, it was a very meaningful change: the Hungarians assigned the responsibility for everything related to the Jews to the Germans. In addition, they appointed extreme anti-Semites to posts in the Ministry of the Interior that was in charge of the police and gendarmerie, with the intent to help the Germans to "solve the Jewish problem" in Hungary.

Despite the occupation, the Germans, in agreement with the Hungarians, maintained Hungary's image as a sovereign country. They leveraged the help and advice of SS officer Veesenmayer who later served as the Reich plenipotentiary[1] in Budapest. Regent

---

[1]   A plenipotentiary is a high-level diplomat whose status is similar to that of an ambassador and even more so. The German plenipotentiary was the highest-ranking German official in occupied Hungary.

Horthy remained the alleged head of state and the country continued to function nearly without change. The preservation of Hungary's image as a sovereign nation and the appointment of senior ministers and officers aligned with the German doctrine improved the cooperation between the two countries, especially with respect to the attitude toward the Jews. Even before the occupation, the army and economy in Hungary were harnessed to support the German war efforts. The German occupiers found Hungary a dedicated, motivated, and passionate partner to exterminate Hungarian Jews as quickly as possible.

There is no doubt that the Germans alone, given the limited human resources and means available to them, could not have identified the Jews, separated them from the general population, concentrated them in ghettos, and put them on the trains to the death camps. Preserving the independent image of Hungary and appointing anti-Semites to key positions in the extermination machine, especially in the Ministry of the Interior, allowed the Germans to harness all the Hungarian governmental branches to the mission of extermination. This included governmental offices, army, police, gendarmerie, and various local authorities. Even those would not have sufficed without the underlying anti-Semitic culture that had been consistently developed in Hungary since the end of World War I. This culture was so ingrained that the number of officials in the various administrative institutions who did not want to partake in the extermination of the Hungarian Jews was very small and played no part in halting the process.

The public perception of Hungary as a sovereign state gave the Hungarians—and especially Regent Horthy, who won great public respect—certain power to influence the course of events. They used this ability to intervene when the Germans were about to begin the extermination of the Jews of Budapest. This intervention came as a response to foreign pressure and threats, and it temporarily prevented the extermination of the Budapest Jewry. Unfortunately, for most of the Hungarian Jews it was too late.

At the beginning of 1944, word about an imminent invasion reached the Jews of Hungary, mostly from the sources of the Relief and Rescue Committee and the Jewish Pioneer Underground (JPU).

According to one of the activists, Menachem (Micky) Frank, "at the end of 1943, the likelihood of Germany taking over Hungary seemed to our friends, the refugees from Poland, real and close."[2] Frank further said that in January 1944 a joint meeting was held in preparation for a possible German invasion of Hungary. The meeting was attended by the representatives of the youth movements from Poland, Slovakia, Carpathian Rus (Micky Frank himself), and Hungary as well as the Rescue Committee representatives. An additional meeting was held in February in which it was said with certainty that the Germans would invade Budapest within a month. Frank adds in brackets: "With time the source of information was revealed—comrade Brand of the Relief and Rescue Committee."[3]

Peretz Révész included in his book a full detailed description of how, on March 16, 1944, in the presence of Révész himself, Joel received an explicit warning from the representative of the Abwehr (the German military intelligence service) in Budapest about an invasion in the "next few days."[4] Joel was warned to take his family out of Hotel Majestic[5] where they stayed, as the Gestapo was about to situate its headquarter in this hotel. The next day, March 17, this information was delivered to a forum of about fifty people (which is consistent with Frank's account, except for the date), but they did not take it very seriously. Joel too did not believe that the invasion was so imminent and did not take his family out of the hotel. Therefore, on the day of the invasion, they needed Biss's help and he was the one who got them out of the hotel.[6]

The warning Joel received from the Germans was not a gesture of humanitarian goodwill but rather a cold business calculation. For many months prior to the invasion, Joel was using his contacts in

---

2   Israel and Lazar, 1994, p. 154.

3   Ibid., p. 155.

4   Révész, 2001, p. 127.

5   This was a small hotel "Kis Majestic" (Small Majestic), next to a bigger Hotel named "Majestic," both of them on Karthauzi Street, in the Svábhegy district of Budapest.

6   Révész, 2001, pp. 127–129; Biss, 1973, p. 25.

the German military intelligence to help with smuggling people, letters, and forged personal documents, in exchange for money. These Germans were not too happy to let go of their secondary source of income and were therefore interested in protecting their Jewish contacts. At that time, it was already possible for the counter-espionage agents, Canaris's Abwehr, to predict that the Germans would not win the war. In addition to the bribe money that these Germans pocketed, they probably also tried to prepare a future alibi for themselves. They may have also known that someone in the upper echelons would wish to exploit the contacts of the Relief and Rescue Committee abroad, as indeed happened not long after the occupation.

Some historians mentioned Kasztner as the one who supposedly received the warning about Germany's imminent invasion from *Abwehr* messenger Winniger on March 14, 1944, five days before the invasion itself. This mistake originates from a misinterpretation of Kasztner's report. In this context, Kasztner used the German expression *teilte uns* that means "shared with us." The text refers to the information brought by Joel, but the wording allows, for those who wish to misrepresent the facts, to present this event as a personal achievement of Kasztner's.[7] The slight difference in the dates is meaningless, none of them had been documented in real time.

The invasion forces were accompanied by the SS including the "advisory" team on Jewish affairs, representatives of the secret service (SD), representative of the economic department, and SS combat divisions. The advisory team on Jewish affairs was headed by *Obersturmbannführer* (lieutenant Colonel) Adolf Eichmann together with his deputy Dieter Wisliceny and two of his senior assistants, Otto Hunsche and Hermann Krumey. The head of the SS secret service in Hungary was *Sturmbannführer* (Major) Otto Klages,[8]

---

[7] There is no independent confirmation to a warning Kasztner received.

[8] There are several versions of the spelling of his name. His real name was probably Gerhard Otto Clagges, but he always used Otto Klagges. Later, before his death, he was promoted to *Obersturmbannführer*.

the representative of the SS economic department in Hungary was Kurt Becher, an officer in Eichmann's rank.

Becher, who joined the negotiations between the Rescue Committee and Eichmann only after Joel had left for his mission, to promote the "Blood for Goods" deal,[9] was Kasztner's main contact with the Germans. On various occasions, Becher helped Kasztner and the Rescue Committee to save Jews.[10] Towards the end of the war, Becher was promoted by Himmler to a higher rank than that of Eichmann.[11] Becher's assistant, a captain by the name of Max Grüson, must have realized only in Hungary the intention of his government in regard to the "Final Solution" for the Jews. As of that moment, he did his best to help Jews. It is possible that his efforts cost him his life.

Klages, the head of the SS secret service in Hungary, was a far more tolerant person than most Nazis. Hansi mentioned him favorably as someone who occasionally helped in times of crisis. He was killed in the fascist revolution in Budapest in October 1944, during the abduction of Regent Horthy's son.[12] Klages and Max Grüson were the only two SS men who were killed or "disappeared" in Budapest during the war.[13] Both had a relatively positive attitude toward Jews—which was probably the reason for their deaths. It is unlikely that an experienced commando, such as Otto Skorzeny, who also freed Mussolini,[14] needed Klages's help in the abduction

See http://www.redcap70.net/A%20History%20of%20the%20SS%20Organisation%201924-1945.html/K/KLAGGES,%20Dr.%20Gehard%20Otto.htm.

9   See the chapter about the "Blood for Goods" deal later on.

10   This was at least the impression of some of the rescue committee members including Kasztner.

11   His positive attitude to the Jews toward the end of the war does not necessarily reflect his earlier activities in the SS.

12   Braham, 1994, p. 948.

13   See Eichmann's trial, Dr. Shlomo Yehuda Ernst Abeles's testimony, session 49 (the name Grüson is mentioned there as Gryson).

14   Mussolini, the fascist leader of Italy, was arrested by the Italians towards the end of the war when Italy withdrew from the war and the alliance with Germany.

of young Horthy. It is more likely that he was called to participate in this abduction attempt only to be "accidently" hurt.[15] This type of quiet elimination was probably a common method of operation for the Nazis. It was used, for instance, to get rid of *Generalfeldmarschall* (Field Marshal) Rommel.[16]

SS combat divisions, known as Waffen SS, were also present in Hungary. They were under the command of senior generals but did not participate in the extermination of Jews.

The German invaders were equipped with lists of names and addresses and immediately started arresting anti-Nazi politicians, public figures, and mainly Jews. The members of the Rescue Committee left their apartments and moved into Biss's office-flat. This is where Biss also brought Hansi and her two sons after having rescued them from the hotel in which Eichmann settled the following day with his headquarters. Joel was previously taken[17] by his Abwehr contacts and was led to the apartment of one of the Abwehr members (probably the apartment of the agent's girlfriend). This is how he survived the first days of the occupation. After a few days Joel left the hiding place and joined Hansi in Biss's apartment.[18] According to Joel, the Germans who hid him strongly suggested

---

[15]   According to Hansi, Klages "was executed in the midst of the war" (Brand, 1960, p. 47). According to the "redcap" website (above): "Himmler had told Clagges to keep his eyes on Eichmann a lot!".

[16]   Erwin Rommel, a decorated German army field marshal, was involved in the June 20, 1944 plot against Hitler. He was given a state funeral after he was forced to commit suicide.

[17]   Probably from a hidden place in Budapest, the address of which is mentioned in the British investigation report — 21 Apály Street.

[18]   The "hiding place" at 15 Andrassy Street is mentioned many times in the literature but no children are mentioned. In no place is it mentioned that Hansi's children stayed there. They may have been there for a few days or a few hours, but probably not for a long time. This was especially prominent in Hansi's descriptions of how the Hungarians invaded the apartment (twice) and took her and most of the other tenants, as she too does not mention her children at these stages. Therefore, it seemed that the children were removed beforehand to the care of the couple of Christians mentioned at the beginning of Brand, 1957, p. 35 (Weissberg, 1958, p. 39), Wilma and Gábor Biro, at 33 Francia Street.

that they "keep safe" the Rescue Committee's money for them, but he evaded this and entrusted them only with his own private money and valuables. Of course, they were never recovered. Kasztner writes in his report that together with Joel, the Germans took a suitcase with the Rescue Committee's money, including foreign currency. None of these statements has been corroborated by other independent sources. Kasztner does not mention any money he entrusted with the Germans but on page 16 of his report he admitted that he had entrusted the secret correspondence of the committee to German agents for their safekeeping. Without trying to determine which of the two was right about the money, it seems that this was of no real importance. If it was justified to entrust the Germans with secret correspondence, it would seem reasonable to entrust them with money.

8. Early Rescue Attempts in Budapest

Background

As we have already seen, information about the fate of Jews in German-occupied territories was not in shortage in Budapest in March 19 when the Germans invaded Hungary. There was no reason to believe the Germans' promises that the Jews would not be harmed if they followed orders and refrained from spreading horror rumors. The Germans' statement that from the time of the occupation they had full authority regarding the Jews in Hungary was supposed to alarm the Jews and increase their distrust in the German promises. In addition, according to Kasztner, a German agent informed him on the very day of the invasion that the fate awaiting the Hungarian Jews would be worse than that of the Jews in Poland.[1]

Uniquely, the Jewish leadership in Budapest had information about the seemingly successful rescue attempts in Bratislava, the outcome of the Warsaw Ghetto uprising, and detailed information regarding the extermination location and process. All of this, together with information about the situation at the front has affected the rescue attempts in Budapest.

The Front Line

Since the battle in Stalingrad in the winter of 1942 the Germans were in continuous retreat. During the summer of 1943 German forces suffered severe losses and were pushed back westwards hundreds of kilometers. In mid-March 1944 the Russians were already in the

---

[1] Kaszter's report, 1946, p. 16.

eastern part of Romania and not far from the Hungarian border. At that time, it must have been clear to those who were as well informed as the leadership of the Hungarian Jews that the war would not last forever and would not end with Germany's victory. In addition, the results of the Warsaw Ghetto uprising and the fate awaiting Jews in German occupied territories were known very well. Thus, it was clear that the Jewish rescue attempt must concentrate on delaying tactics.

The Bratislava Working Group

Most of those involved in the rescue efforts in Hungary were aware of the rescue efforts of the "Bratislava Working Group," which operated to rescue Jews in Slovakia and Europe as far back as 1942. Because rescue efforts in Hungary were heavily influenced by this information, it is crucial to know what happened in Slovakia and how those events were perceived in Hungary.

In the summer of 1942, after more than half the Slovakian Jews had been deported from the country and murdered, negotiations started between representatives of the Jewish community in Slovakia (the "Working Group" led by Rabbi Weissmandl and Gisi Fleischmann) and Eichmann's senior representative in Slovakia, Wisliceny. During these negotiations, fifty thousand dollars were paid to Wisliceny.[2] In exchange, he agreed to stop the deportations at the end of 1942. Deportations from Slovakia indeed halted until an uprising erupted in Slovakia against Germany in the summer of 1944 in which many Jews took part.

Nowadays, some researchers claim that the deportations were stopped following the demand of the President of Slovakia, Reverend Jozef Tiso, after he had been approached by the Vatican. The president (and probably the Vatican too) found out that the deportation was not for "resettlement" or work purposes but

---

2   It is likely that part of the money was taken by the Jewish mediator, Karol Hochberg, who represented the Working Group in the negotiations with Wisliceny.

for murder. This thinking, which was adopted by Kasztner,[3] is predominantly based on available documentation that mentions these demands. There is no documentation mentioning the impact of money. Most researchers ignored the fact that to maintain discretion and secrecy, all of the German understandings with the Jews were always made orally and never written down.[4]

It is difficult to establish with certainty to what degree the money contributed to stopping the deportations, but the chain of events undoubtedly indicate that it had some impact.[5] The deportations were stopped immediately after the first payment was received; they were renewed when the follow-up payment was not received; and they stopped again when the entire payment was made. Following the successful deal to stop the deportations from Slovakia, another deal, known as "Europa Plan" (Europe Plan) was discussed. The intent was to stop exterminations in most of Europe's territories in exchange for two million dollars. The Slovakian Jews failed to raise the required sum (they also had great difficulty raising the previous fifty thousand dollars) and the proposal failed. Most, but not all, of these details were familiar to the leaders of the Jewish community in Hungary as well as to the Rescue Committee, which was in touch with the Bratislava Working Group. Based on the details known at that time in Budapest, the Rescue Committee decided to try the Slovakian method also in Hungary. Given everything known to them, the Rescue Committee believed that it was the money that stopped the deportation. They were not aware of other factors that could have affected the decision. For example, the Rescue Committee did not know and could not have imagined that Reverend Tiso, Slovakia's Nazi anti-Semitic president, would demand the Germans

---

3   Kasztner used to attribute to himself every success and underrate the contribution of others. In this case he also served the interest of the leadership that made its mind in advance that rescue by Jews was impossible and hence successes should be attributed to foreign entities.

4   See, for example, Hadari, 1992, p. 134.

5   Bauer, *Yalkut Moreshet* no. 26, November 1978, p. 27: "It is unclear whether the cessation of the deportaions was the result of the bribe payment or was influenced by other factors."

to stop the extermination. Even today, it is impossible to know for sure what chain of events occurred and what the relative weight was of each of the factors that halted the deportations. What matters is that in real time it was reasonable to believe that money helped.[6]

The Auschwitz Protocols

The "Auschwitz Protocols" did not exist at the time of the German occupation of Hungary, but the real nature and purpose of Auschwitz, at least in general terms, was known in Budapest much earlier, and therefore they will be discussed here.

The Auschwitz Protocols, also known as the Vrba-Wetzler report, is a document composed by the first two Jews who escaped from Auschwitz. They managed to reach members of the Jewish Working Group in Slovakia to report on the real nature of this notorious camp. The report included a detailed description of the camp and the extermination process. It also included information about the scope of murder taking place in Auschwitz. However, it is not known what exactly was written in these protocols, who received them and when. Unfortunately, no copies of the original version exist, though various reconstruction attempts were made. The differences between the various reconstructed copies are substantial. According to some sources, the protocols included a detailed report of the Germans' preparations to receive eight hundred thousand Hungarian Jews in Auschwitz, in order to exterminate them. Similar things, without an explicit reference to the Auschwitz Protocols, are included in Kasztner's report.[7] Actually, Kasztner's report is almost word-for-word identical to certain versions of the protocol as it was reconstructed from memory by one of the original writers.[8]

---

6   Eichmann's trial, Dr. Shlomo Yehuda Ernst Abeles's testimony, session 49: "Our group saw from that that one could use money to work with the Germans, too."

7   Kaszter's report, 1946, p. 30.

8   It is impossible to rule out the possibility that the details have been copied from Kasztner's report to the reconstructed protocol and not vice versa.

Various versions of the protocols, translated into different languages, are available on the Internet, some referenced by the "The Vrba-Wetzler Report" entry on Wikipedia website.[9] An English version of the document claiming to be "the full text of the report" and taken from American governmental sources, does not mention the preparations to exterminate the Jews of Hungary or the number eight hundred thousand.[10] However, a Yad Vashem document, in Hebrew, establishes that the protocol included an explicit warning that "preparations are made to kill about 800,000 Hungarian Jews."[11]

According to Braham and Bauer, Kasztner may have received the report at the end of April 1944.[12] In the Hebrew version of this same book Prof. Bauer added that it was highly unlikely.[13] Other entities received the report during May of the same year. The leaders of the JPU hardly mentioned the report, so it is likely that they did not know of its existence, or alternatively, that its content was insignificant for them as it did not reveal anything new to them. Peretz Révész mentioned the protocols indirectly, but he did not explain his connection to these protocols.[14] The protocols were not mentioned in Sharet's report about his meeting with Joel during his mission[15], indicating that Joel, too, did not know of them or that their content did not add anything new to him. On page 3 of Sharet's report, attached as Appendix 1 to this book, Joel talked about six million Jewish victims until mid-May 1944, the time he left

---

[9]   http://he.wikipedia.org/wiki/%D7%93%D7%95%22%D7%97_%D7%95%D7% A8%D7%91%D7%94-%D7%94-%D7%95%D7%A6%D7%9C%D7%A8.

[10]   See the wording of the document published by http://www. HolocaustResearchProejct.org, based on the transcription of the original protocol by the American Department of Justice and War (Refugee Board Archives).

[11]   http://www.yadvashem.org/odot_pdf/Microsoft%20Word%20-%20406.pdf.

[12]   Braham, 1994, p. 827; Bauer, 1994 (the English version of *Jews for Sale*), p. 157.

[13]   Bauer, 2001 (the Hebrew version of Bauer's book *Jews for Sale*), p. 206.

[14]   Révész, 2001, pp. 164–167

[15]   The meeting took place in early June 1944 and Shret summarized it on June 11, 1944. The mission is discussed in the chapter about the "Blood for Goods" deal later on.

Budapest. Later on, on page 4, he explicitly talked about five years of extermination and about 12,000 deportees per day. The protocols were not mentioned in the report at all.

In his report, Kasztner wrote that the Rescue Committee—and specifically Kasztner himself—had testimonies documenting the Nazis' horrors, including specific reports on Auschwitz, Treblinka, Lemberg, and other places. Therefore, the Vrba-Wetzler report, written in April, was not expected to provide new details to the members of the Rescue Committee, especially if it did not include a specific reference to the preparations for the extermination of the Hungarian Jews.[16] As mentioned previously, the protocols published by American sources include no reference to Hungary. In a recent interview given by Braham and published in Hungary on October 9, 2017, he withdrew his accusations that the Jewish leadership concealed the content of the protocols from the public. He added that there was not a shred of evidence that Hungary was mentioned in the protocol.[17] Regardless of the exact content of the Vrba-Wetzler report, it could not have offered much new information to the Jewish leadership in Budapest. In addition, as previously mentioned, by the invasion date, March 19, 1944, a German official had already informed Kasztner that the fate awaiting the Hungarian Jews would be worse than that of the Jews of Poland.

Some researchers claim that the warning sent by the US government on June 27 to Hungary and the following massive air raid on Budapest on July 2 came in response to the Auschwitz protocols, but this is probably incorrect. The Auschwitz protocols focused on the German activities in Poland and it is unknown whether Hungary was mentioned in them.[18] The American warning was directed specifically to Hungary and not to Germany. Therefore, there is no way to explain a connection between the protocols and the raid on Budapest. Joel's report dealt specifically with the events in Hungary and thus, more likely to have initiated this result.

[16]   Kasztner's report, 1946, p. 16.

[17]   Népszava, October 9, 2017.

[18]   See the chapter about the Auschwitz Protocol later on in this book.

Time-wise, the protocols were sent by Krausz to Switzerland only on June 19, 1944 and disclosed there on June 23.[19] It is doubtful that they reached Washington in time to evoke such a decisive action. Joel's report reached Washington on June 6, and specifically the white house on June 8,[20] much earlier than the content of the protocols. Therefore, it makes more sense that Joel's report resulted in Washington's actions. Hirschman's report dated June 22, 1944 about his meeting with Joel, confirming earlier reports about Joel's mission may have helped persuade the authorities to respond in a prompt and decisive manner.[21]

Five Different Ways for Rescue

Immediately upon the German occupation of Hungary, the local Jewish leadership in Budapest and especially Zionist activists there began to look for ways for rescue. The armed resistance, which was the preferred way for the Zionist leadership in Palestine, was disqualified immediately. There were no basic conditions in Hungary that would allow armed resistance. The men were recruited into the labor service, there were no big forests to hide in, there was no sympathetic population, and, above all, the manpower that stood against the Jews in Hungary was greater than anywhere else. Contrary to the situation in most other places, in Hungary it was not a hated occupying army that organized the deportation of Jews for extermination. This task was undertaken by the Hungarian fascist government established after the occupation, which mobilized all the state mechanisms at its disposal for this cause, in particular the police and gendarmerie. Five rescue methods emerged under Hungary's special circumstances, and four Jewish entities pursued

---

[19]   Nedivi, 2014, pp. 189–192.

[20]   Erbelding, War Refugee Board, Day by Day, June 6, June 8 (http://www. rebeccaerbelding.com/).

[21]   See Supreme Court Judge Shimon Agrant's reasoned ruling on appeal of the District Court's ruling in the Kasztner case (Judgments, vol. 12, 1958, p. 2163).

them, with some coordination as well as disputes, to try to save Jews:

- Organizing the Jewish community, especially in Budapest, given the constraints and restrictions imposed by the Germans and Hungarians to avoid unnecessary loss of life. This was mainly done by the Jewish council.
- Mobilizing the support of the least extreme Anti-Semitic Hungarians who still had influence or power and especially the Regent to intervene in favor of the Jews—"the Hungarian line." This was mainly done by the Jewish Council and the Rescue Committee (specifically, Ottó Komoly).
- Mobilizing the support of neutral countries still represented in Hungary and international organizations such as the Vatican and the International Red Cross in favor of the Jews—"the international line." This was mainly done by Moshe (Miklos) Krausz and the Rescue Committee (specifically, Ottó Komoly).
- Convincing the Germans that extermination of the Jews is not in their best interest and that they may benefit more from keeping Jews alive—"the German line" or "the big line." This was mainly done by the Rescue Committee (specifically Joel and Hansi Brand, Kasztner, and Biss)
- Organizing non-violent passive resistance aimed at preserving Jews' lives, mainly by smuggling them into safer places outside Hungary and producing and distributing fake documents to the Jewish population to enable them to avoid the anti Jewish decrees—"self-rescue" or the "little line". This was done by the JPU (at that time headed by Revesz, Goldfarb and Friedl-Benshalom) with the support of the rescue committee.

All the mentioned ways were used, and each one helped to some extent. But even all together, they could not prevent this disaster and could only reduce it somewhat.

The Jewish Council: Judenrat

When the Germans invaded Hungary, their first two actions in regards to the Jews were to arrest those who were singled out in advance, and to demand the Jewish leadership to establish a "Jewish Council," Judenrat. The intent of the Judenrat was to serve the Germans as a channel to deliver their messages and demands to the Jewish general public. The tasks of the Jewish Council members were neither simple nor pleasant. Essentially, the Germans used them as a form of self-enforcing intermediary to control the Jewish population, as they had done in many other communities in occupied areas. This format of self-enforcement intermediary was part of the Nazis' overall method and served them, among other things, to arrange and accelerate the extermination. The prevention of such process was certainly not within the power of the Council.

As early as the first day of the occupation, Eichmann's representatives appeared at the offices of the Jewish community in Budapest demanding to summon its leadership at 10 am the following morning, March 20, 1944.[22] At the meeting, the Germans clarified that as of that moment, the handling of all Jewish matters was assigned to them. This message was supposed to evoke fear that contrary to the Jewish leadership's expectations, the Hungarian government would no longer ensure their safety. For some reason, however, such concern had not been expressed and there is no evidence that such possibility had been considered. The Nazis' clear message that they now handled all Jewish matters in Hungary could not undermine the Jews' belief in the Hungarian government. The Jewish leadership and the public continued to believe that the Hungarian leadership, and in particular Regent Horthy, would not allow the Germans to deport or exterminate them, as was done in other places in Europe.

Immediately after the Jewish Council was established, the Germans demanded that a reassuring message would be conveyed to the Jewish population throughout Hungary. The message articulated that the Jews would not be harmed provided that they

---

[22]   Braham, 1994, p. 447.

strictly obey instructions and refrain from spreading horrible rumors. This document was distributed by the Judenrat, which consisted of the most senior Jewish leaders in Hungary. It put the population at ease. Specifically, it cemented the public mistrust in the information disseminated by other sources, namely the Zionists. There is no documentation showing that the Jewish Council made any attempt to warn the public about the exterminations, even after they realized that the Germans were indeed sending Jews to be slaughtered. To be fair, there is no proof that such messages were not sent or that there were no attempts to send such messages.

According to Kasztner, on March 20, 1944, when the Germans convened the Hungarian Jewish leadership, he was already aware that the fate awaiting the Hungarian Jews would be worse than that of the Jews in Poland.[23] Yet, there is no reference that this message was forwarded to the Jewish leadership before or shortly after the meeting.

The Jewish Council did not warn the public, but its members did their best to help in many other areas. They did their best to mobilize Hungarian officials, and especially the Regent Horthy, to prevent the deportation of Jews, and did everything in their power to organize community life so as to avoid unnecessary deaths. In one case they were able to prevent the deportation of a group of Jews by approaching the Hungarian government, but this success was short-lived.[24] Eichmann deported the group anyway some time afterwards—he blocked the communication channels between the Jewish Council and the Hungarian authorities by inviting them to a very long meeting in his office.

The Jewish Council painstakingly identified and allocated housing solutions within the area of houses allocated to Jews, both before and after the Jews were confined to the ghetto. This was not an easy task given that the living space allocated to the Jews was considerably smaller than the minimum required to live a reasonable life. The Council also operated hospitals and helped

---

23   Kasztner's report, 1946, p. 16.

24   Braham, 1994, p. 891, the Kistarcsa detention camp incident.

those in need. But all that was insufficient to narrow the dimension of the Holocaust for the Hungarian Jewry.

After four and a half years of war, after detailed reports of the extermination in Slovakia and the vast knowledge accumulated from Polish and other refugees, and after the deportations of summer 1941, it is hard to imagine that the Jewish leadership had no idea about the Germans' plans for the Jews. It is therefore puzzling why the Jewish leadership did not warn the Hungarian Jews and the periphery Jews in particular that the anti-Jewish steps taken by the Germans might be in preparation for extermination. Regardless, there is no certainty that warning the periphery Jews would have contributed to their rescue whatsoever. The overwhelming Hungarian power and the collaboration of the general Hungarian population prevented any large-scale rescues. And it is doubtful that general panic would have helped.

The Palestine Office

Moshe Krausz, Head of the Palestine Office in Budapest, played a significant role in the rescue attempts in Hungary. He was not liked by the Zionist *halutzim* but helped many of them both before and after the German occupation. Krausz provided refugee *halutzim*, who stayed in Hungary illegally in the pre-occupation period, legal documentation affirming their candidacy to immigrate to Palestine. These documents provided a certain legal status which helped with issues such as financial support from the local community. After the occupation, Krausz focused with considerable success on attempts to influence representatives of neutral countries to help Jews. His most important and best-known contribution was his partnership with Switzerland's vice consul, Carl Lutz, to secure seventy-six buildings as Swiss exterritorial holdings that functioned as safe houses. In particular, more than two and a half thousand people survived the autumn of 1944 and the winter of 1944–1945 in Arthur Weiss's[25] old

---

[25]   Arthur Weiss, the owner of the building.

glass plant, the "Glass House," which he put at Krausz's disposal to serve as a refuge for Jews at risk under Swiss protection.

The JPU (Jewish Pioneer Underground)

The political weight of the Zionist entities, including the JPU, until the occupation, was negligible but they became significant afterwards. Their first tasks, immediately after the occupation were to warn their colleagues and the public from the consequences of the occupation and to produce and disseminate fake documents.

All traditional communication channels in Hungary after the occupation were either blocked or censored, and personal mobility of Jews was extremely limited and dangerous. In this situation the JPU sent messengers, mainly young women, to warn their colleagues in the Hungarian periphery.

The emissaries were sent mainly to known Zionists for fear that others would treat them with suspicion and might even regard them as provocateurs because of the negative image of the Zionists in the eyes of the general Jewish population who considered themselves Hungarian.

In one of his lectures, Prof. Yehuda Bauer said that the JPU, in conjunction with the Rescue Committee, sent seventeen representatives to warn the periphery Jews (others claim that 150–200 representatives were sent).[26] The involvement of the committee was imperative because it was the only possible source of financing. It is possible that some of the people who received the warnings did not believe what they heard, but a considerable portion of the recipients kept the information to themselves: following the Holocaust, the recipients who survived conveniently lost all recollection of the facts. David Shin, for instance, denied having been warned but conspicuously escaped without informing others.[27]

---

[26] Kashti, 2014, p. 47.

[27] See, for example, Dinur, 1987, p. 156.

The other urgent mission of the JPU was the production of fake documents. Until the occupation, only refugees staying in Hungary illegally needed fake documents. After the occupation, there was an urgent need to equip the entire population with fake documents in order to help people to avoid, as far as possible, the anti-Jewish decrees that were imposed on them. The JPU document forgery factory was one of the great successes that helped save many lives.

In addition, following the occupation, the JPU enhanced the *tiyul* operations, but this time in the opposite direction, out of Hungary.

The Rescue Committee

After the occupation, the Rescue Committee continued all its pre-occupation activities including the *tiyul*.[28] They helped the JPU with financing and providing resources for the purpose of disseminating information and border crossing. This time, unlike in the past, the aim was to smuggle Jews out of Hungary. In addition, Ottó Komoly (head of the Rescue Committee) and Kasztner tried to enlist moderate political entities in Hungary to intervene in favor of the Jews, but mostly in vain. A few months later Komoly's efforts to save Jews gained two significant achievements, one in the "Hungarian line" and the other in the "international line," which will be discussed later.

The path that quickly became the main course of the Rescue Committee action, was direct dialog with the Nazis. This time directly with the SS instead of the more moderate people of the Abwehr. The intention was to mirror the attempts of Rabbi Weissmandl and Gisi Fleischmann from Slovakia to bribe German officials in an effort to prevent the extermination of Hungarian Jews. This operation was led by Joel and Kasztner. The idea was to make contact with the entities controlling the fate of the Hungarian Jews, namely the Germans, and specifically Wisliceny.[29] The first meeting with

---

[28] At that point, Kasztner attributed it to Menachem Klein and forgot Joel. Kasztner's report, 1946, p. 22.

[29] Eichmann's deputy who was known from his contacts in Bratislava.

Wisliceny was probably coordinated by Joel through his contacts at the Abwehr but he did not mention this explicitly in his book. Kasztner and Joel attended this meeting with Wisliceny which was held on April 5, 1944, about three weeks after the invasion. It was followed by additional meetings with other SS representatives, mainly Hermann Krumey.

The talks with the Germans focused on attempts to prevent the segregation of the Jews from the general population, gathering Jews into ghettos, deporting Jews out of Hungary, and murdering them in the extermination camps. Already at the first meeting Joel and Kasztner had with the SS representative Wisliceny, the request was made to renew the negotiations that began in Bratislava on the "Europa Plan." An additional request was made that the Germans demonstrate goodwill by the release of six hundred Jews who had (at least allegedly) legal immigration certificates and could be sent to Palestine on a ship that was at the disposal of the Jewish Agency in Romania at the time. Wisliceny did not respond directly at the meeting but clarified that the Germans were not interested in the immigration of individuals but rather in that of at least a hundred thousand people. At that meeting he also set the price of two million dollars for these hundred thousand people and demanded that an advance of two hundred thousand dollars (six and a half million pengő) be paid at once.[30] The price that Wisliceny demanded was ten times as much as the price requested about a year earlier in Bratislava, where the two million dollars were the price for one million Jews. Despite the high price, the advance was paid, but because the Germans, and specificity Becher, raised the price it was enough only to pay for the release of the train passengers. This train, which is called the "Kasztner train" or the "train of the privileged," saved about 1700 Jews from Hungary. It will be discussed later on.

The fact that the "Europa Plan" (stopping the extermination in exchange for two million dollars), which was conceived in Bratislava in 1943, was brought up again in Budapest one year later, reinforced the impression that money was an important

[30] Kasztner's report, 1946, p. 25.

consideration and that these negotiations had senior level support. The negotiations involved several German representatives, not just a single person, which further reinforced the impression that they were sanctioned by the German administration. It was clear that this was not a personal bribe to the directly involved negotiators since Eichmann and his entire staff were aware of it. It soon became clear that the Germans demanded military-type goods (trucks) and promised advances in the form of shipments of Jews to freedom[31]. These clearly indicated that this was not a personal initiative of low-level officials but rather it had the support of senior executives such as Himmler. The similarities to the negotiations in Bratislava and the number of people involved instilled the belief that there was a real potential for saving Jews and that money was essential to the plan's success.

Internal conversation within the Rescue Committee brought up a difficult question: which place would be willing and able to absorb such a large number of Jews (one hundred thousand)? According to Joel, this issue was seriously discussed in Budapest since this was the weak point in any negotiation to save a large number of Jews. It was clear that even if all the immigration certificates allocated by the British were to be given to Hungary, the amount would have been insufficient.[32]

---

[31]   First the release of Jews, then the supply of goods and so on.

[32]   Brand, 1957, p. 67 (Weissberg, 1958, p. 80).

9. The Negotiations with Eichmann: The "Blood for Goods" Deal

Joel and Kasztner had several more meetings with officers from Eichmann's headquarters. At some point in April, Joel was summoned to a meeting with Adolf Eichmann, the Germans' senior representative for Jewish affairs in Hungary. The instruction was received through one of the German counter-espionage (Abwehr) people, Winniger, with whom Joel had contact prior to the invasion. It was received with one hour's notice, which limited Joel's ability to consult and coordinate with other members of the Rescue Committee. Joel said that before the meeting he was able to talk on the phone with Kasztner, Komoly and Hansi, and got the approval and blessings of all of them. Different sources indicated different dates for this meeting. In Joel's investigation by the British in 1944, the date April 16, 1944 was mentioned. Joel's book, published in 1957, identified April 25, 1944 as the date of the meeting.

Joel was the natural choice for the Germans. The Abwehr's people knew Joel and worked with him for a long time. They knew he had contacts with the outside world. They hardly knew Kasztner, who was by far less active and less involved in rescue operations until that time and they probably knew nothing at all about other members of the Rescue Committee. In fact, Eichmann told Joel that he had checked on him before summoning him.[1] There is no doubt that Joel's importance to the Germans at that time was much greater than that of Kasztner's. This is why he was warned about the imminent invasion and was hidden by the German military counter-espionage to avoid the first wave of arrests on

---

[1]   Ibid., p. 79 (Weissberg, 1958, p. 91).

the occupation day. In the first meeting of Kasztner and Joel with Wisliceny, Wisliceny thought that Kasztner was Joel's secretary, and Kasztner must have been greatly offended by this.[2] From the Germans' perspective, Kasztner was a poor candidate to negotiate with, for many reasons, mainly because of his political ties with the Hungarian establishment. After all, the Germans wanted to conceal the negotiations from the Hungarians.[3] Moreover, at that time Kasztner did not have children who could be held hostages while the messenger was sent abroad.[4] Bandi Grosz, a converted Jew who probably served as a double agent for the Germans and the Jews, must have had considerable influence on choosing the envoy.[5] But the key to selecting Joel was the support of the Germans with whom he had contact for a long time, well before the invasion.

Joel was not only the Germans' choice; he was the choice of the Jews as well. When the Rescue Committee of the Jewish Agency in Jerusalem needed someone trustworthy to supervise Krausz's activity in the Palestine Office in Budapest, to ensure that the distribution of immigration certificates to Palestine was fair, Joel Brand was chosen, not Kasztner. Joel was the most accepted and respected man by the halutzim in Hungary at that time. Most of them did not trust Kasztner at all. Kasztner was livid that the Germans (and the Jews) did not choose him or his father-in-law, Joseph Fisher, to conduct the negotiations with the representatives of the Jewish Agency in Turkey and later he even claimed that he was "excluded [by Joel] from the talks."

Joel's meetings with Eichmann were described in the British investigation report from 1944,[6] in Moshe Sharet's report of his

---

[2]   Brand, 1960, p. 33.

[3]   Kasztner himself mentioned his contacts with a Lieutenant-Colonel at the Hungarian army, József Garzoly. Kasztner's report, 1946, p. 20.

[4]   Barlas, 1974, p. 114.

[5]   According to Hansi, Grosz initiated the negotiations and persuaded the Germans that the Rescue Committee could be used as a channel for negotiations with the West (Brand, 1960, p. 40).

[6]   Joel Brand files in the British Intelligence, 1944.

meeting with Joel,[7] in Joel's book (1957), and in his testimonies in Israel during the Kasztner and Eichmann trials. The descriptions in all sources are quite similar, with small differences in dates, in the number of Jews that the Germans were supposed to release under the proposed deal as a "prepayment," and other minor details. According to Joel, he was concerned that exposing to the British the large number of Jews the Germans were willing to release as a prepayment would intensify their opposition to the entire rescue attempt. These concerns were well founded in light of Britain's immigration policy or, to be precise, the lack thereof. It is possible that hiding from the British the information about the size of the advance offered by the Germans was already decided in Istanbul immediately upon Joel's arrival there. Support for this opinion is in the discrepancy between the information provided by Wenja Pomeranz (the envoy sent from Istanbul to update the Jerusalem leadership) to the leadership, and the information provided by the leadership (Sharet and Ben-Gurion) the next day to the British High Commissioner in Jerusalem. Wenja Pomeranz reported to the agency's management of a down payment of 10,000,[8] while in the report of the High Commissioner it was 5,000 to 10,000.[9] The reason for the other minor differences was the difficulty to remember accurately the details that were perceived unimportant at the time.

In his book, Joel mentioned a proposal to release one million Jews,[10] but not all the Jews in German occupied territories, in exchange for ten thousand winter-adjusted trucks[11] (for the eastern

---

[7]   The report is included in the appendices to the protocols of Eichmann trial published by the Ministry of Justice. A copy is included here as Appendix 1 (t\1176). See also Porat and Weitz, 2002, pp. 265–278.

[8]   Porat and Weitz, 2002, p. 259.

[9]   WRB_1435, p. 119. Barlas, 1975 (Hebrew translation of the same report), pp. 115–116.

[10]   Brand, 1957, p. 77 (Weissberg, 1958, p. 91).

[11]   Some other goods were also mentioned, but by far less significant.

front). The "conversion rate" was one truck for every one hundred Jews.[12] Consequently Eichmann said[13]:

> When you return from Istanbul and inform me that the proposal was accepted, I will blow up Auschwitz and send to the border ten percent out of the promised million. You will get these one hundred thousand Jews and then you will give us trucks and this is how the business will proceed step by step. For every one thousand trucks—a hundred thousand Jews, and this is a cheap price to pay.

This proposal is known in the literature as the "Blood for Goods" deal.

In his interrogation during his trial in Jerusalem, Eichmann confirmed the details of the deal, including the release of one million Jews and the method of advances described in Joel's book. Eichmann did not confirm in his trial that he had promised to blow up Auschwitz.[14]

According to Kasztner's report, on the day Joel met Eichmann, Kasztner also met Wisliceny in the afternoon.[15] By that time, Kasztner had already been updated on the details of Joel's conversation with Eichmann and was familiar with the entire picture. Kasztner claimed that Joel's meeting with Eichmann was held on May 8 and that this was not their first meeting. Kasztner later wrote that on May 10, 1944 he was arrested by the Germans for the suspicion that he was leaking to the Hungarians details about the negotiations for "selling" Jews. According to him, his arrest was initiated by Grosz in order to ensure that Grosz, rather than Kasztner, would accompany Joel on his trip. This opinion might have sounded reasonable in 1946 when Kasztner wrote his report. Today, more than seventy years later, it is entirely clear that as far as the Germans were concerned, Grosz's

---

[12]   Brand, 1957, p. 86 (Weissberg, 1958, p. 104).

[13]   According to Friedlaender, 2010, p. 582 (and other sources), Hitler was aware of the negotiations and approved them to a certain degree.

[14]   Eichmann's trial, session 105, p. 1531 in the Hebrew transcript.

[15]   Kasztner's report, 1946, p. 34.

mission was separate, independent, and probably more important than Joel's mission. Actually, they may have used Joel's mission only as a cover for Grosz's mission. Given this, Kasztner could not have joined Joel instead of Grosz. Kasztner probably wanted to go instead of Joel, but found it difficult to be upfront about it.[16]

On May 17, parallel to the beginning of the deportation of Hungarian Jews for extermination, Joel and Grosz set off on their way to their mission. They were taken by car to Vienna, and from there, on an official German plane, to Istanbul, where they arrived on Friday, May 19, 1944 at dusk.

[16]   Ibid.

10. The Destruction of the Hungarian Jewry

The Preparations

In parallel to the discussions on selling the Hungarian Jews in the framework of the "Blood for Goods" deal, the Germans, with Hungarians support, rushed with the preparation to destroy the entire Jewish population of Hungary. Preparations for the destruction of Hungarian Jewry were carried out at unprecedented speed. This speed was made possible by several factors unique to Hungary, specifically:

- the intense anti-Semitic propaganda that had been going on in Hungary since the end of World War I;
- the fact that the activity was carried out entirely by the Hungarian (allegedly sovereign) government, which received considerable public support, and not by an external occupier;
- the fact that the deportation of the Jews from the state was supported by a large portion of the general public and by government officials (according to Braham, the effect of the few Hungarian officials who refrained from supporting the deportations was insignificant and did not delay the process whatsoever);
- the infrastructure prepared in Hungary for previous attempts to deport Jews from the country since 1941.

Immediately on the first day after the occupation, the Jews were required to form a "Jewish Council" (Judenrat). On the same day, restrictions on withdrawing money from the banks were imposed and the Jews' access to safes held by them in the banks was blocked. The separation of the Jews from the general public and their marking with a yellow badge was enforced as early as April 5, 1944. Towards the end of April, Jews were required to submit a detailed report on all their property and belongings, and at the same time, restrictions on cash withdrawals by Jews were also tightened. In addition to all of the above, in order to prevent Jews from transferring property to Hungarian friends, the Hungarians issued a regulation eliminating the validity of any transaction of transferring property carried out by Jews since the day of occupation. This effectively completed the legislation that allowed Hungarians to deprive Hungarian Jews of all their property.[1]

The Hungarians were not content with dispossessing the Jews of their property. As part of their efforts to harm Jews in every way possible, they also limited, from the end of April, the food allowances earmarked for the Jewish population within the rationing that existed in Hungary at that time to a level that was far lower than its general population entitlement.

To make matters worse, Hungarians restricted the time allowed for Jews to be on the streets for shopping and errands to two hours, thus making it very difficult for Jews to purchase even the small amount of food they were allocated

With all this done, at the end of April the preparation for the destruction of the Hungarian Jewry had been completed.

Liquidation of the Periphery Jews

The concentration of Jews in ghettos started on April 16, 1944, less than a month after the occupation, and two weeks before the publication of the regulations that legalized this action (April 28, 1944).[2] This process began in north-east Hungary, continued at the beginning of May in north Transylvania (south-east of Hungary), and spread within two months to all parts of the country except for the capital, Budapest.

---

1 Braham, 1994, pp. 543–549.

2 Braham, 1994, p. 590.

It started in the areas that were close to the military front with the Soviet Union. The steps taken were justified by the military's need to remove Jews from the front line, as Jewish loyalty to the state was questionable. This pretext seemed reasonable to the Jews. It continued to mislead them with regards to the extermination plans that were coordinated between the Hungarians and the Germans. This pretext was used also by the Hungarians to justify the removal of the Jews from their homes and their concentration in ghettos even before the legal framework for this action was published by the authorities.

The Hungarian Jews were in the ghettos for a relatively short time, mostly between a few days and a few weeks. This stage was short and quick but exceptionally cruel. The herding of the Jews into ghettos was done violently by large forces of the Hungarian police, the gendarmerie, and the local Hungarian authorities, nearly without any German interference. The ghettos were unfit for human habitation, many of them without any appropriate sanitation facilities and without drinking water or food. While the Jews were in the ghettos, they experienced cruel investigations and brutal body searches by the Hungarians. The Hungarians robbed them of all valuables they had, allegedly in order to transfer them to the State treasury, but more likely, for personal use.

All the ghettos in Hungary, except for the one in Budapest, were merely short transit stations on the way to extermination in Auschwitz. During May and June 1944 approximately four hundred and forty thousand Hungarian Jews, nearly the entire Jewish population outside of Budapest, were sent to the gas chambers. Hungarian forces identified the Jews, gathered them in ghettos, and loaded them onto deportation trains. At that time, the Germans in Hungary had no means to execute a deportation at such scale and speed — about half a million Jews within two and a half months. The Germans harnessed the Hungarians' enthusiasm to get rid of the Jews in any way possible, including systematic murder. The Hungarians were motivated by ongoing anti-Semitic incitement bolstered by their desire to confiscate the property of deportees and victims. While the Germans had applied great pressure on the Hungarian government to deport the Jews for a long time, Hungary refused to do so up until the occupation. Only the fascist government that was appointed after the occupation, and in particular the Ministry of the Interior and its internal security forces, did it with considerable passion, while the Germans merely served as consultants. The fact that the deportation was done by the Hungarians themselves made it particularly difficult to evade or resist since it was perceived "lawful," with great public support, and not by a foreign conqueror as was the case in most of Europe.

The Fate of Budapest Jewry

The initial intention of the Hungarian and German authorities was to treat the Budapest Jews as they did elsewhere in Hungary. This included their concentration in ghettos. This intention was not carried out immediately because of disagreements among Hungarian authorities regarding a specific plan and the involvement of some Hungarians with goodwill who helped to delay this process. The other anti-Jewish decrees (except for their concentration in a ghetto or ghettos) were implemented in Budapest as elsewhere in Hungary, including marking Jews with the yellow badge.

The evacuation of the Jews of Budapest from their apartments began in the second half of June 1944, about three weeks before their scheduled deportation. Unlike other places, a single central ghetto or several large ghettos were not built in Budapest. Instead, nearly two thousand buildings were marked as "Jewish houses" and all the Jews were ordered to move in and crowd in them. The "Jewish houses" were spread over Budapest residential areas in order to deter the Allies from bombing the city.

Since the deportation of Budapest Jews was prevented in early July 1944 following the order of Horthy to cease the deportations, the situation of Budapest Jews who were concentrated in Jewish homes remained stable until mid-October, when the extreme Hungarian fascists seized power in the country and Horthy was removed from office.

At that time, the real disaster of the Budapest Jewry started. Many were murdered by the Hungarian fascists on the streets and on the Danube banks, many starved to death in the ghetto because of the insufficient food allocated to Jews (less than half the calories allocated to prisoners), and many more lost their lives in the death marches, purportedly on their way to forced labor in Germany, but in reality subjected to a ghastly brutal means of extermination.

It was only in the second half of November 1944, about one month after the fascists had taken over the country and after Horthy was removed from power, that Hungary decided to build a big ghetto for the Budapest Jews instead of the Jewish houses scattered across the city. The evacuation of the "Jewish houses" took place over the last days of November and was completed by December 2. At that stage, the city was already under the Soviets' siege, and the Jews suffered from it like the rest of the population. In addition, they also suffered from a series of decrees imposed by the fascist government and harassments from its unrestrained supporters who rampaged through the city and murdered Jews without any provocation or reason, and certainly without any consequences.

11. RESCUE ACTIVITIES IN BUDAPEST AFTER JOEL LEFT FOR HIS MISSION

Continued Negotiations with Eichmann

On Eichmann's demand, Hansi joined the last meeting with him before Joel left on his mission. In that meeting, Eichmann instructed Hansi to report daily on the progress of Joel's mission. He emphasized that she and the children were to stay in Budapest as hostages to ensure Joel's return.[1] She was briefed about the details of Joel's mission and was warned not to expose them since the Germans regarded this mission a state secret.

After Joel's departure, Hansi came alone to the first meetings with Eichmann, but after a short while she decided to bring Kasztner with her. She believed Kasztner would do a better job negotiating with Eichmann than she or other candidates could.[2] In his report Kasztner wrote: "After Brand and Grosz's departure, I reported to Eichmann together with Hansi Brand."[3] He skimped on the details of the first meeting and jumped directly to report on the second meeting: "On May 22 [five days after Joel's departure], Eichmann

---

1   Eichmann's trial, session 58, p. 874 in the Hebrew transcipt.

2   In her opinion, Komoly did not possess the right traits to hold such talks with a murderer; this included, among other things, the ability to pretend, to make a false representation, and to lie. As for herself, Hansi thought it was best if a woman would not officially conduct such negotiations. It is important to remember that this happened before Hansi gained the Germans' appreciation for enduring the Hungarians' interrogation.

3   Kasztner's report, 1946, p. 38.

confirmed, in a second discussion, the immigration permit to the group of 600 people."[4]

Kasztner's negotiating skills were not apparent in his first meeting with Eichmann. They came into play only in follow-up meetings, after Hansi had coached him. According to Hansi's testimony (which is also corroborated by other sources), she convinced Kasztner to act like an equal party to a commercial negotiation and not as a victim fearing his predator. Kasztner was a heavy smoker and had troubles controlling his habit. Hansi equipped him with Joel's golden cigarette case and suggested that he should not wait for an invitation or ask for permission, but simply use the opportunity when Eichmann lights a cigarette to do the same. The results were impressive—according to the way the negotiations were conducted, and according to Eichmann's later testimony. Kasztner embraced the role and, indeed, acted as a negotiating partner who had something to sell and wanted something in return. In reality, of course, he had absolutely nothing to offer.

In his report, Kasztner covered the dialog with the Germans after Joel's departure in a chapter titled "Negotiations in Budapest on a New Basis."[5] Regardless of the implications of such title, the negotiations were a direct continuation of the talks Eichmann previously had with Joel. At the highest level, they continued to talk about preservation of the Jewish community and evacuation of Jews out of the Reich's territories—the same topics Joel discussed with Eichmann, and the same topics Joel and Kasztner discussed with Eichmann's representatives, Wisliceny and Krumey. Nevertheless, Kasztner may have had little hope for a large deal for releasing many thousands of Jews in exchange for trucks, but he saw the opportunity to rescue small groups as part of the advances promised by Eichmann. As such, his "new basis" was to refocus on the little that was easier to achieve instead of trying to progress the

---

[4]   Kasztner's report, 1946, p. 39.

[5]   Kasztner's report, 1946, p. 38.

larger deal that may have saved more Jews but had lesser chance.[6] Specifically, Kasztner focused right away on the relatively small group of immigration certificate holders which included his family and friends. These were the privileged who were supposed to depart by boat but eventually departed by the train that took them to Switzerland through Germany.

As a reminder, the Germans' intention to exterminate the Hungarian Jews was known to the local leadership and to the Rescue Committee, and in particular to Kasztner.[7] Nevertheless, the official leadership—the Jewish Council (Judenrat)—made no attempt to warn the periphery Jews (or the Jews of Budapest) of the dangers ahead. It is possible that in the first days of the invasion the Jewish leadership still believed the Germans' promise that nothing would happen to them if they complied with instructions. At the end of May there was no justification to believe that any more. Regardless of the leadership's behavior, it is likely that attempts to warn the Jewish population or even to call for resistance would not have changed the fate of the periphery Jews and might have possibly worsened the conditions of the Jews in Budapest. The hostility of the Hungarian authorities and the incited public against the Jews was too widespread to expect anyone to help. The Hungarian forces who were gathering and deporting the Jews were too large to leave the Jewish population any real chance of resisting them. And Jewish men who were fit to resist were already taken to labor service, leaving behind only women, children, and the elderly.

The dialog with the Germans did not stop other rescue attempts or aid activities, such as forging documents and transferring information, including warnings, to the periphery Jews and from them to Budapest. The members of the Rescue Committee were intelligent enough to realize that the chances of Joel's mission to fully succeed were minimal. Therefore, it was reasonable for them to attempt to delay the extermination and try to exploit smaller-

6   Mainly due to the adamant objection of the British who did not want Jewish refugees flooding Palestine.

7   Kasztner's report, 1946, p. 16.

scale rescue opportunities while the Germans still believed in the possibility of the "Blood for Goods" deal, and they expected the rescue delegation in Istanbul to behave in the same way. They obviously did not expect total disregard and dysfunction on the part of the representatives of the Jewish Agency in Istanbul and the JDC. At a minimum, they expected these organizations to pretend to be interested in Jewish lives, thus at least engage in a dialog and progress the negotiations. It is likely that they did not really expect the supply of trucks. With this mindset, the two main rescue activities in which the Rescue Committee engaged right after Joel's departure were "Jews on Ice" and "the train of the privileged."

Strasshof or "Jews on Ice"

Eichmann did not commit to pause the deportations until Joel's return. He did promise that the deportees would be sent to "Austria or some other place." This promise was given prior to Eichmann's first meeting with Kasztner.[8] Regardless of the promise, the deportees were sent to Auschwitz and their fate was known in Budapest. Already at a very early stage, Hansi and Kasztner pointed out to Eichmann that he would not be able to fulfill his part of the bargain if he did not keep enough Jewish people alive. This is how the "Jews on Ice" deal was conceived.

Regardless of Eichmann's negotiations with the Rescue Committee, a need arose in Vienna for forced labor to build fortifications. Instead of being sent to Auschwitz, several trains from Hungary with about fifteen thousand Jews were sent to Austria, to a place near Vienna known as Strasshof. Some researchers[9] regarded these transfers as an achievement of the Rescue Committee while others[10] presented the rerouting of the trains as routine procedure to deliver Jewish forced labor wherever it was needed.

---

[8]   Hansi's testimony in Eichmann's trial, session 58, p. 875 (in the Hebrew transcript)

[9]   Schmidt, 1985 (Medvetánc, 1985, pp. 2–3), p. 111.

[10]   Braham, 1994, p. 734; Reichenthal, 2009, pp. 117–121.

In a letter dated June 7, 1944, the Mayor of Vienna, a former SS officer named Blaschke, wrote to Himmler's deputy, Kaltenbrunner, asking for forced laborers. In his reply on June 30, 1944, Kaltenbrunner wrote to Blaschke that he was sending four transports with twelve thousand Jews of whom he believed thirty percent were fit for work. The letter included an unusual instruction: "The women and children amongst these Jews, who are unfit for work, must be ready for special action [extermination] and will be transferred from there one day—they should stay in the camp also during the day."[11] Contrary to the German routine to immediately murder those who were unfit to work, the instruction was to keep them alive in Austria. The Germans, and Himmler in particular, did not have a good track record of keeping their promises—so it is no surprise that they made the comment indicating that the people unfit to work must be ready to be sent to extermination. According to several sources, Himmler told his people: "Promise what you want. We shall fulfill what we want."[12]

The letter ended with a note that referred the letter recipient to Krumey, one of Eichmann's assistants in Budapest, for further details and clarifications. The careful wording of the letter tried to conceal the unusual instruction that required to keep alive Jews who were unfit for work, if only temporarily. The final destination—"special action"—was the German code word for extermination.

In general, the Germans tried to conceal all rescue deals with the Jews, and the letter was no exception. Braham described the Strasshof episode in details. He mentioned that these Jews were treated relatively well and that most of them survived, but he did not consider this transport as an achievement of the rescue activists.[13] Another document,[14] dated August 9, 1944, detailed the rights of the people in this special transport and the manner of handling

---

11   Eichmann's trial, t_1211.

12   Hadari, 1992, p. 133; Kurt Becher's affidavit in Eichmann's trial, section 106, p. 1531.

13   Braham, 1994, p. 734.

14   Eichman's trial, t37_273.

them in the event of transgressions. Here, families and children were mentioned again. It was said, among other things, that the penalties imposed on the offender would also be imposed on his family. From this, it is clear that the forced laborers remained in family units, contrary to the usual procedures.

According to Kasztner's report and Hansi's testimony in Eichmann's trial, during their talks with Eichmann about this particular deal, he agreed to keep alive the Jews who were unfit to work, and especially children, who were Hansi's top concern. However, the Germans refused to feed these people at their expense. As a result, the deal included payment to the Germans to cover the living expenses of the Jews. In her book, Anna Porter claimed that it was Hansi who, in discussions with Eichmann, proposed that the Rescue Committee (and indirectly the Hungarian and international Jewry) would bear the living costs of those unfit to work.[15]

According to Kasztner, the number of Jews the Germans agreed to send to Austria was thirty thousand, half from Budapest and half from the periphery. In practice, all the transports were from the periphery only. The total number of Jews in these transports was a little over fifteen thousand.

The trains that were directed to Austria instead of Poland (Auschwitz) were selected in conversations between Eichmann and Kasztner. The idea was to distribute the rescue across different areas of Hungary—no individuals were selected. One of the trains destined for Austria was mistakenly sent to Auschwitz. After the mistake had been discovered, the Germans sent another train to Austria so that the total number of survivors remained as planned.

Hansi and Kasztner conducted the negotiations for the "Jews on Ice" deal directly with Eichmann. No other representative of the Rescue Committee attended these meetings but everyone was

---

[15] Porter, 2008, pp. 175–176; Hansi's testimony in Eichmann's trial, session 58. Both indicate Hansi's important role in preserving the lives of those unfit for work, and mainly of children. Braham, 1994, p. 733; Kasztner's report, 1946, p 49/50.

briefed about it. In his book, Biss wrote that he was involved in the discussions at Klages's office, but not at Eichmann's.[16] The influence Biss and Klages had on preparing this deal was probably insignificant. It is possible, however, that already at an early stage Biss was involved in looking for funding and supply sources to feed the saved Jews. Biss was involved in funding activities although he was not the treasurer of the Rescue Committee at that time. In his book he described the Strasshof events at great length, but the details were inaccurate.

The Strasshof affair is not directly covered in Hansi's testimony in Eichmann's trial, although she did describe discussions with Eichmann about keeping alive the Jews who were unfit to work. Specifically, she did indicate at the trial that even before Kasztner showed up in front of Eichmann, Eichmann already promised that the Jews would be sent to "Austria or somewhere else." She also indicated that she introduced Kasztner to Eichmann shortly after Joel's departure. Since the transfers to Austria were not mentioned in Joel's book nor in Moshe Sharet's report of his meeting with Joel, it appears that the details of the deal, including the specific destination—Strasshof, were agreed only after Joel left on his mission.

One way or another, the transfers of Jews to Strasshof instead of Auschwitz, and keeping about fifteen thousand Jews alive, was a major achievement of the Rescue Committee.[17] This was corroborated by Hansi's testimony and Kaltenbrunner's letter,[18] and it was also the conclusion of the Hungarian researcher Mária Schmidt.[19]

16   Biss, 1973.

17   Kasztner's opponents, such as Richental, 2010, p. 118, tried to present the Strasshof transfers as a routine event, including the keeping alive of the people who were unfit for work.

18   Kaltenbrunner's letter included the instruction to keep in a guarded camp those who were unfit for work from the transfers arriving in Strasshof. Eichmann's trial, t\1211, t\37_273.

19   Hungarian researcher Mária Schmidt (Schmidt, 1985) also considered the transfer of Jews to Strasshof a rescue operation of the Rescue Committee.

"The Train of the Privileged"

Before and during the discussions about "Jews on Ice," discussions were also held about releasing a limited number of Jews and transferring them outside of the Reich as a goodwill gesture. The topic came up immediately in the first meeting Joel and Kasztner had with Eichmann's assistants, well before the discussions regarding "Jews on ice" started. The latter began only after the quick deportation of the periphery Jews, which raised the concern that the entire Jewish population would be exterminated before any serious negotiations began.

The original request, which was probably initiated by Kasztner, was to allow six hundred people, who allegedly already had immigration certificates to Palestine, to cross the border to Romania in order to board a ship of the Jewish Agency. The ship just happened to be anchored there at the time. After a short deliberation, the Germans agreed to the concept of releasing some number of Jews as a goodwill gesture. However, they objected to the immigration to Palestine due to their commitments to the Muslim Mufti of Jerusalem.[20] In addition, the Germans claimed they were unable to release Jews directly from Hungary where they were "Hungarian property." Instead, the Jews would have to be first transported to Germany where they would become "German property." This is how the idea of the train was conceived. After Joel's departure, Kasztner's main focus turned to these discussions about the train. This train ultimately transported approximately 1,700 survivors and was known as "Muster Zug," "Kasztner's train" or "the train of the privileged."

The report Kasztner wrote after the war was originally written in German. The term Kasztner used to describe the intended passengers of the train was *Prominenten* ("the prominent ones"). The term "privileged" was coined by the translator of Kasztner's report into Hebrew, maybe reflecting his personal opinion. Clearly,

---

[20]   Mohammed Hag Amin al-Husseini, the most important Arab Muslim leader in Mandatory Palestine, who was an extreme anti-Semite and a friend of Hitler. In his meetings with the senior German leaders they reached understandings regarding the liquidation of all Jews in the Middle East.

Rescue activists at the gate of Columbus camp on the eve of the train's departure, June 30, 1944. Right to left: Zvi Goldfarb, Peretz Révész, Israel Kasztner, Hansi Brand, and Ottó Komoly.

such description was not very helpful to Kasztner during his libel trial in Israel. The term used in the course of the discussions with the Germans was "Muster Zug," or in English, "demonstration train." The intent was to demonstrate to the world that there was a platform for negotiating with the Germans. The term also reflected the belief, which prevailed for a certain period of time, that additional trains would follow the first train—a belief that did not come to fruition. At a very basic level, the term reflected the need to see the Germans keeping their promises. After all, until that time, the Germans had a long track record of generously making promises, but rarely keeping them.[21] The term "Kasztner's train" was given to the train at a much later stage, mainly by those who aimed to improve Kasztner's public image following the libel trial.

On April 28, 1944, the Germans reported that Berlin had approved the request to allow six hundred certificate holders to leave the Reich. This was the number initially requested based on the capacity of the ship that was at the disposal of the Jewish

---

21   One of the exceptional cases where promises were kept was the case of the Manfréd, Weiss, and Chorin families, about fifty people in total. In exchange for passing the rights to their industrial concern to the SS, the Germans had them flown to neutral countries as part of the deal with Kurt Becher. Becher subsequently had great influence over the fate of the train passengers.

Agency in Romania, as was known in Budapest. This number was mentioned in the first meeting of Joel and Kasztner with Wisliceny. At the same meeting, it was agreed with the Germans that half the capacity of the train would be allocated to Jews from the periphery and the other half—to Jews from Budapest. At that time, the fate of the Jews in the city was still in question and there was no reason to believe that it would be any better than that of the periphery Jews.[22]

Shortly thereafter, on May 3, 1944, about two weeks prior to Joel's departure, Kasztner managed to organize for himself, with the Germans' help, a trip to Cluj. Kasztner alleged that the reason for the trip was to complain to Wisliceny about the deportation, but there was probably also another reason: to inform his friends and family about the chances of rescue. He wanted to ensure that the people with close ties to him were included on the list of survivors. Upon his return, he reported on his discussions with Wisliceny but he did not say a thing about his talks with some or all of the leaders of the Cluj Ghetto. It seems that he did not warn the general public about the implications of the concentration in the ghetto and the imminent deportation. There is even a disagreement as to what he said or did not say to the leadership. It is uncertain whether, during his visit to Cluj, Kasztner updated the local leadership on the pending departure and anticipated rescue of a small group of Jews. However, it seems that he had. Otherwise, it is very difficult to explain the behavior of the leaders of the community of Cluj, particularly those with close ties to Kasztner, who escaped and joined the group of train passengers immediately after his visit. They, too, neglected to warn the general public, most likely in order not to jeopardize their own chance of success. After the war, in their attempts to explain the reasons and timing for their escape, without warning others, it was convenient for them to feign ignorance and attribute their escape to sheer luck. However, their inclusion among the train's passengers or their escape to the nearby border

---

[22] Kasztner's report, 1946, p. 30. The mentioned agreement was probably achieved without the involvement of other members of the Rescue Committee.

with Romania seem to indicate that they were specifically warned and knew exactly, or at least approximately, what was going to happen.

Cluj was not the only place where denial followed leaders' selfish behavior. Another example of such case is David Shin's story. According to an article in the newspaper *Davar*[23] on June 14, 1961, Shin said in a press conference that in his hometown Nagyvárad (currently, Oradea in Romania), one of the largest towns in the Hungarian periphery, the Jews were unaware of the pending deportation, let alone where they were being deported and what fate was awaiting them. Shin added that the Jewish leadership in Budapest even assured them that everything would be fine and there was no cause for concern.

This accusation was directed primarily at Kasztner because of his unexplained visit to the Cluj ghetto. During Kasztner's trial, which will be discussed later, some of the Cluj Ghetto survivors testified about a rumor that was circulating in the ghetto about an alleged transfer to another settlement (Kenyérmező),[24] where they would work and live. According to those survivors, the rumor was spread by associates of the leadership and was not denied by it. All of that leadership was later included on Kasztner's train passengers list.

In response to the article, Avraham Izbitzki wrote:

> I was amazed and shocked when I read what comrade David Shin said, as I was sent on behalf of the JPU to David Shin in Nagyvárad to solicit his help to make contacts with Hungarians living near the border who might help smuggle Jews to Romania. This was in March 1944,[25] right after Hungary's occupation by the Germans. In this meeting with him which was held in his home in Nagyvárad, I spoke about the death trains to Auschwitz and Treblinka, about the horrors I saw with my own eyes, about the

---

23   The daily of the Labor Union in Israel, in fact, the ruling party.

24   Hungarian: "bread field."

25   Originally written 1943 by mistake.

liquidation of entire communities, and about the planned total liquidation which will surely not pass over Hungary.[26]

Izbitzki was a refugee who fled from Poland to Hungary immediately after the occupation of Hungary by the Germans in 1944. After the war he immigrated to Israel. Izbitzki wrote the response in a postcard sent to Joel and published in Dov Dinur's book (1987). Later in the postcard, Izbitzki added: "Comrade Shin could not forget this meeting and its content since here, in Israel, we talked about it more than once and we both remembered it." Izbitzki also described Shin's reaction to the warnings: "I begged him that he and his family escape with us right away, even without locking the door. He, on the other hand, calmed me down saying I was exaggerating. He added that Hungary was not Poland." Needless to say, Shin found a way to save himself but did not bother to warn the Jews around him.[27]

In the section of his report titled "The train: list of candidates for rescue," Kasztner wrote: "Only a few knew why their name was on the list. The secrecy of the rescue must have been maintained."[28] These words are troubling. While the rescue negotiations with the Germans had to be concealed from the Hungarians, it did not necessarily have to be concealed from the Jews. Generally, there were attempts to distribute information to the Jews: the JPU sent operatives, with the knowledge and encouragement of the Rescue Committee, to warn the Jews about the imminent risks. These operatives, however, were mostly directed to known Zionists. This was done out of fear for the safety of the Zionist operatives since the general public did not trust them and some people might have tipped the authorities to their presence. It certainly was not done in order to conceal information. In the specific case of Cluj, however,

---

[26]   Dinur, 1987, p. 157/8.

[27]   Similar suspicions were mentioned in the Brands' book with regard to Kasztner's father-in-law, Joseph Fisher, one of the leaders of the Cluj community (Brand, 1960, pp. 132–133).

[28]   Kasztner's report, 1946, p. 46.

Kasztner knowingly withheld information from the general public in an attempt to secure the rescue of his hand-picked friends and family members. Years later, during the libel trial, the defense attempted to portray[29] Kasztner's behavior as cooperation with the Nazis and support of their extermination plans. They argued that the Germans informed Kasztner about their consent to release the certificate holders right on the eve of his departure to Cluj, with the intent to dissuade him from spreading information about the extermination. This argument is very lame. If the Germans wanted to prevent Kasztner from spreading the news, they could have simply declined his request to travel, or they could have just as easily arrested him and sent him to Auschwitz.

Assembling the full list of passengers for the train was a complex, endless task. In his report, Kasztner said that a committee was established to assemble the list, but in fact his personal involvement was greater than he has ever been comfortable admitting. The need for a list came up at an early stage—already in his talks with Joel, Eichmann demanded to see it. Kasztner was actively assembling it even before Joel had left on this mission. Joel did not take part in this.

According to Kasztner, in his first meeting with Eichmann, a few days after Joel's departure, Kasztner promised to Eichmann that he would provide him a copy of the list. The text implies that Kasztner already delivered a version of the list to the Germans. This raises two issues. First, disclosing a list of Jewish names to the Germans at that early stage of the negotiations could have equally been a death sentence for the people on the list. And secondly, upon his departure, Joel had no knowledge that such a list even existed, indicating a possibly deliberate attempt on Kasztner's part to withhold information. And he had good reason to do so. It seemed that the original list he delivered consisted mainly of people from Kasztner's hometown Cluj.[30]

29 Judge Halevy in his ruling at the Kasztner trial, Reichenthal 2010 (and more).

30 Braham, 1994, pp. 1089–1090.

The first group of candidates from the periphery for boarding the train came from Cluj to Budapest on June 10, 1944 (and not on July 10, 1944, as Kasztner wrote by mistake). This group included three hundred eighty-eight Jews, mostly senior members of the community. Their number exceeded the "quota" of three hundred seats designated for the entire periphery Jews. The large number of passengers from Cluj reflected Kasztner's personal and family ties in the city—not the size of the Cluj community relative to the Jewish population in the periphery. In fact, the seats on the train were supposed to be divided equally between the Jews of Budapest and the periphery Jews. The number of the Cluj Jews amounted to more than half the original number (six hundred) and to about one quarter of the total number of Jews on the train when it actually departed (although the fact that the total number of passengers ultimately far exceeded the original number of six hundred should be credited to Kasztner). Kasztner wrote about the prioritization of Cluj people in his report: "Eichmann knew that Klausenburg (Cluj) was especially important to us."[31]

Subsequently, smaller groups of Jews arrived from other places in Hungary where deportations had not yet ended. Jews who were already on their way to Auschwitz were not rescued.

The periphery Jews who were brought to Budapest were housed in a special camp, which was hurriedly built by Ladislas Devecseri, also known by his Hungarian nickname Laci. Devecseri was the husband of Joel's niece. Together with a Christian Hungarian partner (who was the registered owner of the company), Devecseri owned a large construction company that built wood structures. The company mainly did construction work for the Hungarian army, which allowed Devecseri relatively large freedom of movement and access to available construction materials. Within a few days, he built three large wooden buildings in the yard of a Jewish institute for the deaf on Columbus Street in Budapest. These buildings were the temporary lodging for the train passengers.

---

[31]   Kasztner's report, 1946, p. 41.

Columbus camp was one-of-a-kind in the history of the Holocaust. It was an autonomous Jewish camp that was guarded on the outside by the Germans. Jews could come and go relatively easily. The German guards were assigned to prevent the entry of the Hungarians to the camp—not to prevent the escape of Jews. The Germans wanted to keep the Hungarians out since they did not want to disclose their business dealings with the Hungarian Jews, who were perceived by the Hungarians as their property.

Prior to coming to Budapest, the periphery Jews already had first-hand experience with the horrors of being confined to ghettos; and some of them even saw the deportations that followed. Therefore, the move to Budapest was, by itself, a rescue for them. The conditions of the Jews of Budapest were different. They had not yet experienced the horrors of the ghetto, deportations, and brutal body searches for valuables. Since there was no certainty that the fate of the passengers would be better than those staying in Budapest (whether they stayed as Jews or lived as Christians under forged documents), some refugees did not believe that the train would lead them to freedom and preferred not to board it. The members of the Rescue Committee, including Ottó Komoly, did believe. They either boarded the train or sent their relatives, albeit with some apprehension, even if only to convince the skeptics that this was a rescue train and not another German manipulation. The passengers included a member of the Rescue Committee representing the RSZ, Zvi (Ernő) Szilágyi, family members of additional Committee members including Biss, Offenbach, Komoly (his wife and only daughter), Kasztner's family, and Joel's mother and his sisters with their families. None of Hansi's family members joined the journey. In one of her meetings with Eichmann Hansi requested to include her children in the planned journey. Eichmann's refusal to this request convinced her that this was indeed a rescue train. She then took her children to Columbus camp to allegedly include them on the passenger manifest, only to reassure the worried passengers.

The passengers included two special groups. One was a group of about one hundred and fifty people who fully bought their right to travel. This group was organized by the Jewish community leaders and the Rescue Committee, and it funded all the travel costs for themselves and everyone else. Fifty additional people also paid for the journey but not through the community or the Rescue Committee. They paid directly to Becher, who "sold" them the seats.[32] The amount of money Becher received from these people was in addition to the price paid to the Germans by the Rescue Committee. The ransom paid to the Germans for releasing the passengers amounted to approximately two hundred thousand dollars or six and a half million pengő. This was the amount Wisliceny had requested at an early stage, as a ten-percent advanced payment for the million Jews offered to Joel, or otherwise the full payment for a hundred thousand Jews.

Becher not only sold seats on the train, but he also set the final price for all passengers, probably in coordination with Himmler. In June, after Joel had already left, Becher increased the price over the amount that Eichmann had previously set. As such, he had a personal responsibility for the fate of the passengers—which later turned to be critical to their safety. When the train left on its way at the end of June, the Germans still believed that Joel's mission might be fruitful and that the train would promote the negotiations. However, In the second half of August 1944, when the first group of passengers crossed the border to Switzerland, it was already entirely clear—at least to Becher himself—that there was only a slim chance of realizing the larger deal of Jews in exchange for trucks or other military goods. In order to allow the first group (originally planned for five hundred Jews, but Eichmann decreased the number to three hundred) to cross the border to Switzerland, someone close to Himmler had to persuade him that the deal might still be worthwhile. Eichmann had no interest in releasing any Jews and he made no effort to promote this deal. Becher was in a position to do it and he was the only one with an interest in it. Had the train passengers been murdered by the Germans, the alibi he built for himself towards the end of the war as a Jew-saver would have been undermined. And indeed, he had a good

---

[32]   Brand, 1960, p. 161; Friedländer, 2010, p. 84.

reason to fear that, once captured by the Allies, he would have been hanged.[33]

After many discussions and stressful moments, the train left on July 1, 1944 in the early hours of the morning. It carried people who were on the manifest but also people who boarded it at the last minute. Some boarded the train on their own initiative and some were motivated to do so by the leaders of the JPU.[34] As a result of these last-minute personal or JPU initiatives, some other passengers were thrown off the train. Such an event was described in Anna Porter's book: "E. S. told me the story of how his father, one of the train's financiers had been thrown off Kasztner train and murdered."[35]

The journey was frightening and the passengers had plenty of concerns, which were certainly not unfounded. On its way, the train stopped at a station called Auspits (a town in Austria). The resemblance of the name to Auschwitz greatly frightened the passengers, many of whom knew the consequences of arriving there. Similarly, when the passengers were requested to take a shower on the way, they were terrified that they were being led to gas chambers similar to the facilities in Auschwitz that were disguised as showers.

Before the train left the Hungarian border, it was stopped for unspecified reasons and delayed at the station in the city of Mosonmagyaróvár. Joseph Fisher, Kasztner's father-in-law, who was the senior public figure on the train, approached Devecseri (the man who built Columbus camp) at midnight and asked him to go back to Budapest to ensure that the journey proceeded. Devecseri went back, contacted Kasztner who checked into the delay, and then made his way back to the station where he left the train. All this obviously took some time, and the train was not in the station when

---

33   Fortunately for him, Becher was caught by the Americans and not by the Russians or the Hungarians. Regardless of the Jews, the Hungarians would have hanged him for robbery of Hungarian property, including that of the Jews.

34   See Ronen, 2011, p. 57; Braham, 1994, p. 1137.

35   Porter, 2008, pp. 3, 198.

he returned. Instead, Fisher left a volunteer to wait for Devecseri, in order to update him as to the direction the train travelled. Devecseri and the volunteer boarded the next train travelling in the same direction and caught up with the correct train. Devecseri boarded it, but the volunteer decided not to board it fearing that, despite all the promises, the journey would end badly. This underscores how uncertain the passengers' fate was and how great their fear was of what was awaiting them ahead.[36]

The discussions about the train had already begun by the first meeting Kasztner and Joel had with Wisliceny on April 5, 1944, slightly more than two weeks after the occupation of Hungary. The original request was to allow the Jews to board a ship that waited in Romania, but this request was denied because of the Germans' commitment to the Mufti and the Palestinians to limit immigration of Jews to Palestine. The train, then, replaced the boat. It was supposed to carry the passengers to Spain via France, and from there to Portugal where they could cross the Atlantic. On June 6, 1944 the Allies landed in France and within two months, any trip to Spain through France became impossible. Therefore, the Germans could not allow the train to proceed. After some delays, the train arrived in Bergen-Belsen concentration camp on July 6, 1944 and its passengers were housed in a special area allocated for privileged inmates. On August 20, 1944 the first group of more than three hundred people left the camp and crossed the border to Switzerland. The others, except for very few, left Bergen-Belsen and crossed the border to Switzerland on December 7 of the same year. In addition to the passengers who left the journey at various stages, the few who were not released included people who committed disciplinary infractions, and Joel's family members. They were left in Bergen-Belsen. Just before the camp was liberated, they were sent by train to another camp to which they never arrived because, while en route, the war ended and they were released by the Russians.

When the first group of passengers crossed the border to Switzerland, negotiations were held on the border of Germany and

---

[36]   The Memories of Ladislas Devecseri (Devecseri, 1944).

Switzerland between Becher's representatives, on one hand, and the JDC representative in Switzerland, Saly Mayer, on the other hand. Kasztner came to the meeting together with Becher. Since Saly Mayer could not arrange an entry visa to Switzerland for Becher, the meeting was held at the border crossing point at the center of the bridge that connects Höchst in Austria to Sankt Margrethen in Switzerland. Due to the restrictions imposed by the governments of the United States and Switzerland, Saly Mayer's negotiating room was minimal. It was very clear to all those involved that the Germans had no chance to receive anything in exchange for releasing the train passengers. When SS officer Max Grüson, Becher's assistant,[37] asked Saly Mayer to promise that the proceeds would be transferred at a later stage, Mayer replied that a Swiss citizen does not promise what he could not keep. Clearly, the rescue operation was not important enough for him to justify lying.[38]

Despite the disappointing results of this meeting on the bridge connecting Austria and Switzerland, when the first group of passengers crossed the border to Switzerland, Becher sent Himmler a highly optimistic report regarding the progress of the negotiation. In his letter to Himmler, Becher indicated that there was no chance to receive trucks, but clarified that it would be possible to receive other strategic materials that Germany had difficulties to obtain. At that stage of the war, several neutral countries such as Sweden, joined the embargo the Allies had imposed on Germany. Becher also noted that continued deportations of Jews would thwart any chance for further negotiations. When he wrote that report he already knew that Himmler ordered to immediately stop the deportations from Hungary and he acknowledged it by saying that "in the meantime the Reichsführer's order in that matter arrived here." There is no doubt that an honest report on the part of Becher about the negotiations with Saly Mayer on the border between

---

[37]   Grüson was probably killed by the Germans after having tried to help Kasztner make inquiries as to the fate of the Slovakian Jews.

[38]   Naphtali Lavie, Hebrew newspaper correspondent, covered the Eichmann trial. See his article, *HaAretz*, April 4, 2011, https://www.haaretz.com/1.5005766.

Austria and Switzerland would have put most of the passengers in grave danger, specifically those who were not included in the first group that crossed to Switzerland in August 1944 and were still at the special camp in Bergen-Belsen. Therefore, the final release and rescue of most of the passengers should be credited to the Germans, and especially to Becher. Thanks to self-preservation instincts at the very end of the war, these Germans found it better to help the Jews, although previously they had worked diligently to murder them.[39]

Transferring the first three hundred train passengers to Switzerland led to an interesting political development. The Swiss government protested before the German Foreign Office that those passengers were transferred to Switzerland without any coordination and visas, and they requested explanations. The German Foreign Office, whose level of familiarity with the matter was unclear, approached the security authorities, namely the SS, and asked for explanations.[40] The Germans, and especially Himmler, were careful to conceal the details and avoid leaving any written documents concerning this event.

In the meantime, Hansi and her children were Eichmann's hostages in Budapest to guarantee Joel's return. Eichmann explicitly objected to allow the children on the train. He also ensured that Joel's relatives, who were on the train, were not released from Bergen-Belsen, unlike the other passengers. Actually, one of Joel's nieces and her family (Bárbárá Devecseri) were released as part of the first group in August 1944, only because her one-year old son had acute meningitis. Subsequently, in December, when all the other passengers were released and crossed the border to Switzerland, Eichmann's personal representative made sure to keep Joel's relatives in Bergen-Belsen. Even when the Germans withdrew from the area due to advances of the Allies, they made special effort to evacuate Joel's relatives to an area that was still under German

39   Eichmann's trial, t\1220.

40   Ibid., session 61, p. 915 (H); session 61, part 2 (E), accessible via http://www. nizkor.com/hweb/people/e/eichmann-adolf/transcripts/.

control. In fact, Joel's relatives remained arrested until the very end of the war when the train they were riding fell into the hands of the Russians. During the entire period Eichmann knew exactly where Hansi and the children were staying, although the children and the mother stayed at separate hiding places. It seems—and Hansi agreed—that Eichmann decided not to harm her and her children, due to the high regard the Germans had for her after she endured the Hungarians' violent interrogation in June, after Joel had left on his mission.

The Forged Documents and Hansi's Arrest

Obtaining forged documents in Hungary of 1942 was not a difficult task. In his book, Peretz Révész explained that the forged documents were usually real papers of living or dead people that could be bought on the black market for a reasonable price of approximately fifty pengő.[41] Other sources also mentioned the widespread availability of forged documents (or borrowed, namely real documents of other people).[42] So much so, that Révész said that he received from Joel an amount of money to buy a large number of documents to equip random people as required.[43]

The simplest and cheapest way to obtain papers was to approach the registration office and impersonate a stranger. Peretz Révész revealed in his book how it was possible to obtain the details of such a person by simply browsing the civil registry books.[44] In order to avoid arousing suspicion, local Jews were required to perform this task due to the refugees' limited knowledge of the Hungarian language and the prominent foreign accent that most of them had.

---

[41] Révész, 2001, p. 82.

[42] See, for example, Huban, 2004.

[43] At the time, the Rescue Committee had not been officially founded and money was not yet received from overseas. Therefore, it probably had been the Brands' private money. Support for this possibility is found in Kornianski's book (1979, p. 187), which described the exploitation of the Brands' kindness to extort money.

[44] Révész, 2001, p. 82.

Hansi was among those who performed this mission.[45] However, this was practical only as long as a small number of papers were required. When the number of refugees increased, and further, when the Hungarian Jews themselves started requiring forged documents, this path was no longer sufficient. It was necessary to find a source of a larger number of papers for the different needs. Some members of the youth movements under the JPU were aspiring artists who could draw and forge stamps. They produced the required papers by filling in forged details on empty, but official-looking, forms. The empty forms were ordered by Hansi from a printing house. Asher Cohen wrote about the JPU's forged paper industry: "The first forms for their papers were obtained from a printing house owner through Hansi Brand, before March 1944."[46] Printing the forms (as well as filling them in) was obviously a major violation of the law, and all those involved were in serious danger.

On May 22, 1944, a few days after Joel had left for Istanbul, the Hungarian police arrested a group of eighteen refugees who tried to flee to Romania. The members of the group had forged documents and foreign currency. The police managed to extract the source of the documents from one of the detainees, and the owner of the printing house who prepared the forms for the documents was arrested.[47] After an extremely violent interrogation it was revealed that Hansi had ordered the forged papers and paid for them.

On May 27, 1944, the police raided the Rescue Committee's hiding place—the apartment of Biss, who at that stage was already fully engaged in the Committee's activities. The police arrested Hansi, Sándor Offenbach and his wife, and Kasztner and his wife. While searching the apartment, they found large sums of foreign currency and forged documents.[48] Luckily, they did not find the

---

[45]   Hansi's interview to Yad Vashem.

[46]   Cohen, 1984, p. 92.

[47]   Kasztner's report, 1946, p. 39.

[48]   In Hansi's testimony at Eichmann trial, she said: "There were two attaché cases. One contained Hungarian papers, and the other, German papers. Since

suitcase containing the underground's forgery tools, which was hidden at the apartment at that time.

After five days of arrest, which was designed to "soften" the detainees before their interrogation, Hansi alone was taken for interrogation. The investigator was Péter Hain, Head of the Hungarian Gestapo, who was notorious for his cruelty (he was executed at the end of the war by the Hungarians). Hain was interested in two things: the forgery of the documents (which was a secondary issue) and the reason for Joel's trip to Turkey (which was the main issue). In light of the printing house owner's admission, Hansi could not deny her involvement in ordering the forged forms and therefore took full responsibility. In doing so, she protected the other team members. As for the reason for Joel's trip, she denied any substantial knowledge of that because of Eichmann's warning that this was a "state secret."

It was of utmost importance to the Germans to keep the Hungarians unaware of the negotiations for releasing Jews in exchange for goods. The Hungarians considered themselves as having first dibs on any profit which could be extracted from the Hungarian Jews, dead or alive. As a result, Eichmann refused to release Jews directly from Hungary. He insisted that they must be transferred first through Germany in order to make them "German property." The Germans were highly sensitive to this issue at the time. Ten days prior to Hansi's arrest, the Weiss-Manfréd deal was signed which heightened their sensitivity.[49] Pursuant to this agreement, the largest Hungarian industrial conglomerate was signed off from its family ownership, mainly Jews who converted to Christianity, to the SS, in exchange for the release of forty-seven family members. The Germans followed through and transferred all of them to Portugal and other places. This deal infuriated the Hungarians, who considered themselves the rightful owner of Hungarian Jews' property.

I saw what the situation was . . . I confessed that I had done it—but only the Hungarian papers." Session 58.

49   Also known as Manfréd-Weiss.

After one day of interrogation, which, according to Hansi's testimony at Eichmann's trial was half interrogation and half beating, she was taken out of the interrogation room and returned to the cell where the other detainees were held. According to testimonies of people who saw her leaving the interrogation room, including Kasztner and Biss, she was cruelly beaten. Her feet were so bruised that she could not stand. Kasztner was taken to the interrogation room after her, but before the Hungarians were able to beat him,[50] the SS people arrived and insisted on taking custody of the detained members of the Rescue Committee.

The Germans did not know about the arrest of the Rescue Committee's members until Biss brought it to their attention. Biss was not at the apartment at the time of the search and arrest. When he found out about the arrest, he contacted Klages, head of the SS security service in Budapest. Klages immediately understood the risk posed to Germany's interests by exposing the negotiations to the Hungarians. The Hungarians were not happy to consent to the Germans' demand to release the detainees. According to Kasztner, it took Veesenmayer, the Reich's plenipotentiary in Hungary, who contacted the Hungarian Prime Ministry himself before the Hungarians released the Rescue Committee members.[51] The detainees were brought to Klages' office where they were released. Klages expressed his shock, real or fake, of the Hungarians' attitude toward Hansi. Biss, who usually did not go out of his way to praise the Brands, described that the way Hansi endured the torture and remained silent, gained much appreciation from Klages and Eichmann. They said she had "the courage of an Aryan" and treated her with respect from that moment onward. Nevertheless, Eichmann never lost sight of the fact that Hansi and her children were his hostages to ensure Joel's return from his mission. According to Hansi, Eichmann told her that thanks to her silence at

---

[50]   According to Kasztner, the Hungarians had time only to slap him once, but other sources disagree with that. Kasztner's report, 1946, p. 40.

[51]   Kasztner's report, 1946, p. 41

that interrogation she earned her life (and by virtue of that, the life of her children).[52]

On July 18, 1944, approximately two weeks after the members of the Rescue Committee had been released,[53] Kasztner was "kidnapped" in a staged show of force by the Hungarians. He was released after about ten days without so much as a scratch. It seems that he used this opportunity to spill the beans to the Hungarians on all the details that Hansi had not given them.[54]

Rescuing the Budapest Jews at the End of August 1944

The extermination of the Budapest Jews, which was originally planned to take place right after the extermination of the Hungarian periphery Jews, was prevented by Regent Horthy's order from July 7, 1944. This order was not due to humanistic considerations but rather a reaction to foreign pressure. Also, the order was part of Hungary's attempt to quit its alliance with Germany. Horthy understood that the Germans were about to suffer a defeat, and that he would be accountable, among other things, for the murder of the Jews. The foreign powers who pressured Regent Horthy included the King of Sweden, the Vatican, and the President of the United States, Roosevelt. Horthy's own son, who was previously updated on the content of Auschwitz protocols, added to the pressure.[55] Roosevelt's threat from June 27 to bomb Budapest if the deportation continued and the massive air raid that followed on July 2 had the greatest impact. This threat, which was probably a reaction to the information brought by Joel, demonstrates the extent to which the Allies could have helped in narrowing the scope of the Holocaust, had they wanted to. Sadly, even in this case, the involvement

---

52   Eicmann's trial, session 58.

53   On June 30, 1944 the Hungarians arrested the members of the Rescue Committee once again (see the next chapter about the paratroopers' affair).

54   Biss, 1973, p. 120.

55   Braham, 1994, p. 806.

of the United States, while preventing the extermination, stopped short of releasing the Jews from the Nazis. This was probably done to avoid conflict with their British allies, and maybe more selfishly — to prevent the Jews from coming to the United States.

During July and August 1944, the Germans continued to apply heavy pressure on the Hungarians to complete the deportation of the Hungarian Jewry which at that time meant the extermination of the Jews of Budapest. The Germans solicited the help of the Hungarian fascist government, whose members mostly supported the continued deportations, to persuade Regent Horthy. On August 14, 1944, Veesenmayer, the Reich plenipotentiary to Budapest, sent a telegram to the Foreign Office in Berlin saying that the Hungarian government agreed to renew the deportation of Jews and that it expected Regent Horthy's approval. Veesenmayer further wrote that this required the Germans to guarantee safe passage through the Reich territory to the seven thousand holders of foreign passports, as previously promised by the Germans to the Hungarian authorities. Many of these passports were obtained and distributed by Krausz with the help of foreign representatives in Hungary (there were about seven thousands of those — not tens of thousands as Krausz's fans claimed). The safe passage required explicit authorization because of the probability that some of the passport holders might reach Palestine, in spite of Himmler's promises to his Arab allies. Veesenmayer attributed great diplomatic importance to those immigration permits to foreign nationals, despite the concern that some might reach Palestine, in order to preserve the image of Germany as keeping its promises. Veesenmayer also wrote that, except for immigration permits to foreign nationals, all the technical preparations for the Budapest operation had been completed. Anna Porter noted in her book that Roswell McClelland, the US representative of the War Refugee Board in Switzerland, wrote that as part of the preparations to exterminate the Budapest Jews at the end of August 1944, sixty-six trains were ready to transport the Jews of the city to Auschwitz.[56] Such number of trains could transport

---

[56]   Porter, 2008, p. 339.

about two hundred thousand people in the crowded conditions the Nazis used to transfer the Jews. The letter from the German Embassy that specified the number of Jews with foreign passports (broken down by countries) made it clear that the Hungarians agreed to the extermination of all the Jewish population, pending the release of the foreign passport holders.[57] Veesenmayer concluded by saying: "Otherwise, everything is technically ready for the [extermination of the Jews of] Budapest operation."

In his letter of August 14,[58] Veesenmayer wrote to the Foreign Office in Berlin that Hungary's Minister of the Interior was about to recommend to Regent Horthy to deport the Jews of Budapest on August 25 with an option to accelerate the deportation by five days. On August 19 Veesenmayer wrote again to the Foreign Office in Berlin stating that the Hungarians were willing to deport the Budapest Jews to camps within Hungary starting from August 25, but they were unwilling to send them to Germany (for extermination), as previously planned. On the following day, August 20, the first group of about three hundred passengers of the famous train crossed the border to safety, from Germany to Switzerland. On August 24 Veesenmayer wrote yet again to the Foreign Office in Berlin that the Hungarians decided to postpone the date of deportation, this time to August 28. The next day, however, Veesenmayer informed Berlin that at 3 am that morning the SS senior commander in Hungary, Winkelmann, received an immediate order to no longer deport any Jews from Hungary to Germany.[59] On the very same day Becher sent his unfounded optimistic report to Himmler about the alleged progress of the negotiations.[60] This report made some interesting points.

---

[57] The protocols of Eichmann trial, t\37_111.

[58] All the documents referred to hereunder were included in appendices to the protocols of Eichmann's trial and most of them were also published in Dinur, 1987.

[59] The protocols of Eichmann trial, t\1222.

[60] Ibid., t\1220.

- There was no chance of receiving trucks (that Himmler may have continued to hope for) but it might have been possible to receive other vital raw materials for strategic needs.
- Continuing with the deportations from Hungary at that stage would thwart any chance of progress in the negotiations.
- An order was already received to halt all deportations from Hungary.
- Becher asked for approval to proceed with the negotiations in the spirit of the report.

According to the context and timetables, it seems evident that Becher already spoke to Himmler, updated him, and requested to immediately stop the deportations that were scheduled to begin any moment. The letter was just an official follow-up to satisfy bureaucratic proceedings and receive an official confirmation to proceed with the negotiations. The confirmation was indeed received almost immediately in a telegram that Himmler sent to Becher on the following day. Together with the confirmation, Himmler also sent, through his senior representative in Hungary, an instruction to Veesenmayer, the Reich plenipotentiary, to halt the deportations as Becher requested. It is likely that there was a connection between Becher's request to stop the deportations for the purpose of promoting the negotiations and Himmler's decision to halt the deportations, but other explanations are possible.

Braham, for example, was of the opinion that this instruction was given because Himmler was concerned that the deportations might enrage the Hungarians and trigger them into leaving the alliance with the Germans, similarly to the Romanians who left at that time and joined the Allies.[61] This explanation was mentioned in Kasztner's report and it was based on information received from Wisliceny who probably received this information from Berlin.[62]

---

[61]   Braham, 1994, p. 916.

[62]   Eichmann's trial, session 60, p. 911; Kasztner's report, 1946, p. 92.

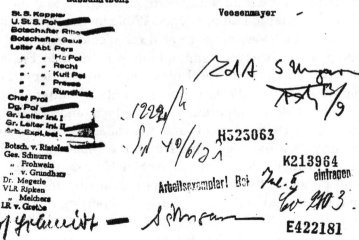

Telegramm
(G-Schreiber)
Verschluss...
zu behandeln
Auswärtiges Amt
Inl II 1775g
eing.   25 AUG 1944
Abt. (... opp. d Eng.

Budapest, den 25. August 1944 11.15 Uhr
Ankunft: "   25.   "   "   11.50

Nr.2379 vom 25.8.   C i t i s s i m e mit Vorrang!
Sofort auf den Tisch!

Für Herrn Reichsaussenminister.

SS-Obergruppenführer Winkelmann teilt mir soeben
telephonisch mit, dass er heute nacht 3 Uhr durch Fern-
schreiben einen Befehl: des Reichsführers SS erhalten hat,
demzufolge jegliche Deportation von ungarischen Juden
nach dem Reich mit sofortiger Wirkung strengstens unter-
sagt wird. Auf meine Rückfrage, ob dieser Befehl amtlich
sei und ich davon Gebrauch machen kann, hat Winkelmann
dies bejaht.
Wäre für umgehende Unterrichtung dankbar, da ich be-
absichtige, diesen Befehl in geeigneter Form weit-
gehend für die Durchsetzung der übrigen Führerweisungen
auszunützen.

                                        Veesenmayer

St.S. Kepp...
U.St.S. Poh...
Botschafter Rit...
Botschafter Gaus
Leiter Abt. Pers
  .   .   Hi Pol
  .   .   Recht
  .   .   Kult Pol
  .   .   Presse
  .   .   Rundfunk
Chef Prot
Dg. Pol
Gr. Leiter Inl. I
Gr. Leiter Inl. II
Arb.-Expl. bel.
Botsch. v. Rintelen
Ges. Schnurre
  " Frohwein
  " v. Grundhar...
Dr. Megerle
VLR Ripken
  " Melchers
LR v. Gre...

Arbeitsexemplar! Bei...   eintragen

H523063

K213964

E422181

Exhibit t\1222_156 at Eichmann's trial: The order to halt the deportation
of Hungarian Jews to concentration camps in Germany.

This explanation is possible but very unlikely, mainly due to the Hungarian public's zeal to deport the Jews. Only a relatively small group around Horthy considered at that time leaving the alliance with Germany. The existence of German documents or declarations from that period that support the claim that the coup in Romania was indeed the reason for stopping the deportation is hardly convincing. Himmler simply could not afford to mention the existence of the negotiations with the Jews without risking his life. If a more fanatical official at the Nazi establishment even got a whiff of what was going on, they would have drawn Hitler's attention to it. It seems that using Romania's departure from the alliance with Germany to explain the halting of the deportations is nothing but a cover story made up by Himmler or one of his cronies in order to conceal his involvement in or even awareness of any negotiations with Jews.[63]

Another possible explanation of the fact that the deportations had not been ultimately carried out may be Horthy's objection. This is a fairly reasonable explanation, but if that was the case, Himmler would not have needed to send an urgent telegram to Winkelmann (the SS commander in Hungary), and Winkelmann would not have needed to contact Veesenmayer at three o'clock in the morning. According to Wisliceny's testimony, as presented in Eichmann's trial, Horthy did in fact cancel his consent to the deportation of the Budapest Jews at the last moment, but only after Himmler's instruction to halt the deportation had arrived, and not vice versa. Once again, the chain of events and all available evidence suggest, quite clearly, that the negotiations with the Nazis did reduce and could have further reduced the scope of the Holocaust in Hungary.[64]

Some pondered the hypothetical possibility that the Hungarians intended to protect the Budapest Jews by deporting them to camps inside Hungary, instead of sending them to Germany. These proposals were made by Hungarian fascists such as Lieutenant

---

[63]   As in previous cases, written documentation regarding negotiations and understandings with Jews was deliberately avoided.

[64]   Eichmann's trial, session 60, p. 911.

Colonel Ferenczy of the Hungarian gendarmerie,[65] who, for a brief period pretended to turn his position around. It seems that these wolves in sheep's clothing even managed to convince Ottó Komoly and possibly Kasztner of their "good" intentions. In reality, Ferenczy's insistence on complete and immediate evacuation of all Budapest Jews to camps inside of Hungary that did not even exist was a telltale sign of his real intentions.[66]

Even if it was not the only reason, evidently, Becher's baseless report to Himmler about the progress of the negotiations and the chance to receive supplies (and not trucks!) in exchange for the release of Jews had considerable weight and made a real impact on Himmler's decision to terminate the deportations. Becher's personal interest in the train deal, that could have turned into a liability should the train passengers not be released, probably triggered the false report. Even if he did not do it for altruistic motives but rather to save himself after the war, the release of the train passengers should be first and foremost credited to Becher. Becher took a huge risk sending his baseless optimistic report. If any information about the real situation reached the extreme fanatics in Germany, such as Kaltenbrunner, Becher would have been in real danger, as indeed one of his assistants, Max Grüson, experienced. Grüson's attempts to help Kasztner check into the fate of the Slovakian Jews came to the attention of a fanatical officer named Brunner who ensured that Grüson disappeared and was never heard from again.[67]

Historians tend to attribute the release of the first group of train passengers to Kasztner. Specifically, they consider him as the leading character on the Jewish side of the negotiations with the Germans. Unfortunately, this is not accurate. The real negotiating partner representing the Jewish side was Saly Mayer, who was

---

[65] László Ferenczy, commander of the gendarmerie, actively conducted the deportation of the Hungarian Jews to Auschwitz and was fully aware of what was happening there. See Braham, 1994, pp. 355, 906.

[66] Ottó Komoly's diary, as published by Prof. Raphael (Bella) Vago, in: Goteszman, Vago and Rothkirchen, 1976, p. 82 onward.

[67] See the testimony of Dr. Shlomo Yehuda Ernst Abeles, Eichmann's trial, session 49, regarding "Gryson."

a poor choice for this task. As already mentioned, Mayer was an inflexible formalist who prioritized his pride over human lives. This posed serious difficulties in the negotiations and on the attempts to save the Hungarian Jewry. Kasztner could not represent the Jewish side because of the simple reason that Kasztner had nothing to offer. Kasztner's most important contribution in Switzerland was his influence on the Germans to finesse their meeting summaries so they would seem as positive as possible. Saly Mayer acted on behalf of McClelland but he lacked McClelland's devotion to saving lives. McClelland was the representative of the War Refugee Board (WRB), established in January 1944 by President Roosevelt. The WRB's mission was to save lives and help refugees in general and Jews in paricular. The WRB as an organization, and its representatives as individuals, were deeply impressed by Joel's rescue mission. They did their very best to exhaust every possibility of rescue while utilizing all legal means at their disposal, and sometimes they may have even pushed the legal boundaries.

Krausz's Rescue Attempts

After Hungary's occupation by the Nazis, Krausz persuaded representatives of neutral countries to take Jews, who were allegedly citizens of these countries, under their wings by providing diplomatic immunity to the buildings where they lived.[68] In addition, Krausz tried to rescue Jews holding passports of neutral countries by lobbying for immigration permits for them. These passports were not always legal. Some of them were obtained from friendly representatives of neutral countries in Budapest, not always with the permission of their governments. The number of foreign passport holders was about seven thousand. After the war, Krausz and his admirers claimed that they convinced the authorities to allow foreign passport holders to take their families with them, thus the

---

[68]   This concept of protected houses was probably an unplanned spin-off from the Hungarian gendarmerie's plan to separate the foreign passport holders from the general Jewish population in an attempt to facilitate the deportation of the Budapest Jewry. See Braham, 1994, p. 908.

number of candidates for immigration was thirty to forty thousand. In addition to passport holders of neutral countries, these rescue attempts were extended to holders of immigration certificates to Palestine, but it is questionable whether such certificates were at all available. These rescue attempts were discussed during Eichmann's trial and were mentioned in German documents filed at the trial.[69]

Many attempts were made to allow these Jews to leave Hungary. These efforts attempted to save Jews only from Budapest, since the periphery Jews had already been exterminated by that time. In practice, these rescue or immigration efforts never materialized, so the arguments around the exact number of potential rescue candidates is meaningless. In retrospect, Krausz's rescue plan had two major shortcomings. First, regardless of decisions at the senior echelons, including Himmler and Hitler's levels, Eichmann was planning to derail the immigration plan using administrative measures at his disposal, even in case his formal appeal against the plan would have been rejected.[70]

A more important yet less known problem was the direct relationship between Krausz's rescue attempts of foreign passport holders and the consent of the Hungarian authorities (namely, Horthy) to send all the other Jews of Budapest to extermination. This was in the critical period between the completion of extermination of the periphery Jews at the beginning of July 1944 and the coup of the Arrow Cross party on October 15, 1944, while Horthy still had significant influence. From the correspondence between Veesenmayer (the plenipotentiary of Nazi Germany to Hungary) and the German Foreign Ministry, it is clear that the Hungarians considered agreeing to the deportation—and in fact extermination—of the Jews of Budapest, on condition that the Germans would provide transit visas to about seven thousand Jews, who, in one way or another, gained the citizenship of neutral countries. For the Germans, these transit visas were intended to pressure the Hungarian government into agreeing to exterminate

69   Eichmann's trial, t37, 92; and t37, 111.

70   Eichmann's trial, session 60, p. 909.

the Budapest Jews. Veesenmayer wrote to Berlin on August 14, 1944: "We can assume that Regent Horthy would agree to that [to the deportation of the Jews from Budapest] only to allow, on my promise, the foreign immigration as proposed and agreed by the Germans."[71] This was clearly a trade in human lives, in which about seven thousand people would have been saved in exchange to abandoning the others whose number at that time was about two hundred thousand. The question to what degree Krausz himself was aware of the connection between rescuing a few and exterminating the many would not be answered here.[72]

At about the same time, July–August 1944, Horthy's offer to release a large number of Jews from Hungary and allow them to travel abroad became known. This initiative saved no one because it was torpedoed by German and British opposition. The importance of the proposal is that before it dematerialized, the US, or at least the WRB, had expressed its willingness to take in all the liberated people without any restrictions. In addition, and with great effort, they even managed to extort at the last minute a British agreement to accept refugees.[73] Unfortunately, the British approval was granted too late, when the offer was no longer valid.

The Jewish Pioneer Underground in Hungary

The vast majority of the members of the JPU were young, members of different Zionist youth movements. They came to Hungary as refugees from neighboring countries and the number of the Hungarians, and especially the post Trianon Hungarians among them was small.

The refugees who arrived in Hungary organized themselves into movements and parties in order to help themselves and their comrades. The cooperation between the various movements,

---

[71]   Ibid., t37_111.

[72]   According to Révész, 2001, p. 207, Krausz was aware of this information.

[73]   Erbelding, 2018, pp. 173–174.

which was limited at first, gradually increased, and in time this organization was called The Jewish Pioneer Underground (JPU).[74]

This underground began its organization in Hungary and especially in Budapest at the beginning of 1942, when Slovakian refugees started arriving. The underground members were mainly refugees, members of youth movements, who identified with the Communist-leaning Zionists' (RSZ) HaKibbutz HaArtzi, with the Social Zionists' (SZ) HaKibbutz HaMeuḥad, and with the Social-Democrat Zionists' (SDZ) Iḥud. They helped their refugee members to survive in Hungary and the surrounding countries. The JPU leadership included Jósef (Yoshko) Baumer who was active in the JPU on behalf of the RSZ party. He was later replaced by Rafi Benshalom (Friedl). Josef Kornianski and Zvi Goldfarb represented the faction identified with the SZ. Eli Shayo and Peretz Révész acted on behalf of the SDZ, the faction identified with Mapai at that time. None of them were Hungarian, in fact, they were all refugees themselves.

The actions of the JPU were described in the memoirs of many of its members, including its leaders, such as Rafi Benshalom (1977), Josef Kornianski (1979) and Peretz Révész (2001). Asher Cohen's book, *The Ḥalutz Resistance in Hungary 1942–1944* (1984), summarizes research work focused on the activities of the JPU underground.

Braham mentioned the JPU favorably as one of the most positive Jewish entities in Hungary during the German occupation but he did not dedicate much attention to it.[75] This is probably due to the limited involvement of this underground with public life and its minor impact on it, at least until the very last stages of the war. The JPU did not engage in military action or physical opposition to the fascist Hungarian regime or the Nazi regime that replaced it in mid-October 1944.

The JPU, like many other refugees in Hungary, were aided by the local Jewish population and especially the Rescue Committee

---

74   For details on the origin and action of this underground see Cohen, 1984; Braham, 1994.

75   Cohen, 1984, p. 9.

for their survival. At first, until the occupation, the presence of the refugees in Hungary contributed nothing to the local population and in fact only made it more difficult and endangered those who helped them.

Until the occupation the JPU merely dealt with caring for the sustenance and welfare of the Zionist refugees in Hungary, each group for its own members. Following the Nazi occupation its activity had expanded. Immediately after the occupation, the JPU distributed warnings to its members and to organizations they had contact with (mainly Zionist entities). They issued forged documents to their members and subsequently to the general Jewish population. They traveled across Hungary under various covers, risking their lives disseminating information and distributing forged documents and other means, including money, to support the smuggling of their comrades. They brought to Budapest considerable, accurate information about the status and conditions of the Jews in the periphery, their assembly into ghettos, and deportation. Messengers of the JPU were an important source of information about the events taking place in the periphery both for the Rescue Committee and for the Judenrat (Jewish Council) appointed by the Germans. The information they brought to Budapest was surprisingly accurate and up-to-date considering the difficulties and limitations of that period. The JPU also prepared several bunkers but these were unsuccessful.

After the extermination of the periphery Jews, the JPU expanded its activity to help the general Jewish public with forged documents necessary for survival. The most popular certificates were "protection letters," indicating their holders were citizens or under the protection of neutral countries, and Hungarian official documents, attesting that their holders were not Jewish.

In the last months of the war, in the period between the Hungarian fascists' takeover of the country in mid October 1944 until the liberation of Budapest in January-February 1945, the JPU continued expanding its activity. It helped establish and maintain orphanages. In addition, it transferred much-needed supplies to orphanages and to the "protected houses" where many of their members took refuge. At that time, the JPU started to initiate operations of military nature: members disguised as local soldiers or as activists of the Hungarian "Arrow Cross" fascist militia helped rescue Jews from local gangs and jails.

The pioneering youth movements at that time showed great interest in children, and each movement endeavored to recruit as many children as possible to bring them to Israel after the war to join the *kibbutzim* with which each movement was politically affiliated. The great interest expressed by the Zionist movement in children as opposed to the limited interest in immigration of adults "without proper (political) selection" can be clearly seen in the Jewish Agency's "rescue policy."[76] In addition to sheltering children, the orphanages served many members of the JPU as safe havens.

The most successful forgery plant was operated by the members of the RSZ. This enterprise proved to be a huge success producing large quantities of various documents for the protection of their holders. According to Ronen,[77] the priority in receiving the documents was for members of the underground, followed by Hungarian communists, and only at the end the general Jewish population.

Additional Achievements of the Negotiations with the Nazis

In the protocols of Eichmann's trial it was stated that Höss, the commander of Auschwitz, said that he had travelled to Hungary after receiving an order to stop the murders of Jews.[78] According to him, following the negotiations conducted by Becher and Eichmann in Hungary, he traveled to Hungary to clarify whether stopping the killings was final or only temporary. Höss further said: "The Jews were adamant that despite the promise to stop the

---

76 Central Zionist Archives, s26/1236 and Porat and Weitz, 2002, p. 389. The document is also attached as Appendix 2.

77 Ronen, 1994, p. 209.

78 Eichmann's trial, session 72, pp. 1102–1103.

extermination, it was still going on. Their pre-condition for concrete negotiations was a complete stop. This is why an order was given to stop the extermination of the Jews." The event Höss described, which occurred after Horthy had been removed from power and the extreme fascists had taken over Hungary, is a result of the negotiations with the Nazis initiated by the Rescue Committee. The main Jewish figures involved in the negotiations at that phase were Kasztner and Saly Mayer. Later on we will elaborate on this topic in the context of the reliability of German documentation from that period.

In his opening speech, Gideon Hausner, the Attorney General and prosecutor in the Eichmann trial, mentioned the "death marches."[79] Hausner described how Eichmann had organized the death marches with the help of his Hungarian fascist friends in order to continue with the extermination of the Jews even following Himmler's order to stop it. He also said that the marches only stopped when Himmler reproached Eichmann for doing so. There is no doubt that this event was also a direct result of the negotiations of the Rescue Committee with the Nazis. These negotiations probably also affected Germany's decision to intervene and prevent the extermination of the Budapest ghetto and its residents by the Hungarians in the last days of the war.

Ottó Komoly and the International Red Cross (IRC)

After Horthy's order to halt the deportation of Jews from Hungary in July 1944, the Hungarian fascists came up with the idea to evacuate the Jews of Budapest to (non-existing) camps within the country, allegedly in order to protect them. During the summer of 1944 Ottó Komoly had been very active in an effort to prevent the implementation of this plan. He managed to solicit the support of some relatively moderate Hungarian politicians, including some

[79] Eichmann's trial, sessions 6–8, p. 93 in the Hebrew transcript of the protocol. The mentioned death marches took place only towards the end of 1944, after the fascists had taken over Hungary and after Horthy had been removed from power.

pro-Nazis, who by then had begun to shy away from the Germans. He succeeded in his efforts, and thanks to him and others who assisted him, the evacuation did not take place. Simultaneously, Komoly attempted to handle another humanitarian crisis: the issue of abandoned children whose parents had been murdered or taken away. At his initiative, the representative of the Red Cross in Hungary, Friedrich Born, agreed to grant such children the protection of the International Red Cross (IRC). To do so, the children had to have a recognized international status, which gave the IRC the legal framework to care for them. Spain and Switzerland declared their willingness to accept five hundred children each, and thus the children became "foreigners" and were eligible for the IRC protection. At the beginning of September, Department A (*A osztály*) of the IRC was formed under the leadership of Ottó Komoly to care for foreign children and take care of their immigration.[80] The people involved in founding and operating Department A, in addition to Ottó Komoly, included Kasztner, Offenbach, Hansi, Elefánt Márton, Rafi Benshalom-Friedl, and Ernő (Efra) Teichman.[81]

The Budapest Ghetto

It was only in the second half of November 1944, about one month after the fascists had taken over the country and after Horthy was removed from power, that Hungary decided to build a big ghetto for the Budapest Jews instead of the Jewish houses scattered across the city. The evacuation of the "Jewish houses" took place over the last days of November and was completed by December 2. At that stage the city was already under the Soviets' siege, and the Jews suffered from it like the rest of the population. In addition, they also suffered from a series of decrees imposed by the fascist government and harassment from its unrestrained supporters who rampaged through the city and murdered Jews without any provocation or reason, and certainly without any consequences.

---

80   Cohen, 1984, p. 205.

81   Benshalom, 1977, p. 171; Kasztner report, p. 108.

Building the ghetto reduced the Jews' living space considerably. The Jewish Council, which underwent several reorganizations since being appointed by the Germans right after the occupation, had to find housing solutions with a population density of about fourteen people per room.[82] The Budapest ghetto existed for only one and a half months, from the beginning of December 1944 until the liberation day in mid-January 1945. The Jews there suffered from extreme poverty in addition to harassments by the Hungarian fascists who often penetrated into the ghetto. Like the general population of the city, the ghetto residents also suffered from the Allies' aerial bombings and from the fighting between the Axis forces (Germans and Hungarians) defending the city and the invading Allied forces (Russians and Romanians), which often damaged the ghetto territory. The authorities allocated food to the ghetto residents at a quota of six hundred and fifty calories per person per day, less than half the allowance for prisoners. In reality, this quota was not always supplied.[83]

As the city descended into total chaos, representatives of neutral countries and aid organizations tried to help. The most efficient and important among them were the Swiss Vice-Consul in Budapest, Carl Lutz, who saved Jews at the "Glass House" and other "protected houses," the Swedish delegation (with American backing) that included Raoul Wallenberg, and Department A of the International Red Cross. Department A's activity in the city was coordinated by Ottó Komoly and Hansi who worked with him as head of the supply department.[84] Since the food supply was far from sufficient, the supply department, run by Hansi and Ernő (Efra) Teichman, tried to augment the supply by purchasing food from other sources.[85] The funds for buying food from local sources were received from local and international Jewish organizations. The complex, dangerous task of buying food and delivering it to the

---

[82]   Braham, 1994, p. 977.

[83]   Ibid., p. 989.

[84]   Ibid.; Kashti, 2014, p. 98.

[85]   On which we shall expand later on.

orphanages and the ghetto was mainly carried out by members of the youth movements and the JPU.[86] This food delivery enterprise even received some help from German soldiers who protected the stock of food from being ransacked by the Hungarian gangs.[87] Helping with feeding the ghetto and orphanages was one of the main contributions of the JPU to the welfare of the general public, alongside the large-scale dissemination of forged documents.

At the very end of the war, just before the occupation of Budapest by the Soviets, the Jewish leadership heard that the Hungarians were about to exterminate the ghetto and its residents, approximately eighty thousand people. They intended to do it quickly before the city fell into the hands of the Soviets.[88] Many people were involved in the successful attempt to save the ghetto, including Hungarians who deliberately leaked information about the plan, international organizations that tried to intervene, and Jews who contacted various officials in Hungary and Germany to solicit their influence and power. Biss attributed this success to Becher's intervention with Himmler. Some claimed that the Germans intervened since they were promised trucks (of a Germany make) from Slovakia with the assistance of a Slovakian merchant named Steger. Révész mentioned Moshe Krausz's involvement, but he estimated that the Rescue Committee (and probably Biss's activity) had crucial weight in preventing the catastrophe.[89]

In a radio broadcast on August 2012, Prof. Shlomo Aronson said that the question of what to do with the tens of thousands of ghetto Jews faced the German commander of Budapest who was entrusted with defending the city shortly before it fell into Russian hands. This commander, Karl Pfeffer-Wildenbruch, telephoned Berlin to find out what to do with the ghetto Jews and "followed the instructions he received" from Himmler. Following these instructions, according to Aronson, he assigned German guards

---

86   Benshalom, 1977, p. 124.

87   Ibid., p. 175.

88   This is mentioned in many sources; see, for instance, Biss, 1973, p. 208.

89   Révész, 2001, p. 255.

to protect the Ghetto and thus prevent its destruction. Himmler, at the time, was still hoping to get something out of Becher's negotiations in Switzerland. He was particularly hopeful about the dialog with the US President's representative for refugee matters, Roswell McClelland. In the broadcast, Aronson did not mention any connection between Himmler's orders and his hopes to get positive results from Becher's negotiations with the Rescue Committee. However, at about the same time most of the "train of the privileged" passengers, more than 1,300 people, crossed the border to Switzerland, and shortly afterwards an additional group of about 1,200 people from Theresienstadt crossed the border as well.[90] These events could not have happened without a specific order from Himmler who was desperately looking at the time for ways to make contact with the West.

Following the release of the first group of the train's passangers, the contacts between Saly Mayer and Becher continued into the summer and fall of 1944. The Germans, and particularly Himmler, were interested in contact with the Americans, in pursuit of a separate peace with the West. On November 5, the representative of the American War Refugee Board in Switzerland, Roswell McClelland, attended a meeting with Mayer and Becher, to discuss transactions to ease the Jews' situation. By attending this meeting, McClelland blatantly violated the instructions of his own government, taking a major risk. From Himmler's perspective, this meeting was a confirmation that the path to the Americans was through the Jewish organizations. In addition, the very facilitation of this meeting enhanced Becher's image in Himmler's eyes. This confluence of events is what led to the rescue of the Budapest Ghetto and other actions that were taken to ease the Jews' situation, as Himmler believed that these actions could be useful for a peace dialogue with the Americans.

---

[90] The rescue operation of the Sternbuch family with the help of Jean-Marie Musy.

12. The Paratroopers' Affair

The Paratroopers' Mission

The paratroopers' undertaking was a painful episode in the history of the Hungarian Jews and of the Jewish community in Palestine. There is no question as to the good intention, courage, and selflessness of all the paratroopers, including the three who arrived in Hungary—Hannah Szenes, Peretz Goldstein, and Yoel Palgi (Nussbacher). There is, however, much doubt as to their proper training for an unbelievably difficult mission.

The paratroopers are often portrayed as envoys of the Jewish community in Palestine who came to help the Jews in German-occupied territories. This description is far from complete. In his book, Palgi talks about his dilemma: "It is not easy to assume a double mission: military in nature, for the British; and of national identity, for rescue purposes."[1] Palgi pointed out that some of the candidates for the mission withdrew. They could not find it in themselves to commit loyalty to the British because they realized that this would undermine their ability to help the European Jews.

In the first eddition of Palgi's book (1946) there is no mention of specific rescue mission guidance the paratroopers received. In a later edition of his book, dated 1977, Palgi added descriptions of meetings with leaders of the Jewish community in Palestine (in the 1946 edition only Berl Katznelson[2] is mentioned on p. 141, and even that indirectly). The leaders offered clarification of the paratroopers'

---

[1] Palgi, 1946, p. 13.

[2] An important public figure in Palestine. One of the architects of Zionist ideology at the time.

main role: "to teach Jews to fight"—according to Eliyahu Golomb;[3] "so that the Jews would know that Palestine is their homeland and refuge"—according to Ben-Gurion;[4] to "save Jews, everything else—later. If no Jews will be left, Palestine and the Zionist vision would vanish as well"—according to Berl Katznelson.[5] In addition, Palgi mentioned a meeting with Golda Meir, but, according to the text, she only shed tears worrying about the paratroopers' fate.[6]

A more accurate description of the meetings the paratroopers had with the leadership of the Jewish community in Palestine is offered in Asher Cohen's book.[7] Cohen used the testimony of paratrooper Ḥaim Ḥermesh to explain the leadership's position in regards to the paratroopers' Jewish mission. Ben-Gurion stated that the paratroopers' mission would be to prepare the Diaspora Jews to immigrate to Palestine after the war. In Ben-Gurion's mind, that would have helped to open the doors to Palestine after those had been closed by the British. At that time, the end of 1943, nothing was said about the need and ways to preserve the very existence of the Jews. The paratroopers met and spoke with several refugees who had arrived from occupied Europe, including Josef Kornianski who came through Hungary. According to Palgi, the paratroopers believed that the situation in Europe was difficult, but they also

---

[3]   Head of the illegal Jewish defense force, the Haganah.

[4]   This is consistent with the content of a memorandum regarding the rescue policy of the leadership of the Jewish community in Palestine introduced in Morgenstern, 1971. See also Appendix 2.

[5]   The need for the rescue is mentioned here as an interest of the Jewish community in Palestine and not as a humanitarian Jewish cause. Note that even years later Zvi Goldfarb found it fit to justify the rescue as follows: "The Zionist movement believed that as many Jews as possible should be saved for the sake of Palestine" (Goldfarb, 1980, p. 101).

[6]   Forth prime minister of Israel. At that time, Meir was a member of the Executive Committee of the Histadrut, and in 1946 she was acting head of the Political Department of the Jewish Agency

[7]   Cohen, 1984, p. 153.

believed that the refugees were exaggerating. The very essence of extermination was inconceivable to them.[8]

The high-level directions given to the paratroopers by the Jewish leadership in Palestine did not include any practical instructions on how to save the Jews. In his book, *Arrows in the Dark*, Tuvia Friling introduced the reaction of one of the paratroopers:

> I also remember our disappointment with the briefs we received in March, at the preparatory course in kibbutz HaZore'a. We were visited there by the leaders of the Jewish community, and the eighteen candidates were asked many questions but received little guidance. Ben-Gurion talked with us too. We were hoping to hear a review about the political situation, but he told us nothing. Instead, he asked each of us how we saw our mission and how we intended to act in order to achieve it. He heard fantastic plans from us for hours. The truth is that we were hallucinating and our plans had nothing to do with reality. . . . At the end of the meeting he summarized: "At the end of this war we must found a Jewish State. The British government closed the door and we are unable to open it by ourselves from the inside. You must prepare the Jews wherever they are. On the day after the victory, all the paths in Europe, all the railroads and all the rivers will witness a huge flood of Jews coming to Eretz Israel. Remember: this is your role".[9]

Nobody addressed the basic question of how to help the Jews to stay alive until the victory came.

The paratroopers' arrival in Hungary had very unfortunate timing, as far as the rescue attempts in Hungary were concerned. It was merely one week before the scheduled departure of the train that was supposed to carry approximately one thousand seven hundred "privileged" to safety. The paratroopers received a list of potential contacts in Budapest. Some of the contacts were Zionist Jews who were overly busy at that time in an effort to get the train and its passengers on their way. Other contacts were simply no

---

8   This was after endless reports from Budapest to Istanbul and all the other information that was already available.

9   Friling, 1998, p. 482.

longer viable. The paratroopers had, among others, the address of Moshe Schweiger, who had already been arrested by the Germans; Sámuel Springman, who had already left Hungary and was on his way to Palestine; Joel, who had already been arrested by the British; and Kasztner, who focused all his energy on making it possible for the train to depart. They also had the telephone number of Mrs. Erzsi Kurtz (Elizabeth Elisheva), who hung up on them when they called to ask about the arrested Schweiger. As all others, the JPU was also busy preparing its representatives for the train's journey.[10] These contacts were given to the paratroopers, not necessarily in order to help the local Jews, but first and foremost to help the paratroopers themselves execute the mission imposed by the British. The paratroopers, or at least Yoel Palgi, did not consider to what extent they were risking the local Jews, and in particular the people they contacted and their families. These people were not asked for their willingness to serve as contacts for the foreign paratroopers—they volunteered. Palgi's insistence on residing in the Brands' apartment was a real threat to Hansi and her two children. This consideration is not mentioned in any edition of Palgi's book.

The Paratroopers

Hannah Szenes was born in Budapest in 1921, immigrated to Palestine in 1939, and was one of the founders of kibbutz Sdot Yam. In 1943 she volunteered to enlist in the British army to fight the Nazis. She parachuted in Yugoslavia (currently Croatia) on March 15, 1944 (four days before the occupation of Hungary by the Germans). Szenes crossed the border from Yugoslavia to Hungary on June 9,[11] and was immediately caught by the Hungarians. In her possession was incriminating equipment, including parts of British uniform, a transmitter, and a borrowed identity. No Jewish entity in Hungary knew of her planned arrival, so obviously they could not have helped her nor could they have been involved in any way in

---

[10]　See, for instance, Révész, 2001, p. 195.

[11]　Gilad, 1949, p. 402.

her capture. Szenes revealed her true identity to her Hungarian capturers.[12] As a Hungarian-born, she was no longer entitled to war prisoner status but was rather considered a traitor (that is the law of most countries, including Western countries). Under these circumstances, the possibility of releasing her from imprisonment using normal legal proceedings evaporated. On November 7, 1944 she was executed at the prison in Budapest, about two months before the city was liberated by the Russians.

Peretz Goldstein was born in Transylvania, Romania, in 1923, immigrated to Palestine in 1940, and was a member of kibbutz Ma'agan. He parachuted into Yugoslavia on April 13, 1944 and crossed to Hungary on June 19 together with Palgi. At the border they met their Hungarian contacts, who were in fact secret agents of the Hungarian police that followed them. When Goldstein came to Budapest, he sensed that he was being followed and hid in Columbus camp where his parents had been waiting for the privileged train to leave. At the end of June, following Palgi's arrest at the Brands' apartment, Goldstein decided (or agreed) to turn himself in to the Hungarians who were looking for him, in order to prevent Palgi's immediate execution[13] (and for other reasons). He was last seen in Oranienburg, Germany, on December 8, 1944. According to the British army, "it is likely that he was killed on March 1, 1945 or shortly thereafter as a war prisoner."

Yoel Palgi was born in 1918 in Cluj, Transylvania (formerly Hungary and currently Romania), immigrated to Palestine in 1939, and joined kibbutz Ma'agan. He parachuted into Yugoslavia together with Goldstein on April 13, 1944. In preparation to enter Hungary, Palgi made a short cross-border excursion on June 13 to meet his Hungarian contacts (who were actually undercover police agents) and collect the falsified papers. On June 19, Palgi and Goldstein crossed the border and entered Hungary with the assistance of their

12   Palgi, 1946, p. 244.

13   According to Gilad, 1949, p. 469, Palgi was arrested at the Brands' house on Bulyovszky Street. Peretz was arrested on July 1, 1944, right after the train had left.

Hungarian contacts, the secret agents. In his book, Palgi writes that he suspected these Hungarian contacts from the very beginning but cooperated with them nonetheless. Palgi also used the forged papers they had given him and Goldstein. Goldstein and Palgi left their weapon and communication equipment with a Yugoslavian partisan for safe keeping. The plan was to send the equipment and weapon with the aid of their Hungarian collaborators after they had settled down in Hungary. According to Palgi, the Yugoslavian collaborator was only supposed to send the equipment upon receiving an agreed upon code word. When the Hungarians requested to receive the equipment, supposedly on behalf of Goldstein and Palgi, the Yugoslavian forgot he needed to ask for the code word and gave the equipment to the Hungarian contacts, who arrested him immediately. While Palgi claimed that he had suspected the Hungarians from the first moment, his commander, Reuven Dafni, wrote: "We received a message by a partisan messenger from the VI Corps that Yoel and Peretz found ways to cross the border and are proposing that Yona[14] and Abba[15] should come over and try their luck there."[16] Palgi had never mentioned that he sent such a message. Such a message, if sent, was inconsistent with having suspected the Hungarians. In his book, Palgi made another inconsistent statement that, during his interrogation by the Hungarians and the Germans, he actually suspected the Yugoslavian collaborator named Stifa, who was also caught by the Hungarians.[17]

Palgi remained under arrest until he was sent by train, probably to Germany on November 23, 1944.[18] He escaped from the train with others and came back to Budapest on the next day. At first, he hid at the French Consulate where he arrived with a French friend

---

[14]   Jona Rozen (Rosenfeld).

[15]   Abba Berdichev.

[16]   Dafni, in: Gilad, 1949, p. 403.

[17]   Palgi, 1946, p. 191.

[18]   Palgi, in: Gilad, 1949, pp. 423-424.

who escaped with him, and later he joined the JPU.[19] Palgi survived the war in Budapest and stayed to help organizing immigration to Palestine for some time after Budapest was liberated, until he was called back home by his British commanders. Palgi died in Israel in 1978 after having served in the Israeli Defense Force (IDF) and in various public positions.

The Paratroopers' Activities in Hungary

Hannah Szenes crossed the border with a group of people who intended to cross to Hungary and agreed to take her with them. Prior to crossing, the Yugoslavian partisans agreed to take them only to the Drava river that marked the border and did not agree to help them in the crossing itself or in finding a contact person on the Hungarian side. The group crossed the river by swimming, which required a considerable amount of time since they had to swim back and forth several times to fetch all the equipment, mainly that of Szenes, which included a radio transmitter. Szenes gave the partisans who accompanied her the uniform she wore[20] except the military trousers.[21] Two members of the group, Kloss and Fleischmann, took a detour to the nearest village to look for a smuggler they knew, but he was not at home. On their way back the two ran into a border guard who escorted them to the police station since he was suspicious of their wet clothes. One of them, Kloss, shot himself on the way.

Szenes and her travel companions did not notice a thing up until the border guards surrounded them. The Hungarians found the radio headphones and Szenes admitted in her interrogation that the radio belonged to her. She even showed them where she had hidden the radio itself at the border crossing area. In spite of the violent interrogation, Szenes did not give away the code so that the

---

19   Palgi tried to take temporary shelter at the house of a Jew whose son he met in prison but that person refused to harbor him (see: Palgi, 1946, p. 341).

20   Gilad, 1949, p. 402.

21   Ibid., p. 454.

Hungarians and the Germans could not use the radio. Within a few days, Szenes and her accomplices were transferred to Budapest for further interrogations.

Yoel Palgi met and talked to Szenes during his arrest in Hungary. In his book, he said that Szenes met her mother on the day she was brought to Budapest.[22] This was only one week after she had crossed the border, probably sometime June 15–17, 1944. Already on the way to Budapest Szenes was violently interrogated. In an attempt to earn some relief and stop the torture, she revealed her identity to the Hungarians, but only her false identity. When the Hungarians figured it out, the interrogation turned even more violent. Szenes decided to reveal her true identity, possibly because she was led to believe (by the Jewish agency representatives in Palestine, before she left) that her family had already received immigration certificates and would have left Hungary before she arrived there,[23] a promise that, even if given, was not honored. However, Palgi claims that the paratroopers did not take seriously the promise to evacuate the families.[24] Even if Szenes believed that her mother was still in Budapest, her haste to cross the border, which resulted in her capture, was not necessarily because of personal reasons. It is reasonable to assume that it was due to a genuine attempt to advance the mission, and had nothing to do with her mother.

In legal terms, Szenes's fate was doomed: she was caught with British military equipment, admitted to possessing a radio transmitter, and confirmed that she was a Hungarian citizen. No legal proceedings could have helped her as long as Hungary was in a state of war.

Goldstein and Palgi left for Budapest with documents provided to them by undercover Hungarian police agents pretending to be partisans. Goldstein's false name was Varga and Palgi's name was Pinper. While en route, a message was sent to them saying that

---

[22]   Palgi, 1949, p. 447.

[23]   Palgi, 1946, p. 244.

[24]   Ibid., p. 91.

Springman had already left Hungary on his way to Palestine and that Joel Brand, who had already left on his mission to Turkey, was not to be contacted. It seems, however, that these details did not reach them on time. The possibility that envoys from Palestine would arrive at some point was known in Budapest. According to Palgi, there were even agreed-upon authentication codes. However, the method and time of arrival, and the identity of the envoys were not known, nor did everyone agree on the need for envoys from Palestine.[25]

The two arrived in Budapest on June 21, 1944 at 8 am. The Hungarian police secretly took photos of them disembarking the train, as Palgi found out later.[26] They called the office of the Jewish community and spoke with Mrs. Kurtz.[27] Yoel asked to speak with Moshe Schweiger who, they believed, was in charge of the Haganah (Jewish self-defense force). Mrs. Kurtz immediately understood that the callers were not aware of the events in Budapest as Moshe Schweiger had been arrested upon the Germans' invasion of Hungary. She suspected that they might be police agents. As a result, she hung up the phone. Instead, Palgi went to Kasztner's office, whose address was in his possession.

On the day Palgi arrived in Budapest, before going to Kasztner's office, he noticed for the first time that he was being followed. After several evasive maneuvers, when he was under the impression that he lost his tail, he arrived in Kasztner's office. The two decided to meet again the following morning, and Palgi left Kasztner's office. According to Kasztner, shortly after their meeting, detectives came to the place looking for him, making it clear that both of them, Goldstein and Palgi, were wanted[28]. Goldstein and

---

25 Révész, 2001, p. 191. According to Kasztner (15a), the paratroopers were supposed to arrive in February.

26 Révész, 2001, p. 192.

27 Mrs. Kurtz talked to them (as stated in Gilad, 1949, p. 416), but probably not from the Jewish community's office since she worked at the representatives of a Jewish-Swiss aid organization and not for the Jewish community (see Révész, 2001, p. 192).

28 Judge Halevy in his verdict in the District Court doubted if this had really happened.

Palgi spent the first night in hotels. When staying at the hotel they needed to present their identification provided to them by the Hungarians, which allowed the Hungarians to continue to follow them. In another meeting Palgi had with Kasztner, it was decided to meet again at the Jewish community's office, this time together with activists from the JPU. Before the meeting Palgi noticed again that he was being followed by detectives, whispered to Hansi to disappear, and escaped.[29] Palgi met with a member of the Rescue Committee, Sándor Offenbach, who coordinated a meeting for the next day at Mrs. Kurtz's house. Palgi realized that he could not go back to the hotel. Instead, he spent the night loitering on the train system. During the meeting at Mrs. Kurtz's house, it was clear to everyone that the Hungarians were aware of the paratroopers' presence in the city. It was proposed that Palgi would go to the Gestapo and introduce himself as Joel's substitute for continuing the negotiations. It was also proposed that Goldstein, who looked too young for such mission, would escape to Romania.

The Jewish activists in Hungary insisted on the prompt return of Joel but at that point in time it was already clear to the Jewish leadership abroad that Joel could not go back to Hungary. It was proposed to send Menachem Bader from the delegation in Turkey instead of him. Bader agreed and it was brought to the attention of the Germans who promised to arrange the required visa.[30] Other names that came up as potential substitutes for Joel were Joe (Joseph) Schwartz, the JDC representative in Lisbon, and Eliyahu Dobkin, an executive at the Jewish Agency.[31] These plans, which were coordinated with the Germans, eventually did not materialize since the British and the Americans prohibited their citizens from making any contact with the Nazis. Jewish office holders were unwilling to take the risk of violating these orders.

---

[29]   It seems that Hansi was also present at the early meeting of Yoel and Kasztner and accompanied him on his way. There is no other way to explain how he could have known her at that stage. See Brand, 1960, p. 59.

[30]   Braham, 1994, p. 1257.

[31]   Hadari, 1992, p. 223.

Given the situation, introducing the paratroopers as Jewish Agency representatives seemed like a reasonable option both to save them and to further the negotiations on rescuing Jews[32].

Introducing a paratrooper as a substitute for Joel could have worked only if a single envoy had come (two would contradict each other in an interrogation), if Szenes had not been captured at an earlier stage, if Palgi's and Goldstein's radio and weapons were not given to undercover Hungarian police agents, and if the ongoing collaboration of the paratroopers with the Yugoslavian partisans had not been known to the authorities. All these details were not known to Kasztner, Hansi, and the members of the Budapest Rescue Committee. They were known, at least to a certain extent, to Palgi. Common sense and responsibility dictate that he should have rejected the cover story that was suggested. However, he may have had no other choice. In the second edition of his book, Palgi wrote that during the meeting at Mrs. Kurtz's house, Kasztner told him: "I informed them [the Gestapo] of your arrival."[33] Confirmation of that also appeared in Kasztner's report.[34] Further verification that Kasztner reported the presence of the paratroopers in Hungary to the Germans is in a 1946 document written by a Jewish Agency committee that was tasked with investigating whether blame should have been assigned to him.[35] According to Biss, a self-proclaimed avid supporter of Kasztner, Kasztner updated both the Germans and the Hungarians about the connection of the paratroopers to him and to the Rescue Committee. Thereby, Kasztner confirmed to the authorities that he and the Committee were collaborating with British spies who held radios and weapons.[36] For Kasztner himself, this did not represent a major problem since the Hungarians considered him to be their agent. Kasztner left all the others, and

---

[32]   Revesz, p. 193.

[33]   Palgi, 1977, p. 104.

[34]   Kasztner, 1946, p. 71.

[35]   Translation of this document is available in the chapter about Kasztner's report later in this book.

[36]   Biss, 1973, p. 145.

especially Hansi, to their own fate as collaborators with enemy spies. According to Biss, Kasztner's reports to the Hungarians reached Klages, the Head of Security for the Germans. This proved to the Germans that Kasztner was serving not only them and the Jews, but also the Hungarians, whom the Germans wanted to exclude.[37] As far as the paratroopers were concerned, Kasztner's report to the Hungarians and the Germans did not affect or add to the risk they faced anyhow.

The idea to introduce the paratroopers to the Germans as representatives of the Jewish Agency was probably Hansi's.[38] She was tasked with bringing them to the SS headquarters in Budapest (in fact bringing Palgi only). When Hansi and Palgi appeared in Klages's office (who was not there at the time), Palgi was taken for an initial interrogation. In the 1977 edition of his book, Palgi complained that Hansi did not wait for him with her car.[39] He clearly did not know that Hansi never had a car or a driver's license. She also could not walk at the time due to the injuries she had suffered a short time beforehand during the Hungarian interrogation. Therefore, she had to return in the same taxi in which they came. In the first edition of his book, Palgi explicitly indicated that he returned to the city on foot (and not due to a shortage of cash), a walk which was well beyond Hansi's ability at that time. Palgi mentioned that the Gestapo officers proposed to take him to the city by car, but he declined and preferred to return on foot.

Palgi's first meeting with the Gestapo representatives was held on Saturday (probably June 24, 1944). He left the meeting unharmed

---

[37]   Ibid., p. 145.

[38]   Révész, 2001, p. 193.

[39]   Palgi's book, *And Behold a Great Wind Came: The Story of a Jewish Paratrooper*, has three main versions. In the first one, published in 1946, he is appreciative of the members of the Budapest Rescue Committee and their activity. The second version, published some time later (1948), includes some complaints (such as the one about Hansi). The third version, which was published years after Kasztner's murder (1977), is similar to the second edition but contains an epilogue in which he withdraws his allegations.

and returned to Hansi's apartment.[40] He insisted on staying there although Hansi explained to him that the apartment was "marked" and under surveillance. Palgi stayed in the apartment, probably anticipating that Szenes would arrive there at some point. According to him, he planned to return to the Gestapo offices two days later. His intent was to meet Klages and receive the Gestapo's protection certificate that would prevent his arrest by the Hungarians. He did not have the chance to do that in the morning due to an air raid that lasted until the afternoon. According to him, by the time the air raid was over, "it was no longer worthwhile to climb the Schwab Hill."[41] Despite that, Palgi found the time to buy a new suit, return to Hansi's apartment, alter his appearance—all before the arrival of the Hungarian police who arrested him at the apartment on Monday, June 26, 1944, at 4 pm.

In her testimony to Yad Vashem, Hansi said that when she first met Palgi, she asked him about the rescue action plan. In response, he showed her a handful of gold coins.[42] According to Hansi, this seemed to her so unreal that she burst into laughter. Hansi further said that Palgi asked for help locating British and American pilots who parachuted in Hungary in order to help rescue them. Palgi had no idea how to find these pilots as all the communication channels in the country were disconnected or censored.

Peretz Goldstein was supposed to leave Budapest and indeed Hungary in order for Palgi's impersonation to have any chance of success. However, not only did he not leave, but he also did not find a decent hiding place. Somehow, he reached the Columbus camp where the privileged, who were waiting to board the train to freedom, were housed. This was confirmed in Kasztner's report, which stated: "We brought him," without specifying who brought

---

[40]   Hansi explicitly said that Palgi had been arrested in "our old apartment" on Bulyovszky Street (see Brand, 1960, p. 61). At that time, she was supposed to be living in Biss's house at 15 Andrassy Street. For some reason both Joel and Grosz gave the British a different address with which I am not familiar.

[41]   Palgi, 1946, p. 171.

[42]   This gold is also mentioned in Palgi, 1946, p. 168.

him and how.[43] One way or another, this was done with Kasztner's knowledge and consent, although this was completely contrary to the previous decision that Goldstein had to flee to Romania. Kasztner's new plan seemed to have Goldstein board the train that was about to depart in the next few days.[44] The plan collapsed when the members of the Rescue Committee were arrested by the Hungarian police on the day the train was about to leave, June 30, 1944, and were interrogated as to Goldstein's whereabouts.

According to Révész,[45] the Hungarians threatened Kasztner that unless he gave away Peretz Goldstein's location, he would risk the members of the Rescue Committee, the train, and the entire rescue operation. Under these circumstances, Kasztner had no choice and he informed the Hungarians that Goldstein was hiding in the Columbus camp where the future passengers of the train were staying. In a letter sent by Kasztner to his friend Hillel Danzig in kibbutz Ma'agan on February 6, 1946, he claimed that the Hungarians interrogated all the members of the Rescue Committee, and that "[Hansi], who was broken mentally and physically [due to the tortures at the beginning of the month] . . . promised the five detectives that she would lead them to Peretz." In fact, it was Kasztner himself, personally and at his own discretion, who exposed the presence of the paratroopers in Hungary to the Germans and the Hungarians. And it was Kasztner who knew where Goldstein was hiding and most probably disclosed that to the Hungarians. Hansi did not know where Goldstein was. She received this information from the detectives who were sent by Kasztner to arrest him.

There is no support for Kasztner's description that Hansi was allegedly "mentally broken." Her activity during that very period, including her appearance with Palgi at the Gestapo offices, is inconsistent with Kasztner's characterization. According to both Révész and Hansi, when the police came looking for Goldstein, Kasztner was not among the detained members of the Rescue

[43]   Kasztner, 1946, p. 71.

[44]   Révész, 2001, p. 195.

[45]   Ibid., p. 197.

Committee. While Hansi, Biss, and Offenbach were taken into custody, Kasztner stayed at the apartment together with the Hungarian detectives. It was then that he could have given away Goldstein's location to the Hungarians. He sent the Hungarian detectives to pick up Hansi, who was under arrest, to escort them to the Columbus camp (since the Hungarians were barred from entering the camp by the Germans). At that stage, Hansi had no idea of Goldstein's whereabouts and she learned about it only from the Hungarian detectives who came to pick her up. Kasztner, on the other hand, knew where Goldstein was hiding, as he explicitly stated in his report.

When the Hungarians arrested Hansi and the others, and while Kasztner stayed behind at the apartment to discuss things with the chief detective, the Hungarians showed Hansi that Palgi, whose arrest she was aware of, was alive. Shortly thereafter, the Hungarians came back and made it clear to her that Goldstein was at Columbus camp,[46] and that if he did not turn himself in, Palgi would be executed. When Hansi was taken to the camp, she updated Goldstein of the situation. Kasztner claimed for years that he was not only arrested with the rest of the members, but that he also was present during Hansi's conversation with Goldstein. Hansi refuted this to be false. She claimed that Kasztner, colluding with the Hungarian secret police, staged the arrest of the members of the Rescue Committee for the sole purpose of the alleged "finding" of Goldstein.[47]

Until the train departed, the Germans had placed guards around Columbus camp in order to prevent the Hungarians from entering the place. The Hungarians did not know that when the passengers left the camp that night, the German guards were removed and they could in fact enter the camp without Jewish assistance and arrest Goldstein on their own.

Regardless of Kasztner's conduct, it is reasonably certain that both Palgi's life and the train's departure depended on Goldstein

---

[46]   Brand, 1960, p. 65.

[47]   Ibid., pp. 66–67.

being caught by the Hungarians. Whether the Hungarians knew in advance that Goldstein was in Columbus camp or whether Kasztner informed them of his whereabouts, it is clear only that Goldstein's escape at that stage would have put Palgi, the train passengers, and possibly the members of the Rescue Committee in severe danger. The Hungarians were capable of stopping the train on its way out of Hungary. It would not have been the first time they interrupted a German deportation.[48]

At that time, Goldstein stayed in the Columbus camp until the train went on its way. The next day, he went out of the gate of the camp and was immediately arrested by the Hungarians who had been waiting for him. This heroic act by Peretz Goldstein, a Jew who turned himself in to save other Jews, was not unusual during the Holocaust. The literature and the testimonies in Eichmann's trial mentioned additional cases where one man knowingly agreed to sacrifice himself in order to save others. Not to minimize his bravery, Goldstein's chances to evade the Hungarians were little. They had his exact location, his picture, as well as the details of most of the people who had any contact with him.

The Reasons for the Paratroopers' Failure in Hungary

Many reasons thwarted the paratroopers' mission. The most prominent factors are listed below.

- The paratroopers were not sufficiently prepared for their mission, which reflected a complete absence of a real action plan (both to assist the British military and to rescue Jews, as Hansi described in her testimony to Yad Vashem).[49]

---

[48] The Germans subsequently sent the same people on trucks of their own and the Hungarians could do nothing about it.

[49] Hansi's position regarding the failed preparations of the paratroopers to their mission was fully corroborated by Révész's book (2001) and in his recordings in Yad Vashem.

- The lack of preparation was also evident in keeping the British equipment and uniform after border crossing. According to British military procedures, these were intended for the parachuting and border crossing stages only, in order to guarantee the paratroopers a status of war prisoners should they be caught when penetrating enemy territories.[50]
- The preparations for the mission were made a long time before the actual date of crossing into Hungary. During the preparations, Hungary was still independent and the Jews were relatively safe and free there. The paratroopers knew nothing about the situation in Hungary following the Nazi invasion.
- The paratroopers' lengthy stay in Yugoslavia must have drawn the attention of the many informers around there. Their presence was especially prominent, as Révész emphasized, due to the presence of a young, attractive female paratrooper who attracted much attention. Hannah Szenes was arrested while in possession of a radio transmitter and a weapon. Goldstein and Palgi were able to enter Hungary carrying documents provided to them by the Hungarian police. From the Hungarians' perspective, the sole purpose was to catch their contacts in Hungary. The Hungarians' tactic was highly efficient since it allowed them to also catch the Yugoslavian smuggler, who handed over the weapon and radio equipment to the Hungarian impersonators. When he was arrested, he was in possession of the addresses where Palgi and Goldstein were headed, including the Brands' address.
- The paratroopers knew nothing about the warnings that came from Budapest about the risks associated with crossing the Hungary-Yugoslavia border (as opposed to

---

50 Révész, 2001, pp. 192–193. In a recording made at a home gathering, Révész explicitly mentioned a British military sweater that one of the paratroopers continued to keep in Budapest.

the borders to Slovakia and Romania). Their senders did not take these warnings seriously. A similar warning was voiced by Joel[51] and it was mentioned in Sharet's report which summarized their meeting, but no one forwarded it to the paratroopers.

- The three paratroopers who arrived in Hungary had parents and other family members in Hungary. Palgi indicated this in his book and mentioned that he was promised that their parents would receive immigration certificates before they entered Hungary.[52] This did not happen prior to the German occupation and was no longer possible after it. The desire to meet their parents and possibly help them, may have led them to assume the mission in the first place. There is no doubt that it affected them during the mission and clouded their judgment. In general, personal attachment of this kind is undesirable in such a difficult, complex military mission[53].

- The paratroopers did not realize the severe implications of exposing their real identity, which changed their status from war prisoners to traitors.

- The rescue efforts made by the members of the Istanbul delegation may have been harmful, albeit marginally, to the paratroopers' mission. These efforts focused on helping the British in Europe (and were largely coordinated with them), while facilitating illegal immigration to Palestine. Tuvia Friling wrote that the activities of the Jewish Agency representatives in Istanbul, Eḥud Avriel and Teddy Kollek, in cooperation with the British, included intelligence gathering and

---

[51]   See p. 7 in Sharet's report, attached as Appendix 1; Eichmann's trial, t\1176.

[52]   Palgi, 1946, p. 17 (the promise is not mentioned in later additions).

[53]   Szenes met her mother in the prison, Goldstein met his parents in the Colombus camp, and Palgi was furious because his family was not included in the manifest of the train passangers (Palgi, 1978, p. 244, see the epilogue).

espionage, propaganda, sabotage, and rescue activities.[54] The rescue activities Friling specified included smuggling Allied pilots, air force crew members, prisoners of war, and other people who evaded captivity out of enemy territories. These rescue attempts had clear military focus and were not related to rescuing the Jewish population. These military actions relied on double agents who served the Germans and not the Jewish Agency, just like the agents who "helped" Peretz Goldstein and Yoel Palgi to enter Hungary. According to Friling, these agents also knew about the paratroopers' planned action. However, the method, location, and time, of the paratroopers' crossing the border from Yugoslavia to Hungary were not known in Istanbul. Therefore, no details could have been leaked from there.

Moreover, in an article dedicated to Hannah Szenes, her commander in Yugoslavia before she left for Hungary, Reuven Dafni, wrote:

> I admit, I have no rest. I did not feel at ease with the preparations we made for Hannah's leaving, but we could no longer delay it. She completely refused to wait any longer. All my efforts to convince her to wait a bit longer were in vain. She was adamant to go this time, even without escort and papers. There was no hope to convince her otherwise. The decision was made. In a short time, she would leave. . . .[55]

Such decision-making process was inappropriate for a Zionist-Jewish-military mission of such great importance and it may have also contributed to the failure of the mission.

The paratroopers' operation was poorly prepared. The paratroopers, on their part, did their best, demonstrating courage and dedication, under the impossible circumstances into which

---

54   Friling, 1998, p. 381.

55   Dafni, in: Gilad, 1949, p. 436.

they were thrown. This was not enough to offset the lack of preparation. Unfortunately, the operation failed before it even started and cost the lives of Hannah Szenes and Peretz Goldstein. The question why the Hungarians decided to execute Szenes while the other paratroopers were handed over to the Germans will probably remain unanswered.

It was impossible to release the paratroopers from the Hungarians and Germans by ordinary legal proceedings. This is why Kasztner, according to him, did everything that could have been done using political means. At that stage of the war, July 1944, the Hungarians sought ways to quit the war and surrender to the Allied forces; therefore, they did not rush to execute the paratroopers. In fact, they were planning to release them once Hungary would have extracted itself from the Axis powers. Leaving the Axis powers failed due to a pro-Nazi coup. This sealed the paratroopers' fate. The fact that one of the three survived is in itself a miracle. The European Jews who fell into the hands of the Nazis did not enjoy a similar ratio of survival.

Some allege that the paratroopers' mission failed because of their extradition to the Germans.[56] Hannah Szenes was caught without the knowledge of any Jew in Hungary, including the members of the Rescue Committee, about her arrival in Hungary. While Kasztner informed the Germans and the Hungarians about the presence of Palgi and Goldstein in Budapest, it is clear that this was not new to the Hungarians. It is doubtful that this could have affected their fate.

Unlike other members of the Rescue Committee, Hansi had no relatives on the train. Thus, she had no personal interest in the train's departure, short of her desire to save as many people as she could. In an attempt to ensure the train's departure, it seems that it was Hansi's idea to introduce Palgi as a representative of the Jewish Agency who came to replace Joel. She had no ulterior motive since her two sisters, brother, brother-in-law, and mother were all

---

[56]   Judge Benjamin Halevy at the Kasztner (Grunewald) trial. Weitz, 1995, p. 246; Reichenthal 2009, p. 115.

in Hungary at the time, and were not on the list of passengers. As to the rationale behind the idea proposed by Hansi, Peretz Révész said: "The chain of events after Joel Brand's departure would have allowed such an improvised proposal."[57] Unfortunately, the paratroopers, probably for reasons deemed important to them at the time, opted to conceal pertinent details from Hansi and the other members of the Rescue Committee. Knowing these details would have disqualified the idea out of hand.

Notwithstanding the paratroopers' and their senders' best intent, they totally ignored the immense risk their presence posed first and foremost to Hansi, but also to Kasztner and others. The Hungarians knew, almost from the first moment, the names and addresses of the paratroopers' contacts. The Yugoslavian partisan who smuggled them handed these contacts, together with weapons and equipment, to the Hungarian undercover agents masquerading as partisans.

Since the Hungarians and the Germans knew that the members of the Rescue Committee were cooperating with paratroopers of the Allies, it is surprising that they were not arrested and executed. For unknown reasons, this was not the case and there is no clear explanation for that. It seems that the Hungarians did not arrest Hansi and the other members of the Rescue Committee because they feared similar humiliation as in the forged documents incident, when a release was forced on them by the Germans as described in the previous chapter. Why the Germans looked the other way is even less clear. Perhaps, they did not want to jeopardize the negotiations which were probably more important to them.

Hannah Szenes's mother, Katerina Szenes, who survived the war, testified during Kasztner trial in Jerusalem. In her testimony, Mrs. Szenes complained that she had looked for Kasztner many times to ask him to intervene on behalf of her daughter, but had never been able to talk to him. According to her, she looked for Kasztner on Vadász Street. Mrs. Szenes added that Kasztner's assistant,

[57]   Révész, 2001, p. 193.

a man she named Groszmann, even made financial demands of her.[58] In reality, Kasztner office was not on Vadász Street—this is where Krausz's office was, and Groszmann did not work with Kasztner— he actually worked with Krausz.[59] Krausz was the more familiar, involved with the community, and experienced person, who would have been a natural contact to help in releasing detainees. It makes sense that Mrs. Szenes approached him and not Kasztner. Further proof to the mistaken identity is a statement made in 1947 by R. Benshalom, the leader of the RSZ in the JPU, who testified that Katerina Szenes tried for a long period to approach Krausz (and not Kasztner) but he refused to see her.[60] This false presentation in Kasztner trial, which was probably made in good faith, further unjustly contributed to the blemished reputation of Kasztner and the Rescue Committee in general, and specifically with respect to handling the paratroopers' episode.[61]

---

[58]   Nedivi, 2009, p. 304. Both names, Vadász Street and Groszmann, are mentioned there as related to Krausz and not Kasztner. Groszmann was a RSZ activist who received the Jewish Rescuers Citation from Bnai Brith.

[59]   Kasztner, according to his report, tried to save the paratroopers through his political and military contacts in Hungary who were already thinking of quitting the war. See Kasztner's report, 1946, p. 72.

[60]   Weitz, 1995, p. 56, Rosenfeld, 1955, p.154

[61]   Brand, 1960, p. 144.

13. Hansi: "The Heart of the Consortium"

Hansi's contribution to the rescue attempts in Hungary has never been researched and documented systematically. She did not write memoirs and was not interrogated in real time or even close to real time by the British and others like Joel. There are several recorded interviews with her but none are complete or systematic and thus we have to rely mainly on books and testimonies of others. The most important sources are those based on personal knowledge of the people closest to her: Joel's book, *Emissary of the Doomed* (1957, also published as Weissberg, *Desperate Mission*), Andreas Biss's book (1975), Révész's book (2001) and recordings, and Kasztner's report. These sources are problematic, however. The testimonies of Biss and Kasztner are tainted with personal considerations, thus, they are not reliable historic documentation. Kasztner wrote his report after the war when the risk of moral lynching, initiated by Yoel Palgi, was hovering over his head (as stated in the second edition of Palgi's book). Kasztner already knew in Hungary, and certainly when he wrote his report, that he would be criticized for his actions.[1] Therefore, he carefully phrased his report to be palatable to the political leadership, at the cost of deviating from the truth. He made extra effort to assume credit for every success, leaving others in the shadow, especially the Brands. Biss was hurt when Joel, in his book, did not highlight his contributions to the rescue efforts in Budapest. Later on, Biss was badly hurt when he was not summoned to testify in Eichmann's trial. Somehow, Biss believed that Joel was a very influential person in Israel and he prevented the testimony. Biss wrote his book almost thirty years after the events with the declared

---

[1] Regarding the way he treated the paratroopers and his behavior during his visits to Cluj.

purpose to undermine and discredit Hansi as well as Joel.[2] Révész knew Hansi for a longer period than other refugees and he worked for a longer time with her and with Joel, but he wrote his book more than fifty years after the events. Under these conditions it is clear that these sources should be treated cautiously.

Kasztner tried to portray Hansi as his assistant. She was offended by that. In her testimonies she said that she embarrassed Kasztner after he said in her presence that he managed the Rescue Committee—she immediately asked him: "When did you manage me?"[3] In a few places in his book, Biss used offensive names to describe Hansi. He tried to undermine her contribution to the rescue efforts, and in one case he even claimed she damaged them. Specifically, he claimed that Hansi prevented the contact between Kasztner and Eichmann and delayed it for many weeks. In reality, Kasztner attended his second meeting with Eichmann on May 22, 1944, only five days after Joel left on his mission. Kasztner did not mention that it was Hansi who connected him with Eichmann, of her own initiative.

Hansi's influence on all those who were involved in the attempts to rescue the Hungarian Jews was much greater than the credit she has received. Joel's book clearly highlights her crucial role initiating the first rescue operation to save her sister and brother-in-law from the deportation of the "alien" Jews in the summer of 1941. In the book, Joel explicitly indicated that without her decisive intensive involvement, nothing would have happened. Hansi had an active involvement in helping Joel evade the Hungarian labor service. Hansi's activities after Joel left on his mission were not documented to the same degree. The little information in survivors' memoires, research books, and other contemporary documents[4] suggest that

---

[2]   Biss, 1975, p. 34.

[3]   Brand, 1960, p. 117.

[4]   Hansi did not talk a lot about her activity, and the book she wrote together with Joel, The *Devil and the Soul*, does not contain a lot of information about her own actions.

Hansi was deeply involved in all the rescue activities and that she had great influence on the events and the people involved.

Two sources explicitly point out Hansi's influence on Kasztner's activities in Budapest. In the introduction to her book, Anna Porter wrote that Sári Reuveni, a Holocaust researcher at Yad Vashem, told her that "Kasztner could not have negotiated with Eichmann without the support of Hansi Brand. 'She was his soul', his partner in saving lives."[5] Porter quoted Prof. Egon Mayer, who was born in Switzerland to parents who had been among the survivors and financiers of the train of the privileged. According to Mayer's research, Hansi helped Kasztner believe that the gamble was about to pay off. Mayer added that if it were not for Hansi, he would not have been born.[6] Following the publication of the Hebrew version of this book, Yehuda Bauer wrote about her as follows: "It is true, in my opinion, that she is the true heroine: she was the one who pushed Kasztner to do everything he did, she was the one who was tortured by the Hungarians (and not Kasztner) and she stood behind her husband even when she did not live with him. Someone should gather the pieces some day and write her biography."[7] Unfortunately, these words are not reflected in his book *Jews for Sale*, where she is mentioned only three times, one of them (p. 198) is very far from easily proven factual truth. Hansi was probably the passion, moral compass, and engine behind the rescue activities of Kasztner. Kasztner was by nature a calculated politician and possessed many important and valuable mental traits that helped him save people, but he lacked the emotional capacity and love for the common people. Hansi's (and Joel's) love and compassion for others helped and empowered him. When Kasztner acted on his own without seeking advice (for instance, during his solo visit to Cluj) or when he refrained from accepting Hansi's

---

5   Porter, 2008, introduction.

6   Ibid., chapter 36.

7   *Ma'ariv* (daily newspaper), October 13, 2017. This has no trace in Bauer's books and articles.

advice (during his trial in Jerusalem), he was hurt and the fallout hurt his friends and acquaintances as well.

Kasztner's lack of empathy was bluntly evident when he visited Bergen-Belsen towards the end of the war where he met Joel's blind mother and her daughters (Joel's sisters) whom he knew very well. Yet, he entirely ignored them and their implorations.[8] Similar examples for Kasztner's inability to relate to people are included in Hansi's testimonies and in Biss' book.[9] Hansi addressed, in general terms, Kasztner's inconsideration to the average person, while Biss described specifically Kasztner's indifference to his wife's plea. Biss' wife approached Kasztner to help his release.[10] Kasztner ignored the plea for help, even though previously Biss helped the release of Kasztner and others, including Hansi. These remarks about Kasztner's personality was made by a couple of his greatest supporters—Hansi and Biss—not by his opponents.

Despite Biss's unfriendly attitude to Joel and Hansi, he confirmed that Hansi participated in many meetings with the senior Nazi leaders in Budapest, especially with Klages (Head of Security) and Eichmann (Head of Extermination). These meetings were held both before and after her release from prison by the Hungarians, when she was brutally beaten and had difficulties standing. According to Biss, Hansi participated in the meetings thanks to her calming effect on the Germans. More likely, Hansi participated in the meetings thanks to the respect the Germans had for her, both for her practical problem-solving approach and for having endured the torturous interrogations of the Hungarians who tried to beat out of her information about Joel's mission. As a testament to her practicality, Anna Porter wrote that the entire "Jews on ice" project was in doubt until Hansi, at the meeting with Eichmann, proposed

---

[8]   Full details of the event are included in Porter, 2008, p. 289. I received an additional confirmation to that from Joel's niece, Margit Fendrich, and Joel's sister Hanna (may they rest in peace); both were at the place and were present during the event. Also see Brand, 1960, p. 82.

[9]   Brand, 1960, p. 31; Biss, 1973, p. 67.

[10]   Biss, 1973, p. 67.

that the Jews would finance the sustenance of the fifteen thousand Jews who survived.[11]

Hansi's activism to help those in need started at an early stage, much prior to the foundation of the Rescue Committee and prior to Kasztner's arrival in Budapest. Back in 1932–1934, she took part in fundraising for a restaurant for underprivileged Jewish children in the yard of the synagogue on Páva Street, currently the Jewish Museum.[12]

In Vác, a city near Budapest, an orphanage operated from 1942, with the sponsorship of the Polish Committee.[13] The Polish Committee was an entity caring for Polish refugees in Hungary. Normally, they refrained from helping Jews. The institution was allegedly Christian, but in reality, it hosted Jewish children. It employed assistants from Poland as well as local tutors and volunteers from the various youth movements. When families immigrated to Palestine, they took a few orphans from this institute, pretending they were family members. According to Kornianski,[14] Hansi and Haya Springman (wife of Sámuel Springman, member of the Rescue Committee) used to visit the place, bringing presents to the children. They also purchased supplies for them using an allowance of ten thousand pengő allocated by the Women's International Zionist Organization (WIZO).

Hansi, the only mother among the rescue activists in Budapest, was concerned for the fate of local children from very early stages of the Holocaust in Hungary. In her testimony in the Eichmann trail she said: "I only insisted on the children—at least the children should not be sent to Auschwitz, at least the children should remain in Hungary, and we would ensure that they were looked

---

11   I could not identify the source for this specific remark but it matches similar patterns of behavior documented in survivors' memoires. Hansi always preferred relinquishing money in favor of life.

12   Israel, 1999, p. 181.

13   Cohen, 1984, p. 205.

14   Kornianski, 1979, p. 190.

after by us."[15] This was said in reference to the deportation of the periphery Jews, after which caring for children had become a top priority for all those involved in the efforts to save Jewish lives in Budapest. The periphery Jews were sent to extermination as whole families, maintaining family unity, which made it difficult to exploit opportunities that may have existed to save individuals, including children. In Budapest there was no systematic extermination of families but rather occasional kidnapping of adults for alleged work purposes. The kidnapped were mostly women as the men who were fit for work had been previously recruited for the notorious labor service battalions. With the men enlisted and women abducted, many children remained unsupervised and the need arose to take care of them. Department A of the International Red Cross started caring for children immediately upon its establishment in September and its work intensified in October after the country was taken over by the Hungarian fascists (the Arrow Cross party). Within a short time, apartments and houses were found; they were borrowed, rented or donated by various entities and used as orphanages under the protection of the Red Cross. There were about thirty such orphanages in total and they housed between two to three thousand children, as well as one thousand five hundred to two thousand adults. These buildings were not designed, equipped or organized for the purpose of housing so many people, and especially children of all ages. As a result, there was a need to better equip the buildings and provide an ongoing supply of food. The activity was mainly financed by the Rescue Committee's sources, thanks to its treasurer Sándor Offenbach, who did a great job in fundraising. Hansi, as the head of the supply department, and Efra Teichman were entrusted with the management of the entire project, including finding sources of supply, procuring equipment and food, and allocating the means and supplies to the various places.[16]

These "protected houses" provided only partial protection since the Arrow Cross party did not honor any internationally

---

[15]   Eichmann's trial, session 58, p. 879.

[16]   Benshalom 1977, p 171; Cohen, 1984, p. 207; Braham, 1994, p. 989.

recognized conventions and organizations. For example, the last prime minister of Hungary before the coup, Miklós Kállay, was abducted from the Turkish Embassy where he had found refuge. The Hungarian fascists also invaded the French Embassy of the pro-Nazi Vichy government.[17]

The total anarchy which reigned from mid-October created a severe shortage of everything, especially food products. This led to ongoing supply problems in the orphanages, the ghetto, and the "protected houses" (such as the "Glass House"). Almost simultaneously with the Hungarian fascists' take over, the Soviets began their attack on Budapest. It lasted from October 24, 1944 until the liberation of Pest in mid-January and of Buda in mid-February. Throughout this time, the city was under siege, and some of the gravest battles of World War II took place inside and around it. The Arrow Cross fanatics, robbers, soldiers, and simply hungry citizens, were desperately looking for food and did not hesitate to steal it when an opportunity presented itself. Obtaining and delivering food to the orphanages was, thus, both complex and dangerous. Therefore, most of the transfers and deliveries of products were made by the JPU underground which at that stage was involved in aiding the general population.

In January 1945, immediately upon the liberation of Pest and before the liberation of Buda, Hansi received from the Russians an authorization to buy, hold, and transfer food to the residents of Budapest. The city was famished after long weeks of siege during which the population, both general and Jewish, was disconnected from all external sources of supply. Food was at the top of the priority list of anyone who wanted to help the general population and the Jewish population, whose condition was especially dire. At that stage Komoly had already been murdered, Kasztner was out of the city, and Hansi was the only one who could arrange that kind of authorization.[18]

---

[17]   Palgi, 1946, pp. 338, 347.

[18]   The original is situated at the Memorial Museum of Hungarian Speaking Jewry.

On July 31, 1944 the leadership of the JPU sent a letter summarizing the situation in the city at that time. The letter was signed by the three senior leaders of the JPU: Rafi Benshalom (Friedl), representative of the RSZ; Zvi Goldfarb, representative of the SZ; and Peretz Révész, representative of the SDZ, namely Mapai. In this letter it is said of Hansi: "Hansi (Joel Brand's wife) performs well. She has assumed some of Joel's responsibilities and handles very difficult situations. She is the heart of the entire consortium, and we often need her."[19] We do not have detailed information about the nature of Joel's responsibilities that Hansi took on. The subject is mentioned in Sharet's report on his meeting with Joel, where it says that the issue of the *tiyul* was transferred over to Hansi and Révész. Another far more important and complex mission was the continuation of the contacts with Eichmann. After Joel's departure and in light of the lack of a significant reaction from Istanbul, Hansi, together with Kasztner, faced the embarrassing task of explaining the reasons for Joel's failure to return and the absence of any meaningful response from Jewish entities in the free world to Eichmann's offer.[20] Although Joel reported to Budapest about the existence of an "interim agreement" towards the end of May, the document itself was delayed in Istanbul until July. The document arrived in Budapest on July 7, after all the Jews except for those in Budapest, were sent to extermination camps and the Regent Horthy ordered to stop the deportation. Thus, when the document arrived, it was already absolutely useless.[21]

There is probably no other Jew who acted to save Jews during the Holocaust and gained such appreciation both on the part of the JPU and on the part of the Nazis. As explained, Hansi gained the Germans' respect following her silence during the Hungarians' interrogation which entailed severe tortures. Biss wrote:

---

[19]   Communication Office Archive (the Istanbul delegation) - GFH.

[20]   Braham, 1994, p. 1088.

[21]   Kasztner's report, 1946, p. 74.

Despite the tragedy of the situation, the declarations of Eichmann and Klages about Mrs. Brand's courage, which they compared with that of an "Aryan", were slightly amusing. They regarded Mrs. Brand with a certain amount of respect from then on. They had paid her no doubt the highest compliment these men could make to a woman.[22]

It is difficult to establish with certainty what the writers of the JPU's letter meant by saying "She assumed some of Joel's responsibilities," but it is clear that she became the destination for refugees and their leadership whenever they faced an unsolvable humanitarian problem, as Joel had been until that time. She was involved with financial issues, with supply issues, with "production" of documents, with *tiyul*, and with everything that required her involvement. She continued to be the "go to" for any problem that required personal sensitivity as demonstrated in the memoires of others. Hansi was not an official member of the Rescue Committee but used her place and influence to help in every issue where human sensitivity was needed. Hansi was generous with her food, money, and clothes from her own wardrobe. She offered her home to strangers and hid dangerous materials such as the forgery lab, all in the name of helping others.

Toward the end of the war in Hungary, and particularly after mid-October 1944, a few unusual rescue opportunities became possible. The complete collapse of the government and the total chaos that ensued made it possible, at least sometimes, to buy life in exchange for financial bribes. Prices were high and success was never guaranteed, which made it difficult to find and persuade financers to provide the means. While Hansi was not a member of the Rescue Committee, she was the best person to convince people with means to risk money in the hopes of saving human lives. There are several documented cases supporting that, probably out of many undocumented and forgotten cases.

One of these cases describes an effort to bribe a camp commander to release seven *halutzim* who were caught and arrested in Budapest.

---

[22]   Biss, 1973, p. 58.

A woman came and claimed that she would be able to release the group in exchange to a camera worth seven thousand pengő. The JPU activist said:

> I contacted Sándor Offenbach, who was a member of the "Rescue Committee." He was kind and amicable but said that it was uncertain that the plan would succeed. He went over to Kasztner with me, and he too said that he was uncertain and that it would be a shame to waste 7,000 pengő. . . . I went to Offenbach and Hansi Brand again. . . . Eventually, after all the troubles, I got the money. . . . I gave it to that woman right away and she passed it on. Unfortunately, three of the seven were sent to Auschwitz the previous day. . . . The remaining four were released and the two women were immediately sent to Romania.[23]

Offenbach's and Kasztner's reactions that "success was uncertain and it would be a shame to risk the money," were the kind of reactions that Hansi often heard from friends and relatives, for example when she decided to risk her own money to save her sister in 1941.

Asher Cohen described another case that required Hansi's presence not only to convince Offenbach, the treasurer, to give the money, but also to secure supplies that even the Germans were unable to achieve at that time:

> The champion of escapes from arrests in Hungary, Rut Judenhertz (Bajok), was arrested for the twenty-sixth time and was detained at a prison in Pest. In December 1944, when the prisoners were about to be deported to Germany, Tushiya managed to strike a deal with the Gestapo people: they were going to leave town before it would be ultimately sieged, but needed fuel to go on their way. Tushiya was able to convince Hansi Brand and Sándor Offenbach to get fuel for the Nazis in exchange for Rut Judenhertz's release, and this time it was the last release before the final liberation that came shortly afterwards.[24]

---

[23]   Cohen, 1984, p. 160.

[24]   Ibid.

In her interview with Asher Cohen in March 1979, Hansi told a story about a refugee from Poland who had asked to go back to her homeland to retrieve her children. The official leadership would not finance such a trip. The problem was eventually solved when Hansi, who always put life before money, intervened. This story is included in Peretz Révész' book.[25]

These three events are representative of the compassion and care given to each and every refugee who went through the Brands' House. There were hundreds of these stories.

Hansi exhibited extraordinary courage. In 2000, following her death, the Israeli daily newspaper 'Yediot Aḥronot published a long article about her, titled "The Woman Who Had No Fear."[26] The headline did not exaggerate. Earlier, in 1987, journalist Yael Fishbine published an article about Hansi titled "The Woman Who Played Poker with the Devil".[27] The stakes were high—at a minimum, her and her children's lives. Hansi's courage was exhibited daily: in assisting refugees who had been living in Hungary illegally, in hosting many of them over night in her home, and in employing them in her knitting workshop. It was Hansi who ordered the first forms used by the Zionist underground to falsify residency documents for illegal refugees. And when the Hungarians were looking for the document-forging laboratory, she agreed without hesitation to keep the suitcase with the incriminating material in her home. Hansi was also among those who went to the census office to trick the clerks to provide official documents to refugees. After the occupation of Hungary by the Germans, she played a significant role in the negotiations with Eichmann in order to try to save the Hungarian Jewry. As if it was a fictional spy novel, she hosted in her home the parachuter Yoel Palgi, an enemy combatant actively sought by the Hungarian police. She further took Palgi to the Gestapo offices in Budapest and falsely presented him as an emissary of the Jewish Agency who came to Hungary to continue

---

25   Révész, 2001, p. 122.

26   Moshe Ronen, 'Yedioth Aḥronot, April 11, 2000.

27   Davar HaShavu'ah, weekend's supplement to the daily Davar, June 19, 1987.

A certificate in Hungarian and Russian that was given to Hansi by the Russian occupation authorities in January 1945, during the battle for the city. The certificate grants Hansi freedom of movement across and around Budapest for the purpose of obtaining food for the city's inhabitants

the negotiations that Joel started. Hansi's unbelievable courage was demonstrated also after liberation. At that time, the presence of a woman within sight of the Russian soldiers involved the danger of robbery and violent gang rape. The attitude of the Russians to locals who welcomed them in Budapest was described by one of the leaders of the Jewish underground, Zvi Goldfarb (SZ), in his book *Until the End*. He described how the first Russian soldier he met robbed him of his coat and his watch. In this chaotic situation, when Budapest was in turmoil, Hansi somehow found her way to the Russian occupation authorities in an attempt to provide food for the starving population of the city and especially for the Jews.

Part III

INDIFFERENCE

14. ISTANBUL[1]

Indifference and Negligence

On May 17, 1944, Joel and Bandi Grosz, who probably conceived the entire deal, left on their way from Budapest to Vienna and from there via Bulgaria to Istanbul.[2] They arrived in the city on May 19. To his astonishment, Joel discovered that no one was waiting for him in Istanbul and that a stay visa was not prepared for him. More disturbing, Bandi Grosz drew his attention to the fact that representatives of the Palestine delegation to Istanbul were present at the airport, including Ḥaim Barlas himself, but they left the place as soon as they saw Joel disembarking the airplane. There are many versions to this peculiar event and many explanations and excuses to it, but the unequivocal substantial detail which is undisputable is that a stay visa in Turkey had never been prepared for Joel.

During his interrogation by the British, Joel mentioned that Barlas, the head of the Jewish delegation there, showed him a letter from the British authorities asking for Joel Brand (not Eugen Band as was written in his passport) to be allowed to enter the country.[3] There is no evidence that such a letter ever existed. Such a letter would have contradicted all the documentation describing the reserved attitude of the British towards Joel and his mission. Furthermore, the existence of such a letter would completely contradict the descriptions of Eḥud Avriel,[4] who at the time was

---

[1] There is a good description of what Joel had been through in Istanbul and Cairo in Amos Elon's book *Timetable 1980*.

[2] Brand, 1960, p. 40.

[3] The British investigation report, p. 29, par. 158.

[4] Avriel, 1975, pp. 179–180.

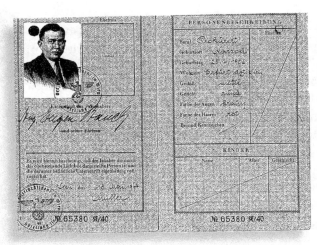

Joel's German Passport
bearing the name
of Ing. Eugen Band

Exhibit t\37_151
at Eichmann's trial:
German document
showing that Hansi is
under surveillance, and
that on July 22nd, 1944
the Germans still hope
for results from Joel's
mission.

the liaison officer of the Jewish Agency delegation in Istanbul to the British intelligence. The British began Joel's interrogation only about a month after his arrival in Istanbul, during which he was in a state of extreme tension, anxiety, and disappointment. Considering these circumstances, it is most likely that such a document had never existed and never presented to Joel and was just a story someone told him in Istanbul to calm his anger at the absence of the visa.

The Istanbul delegation received an update on the planned travel and its objectives, and it was requested to prepare a stay visa for Joel.[5] For preparation of visa, the delegation knew both the emissary's real name and his name as registered in the German passport. The delegation team responded that they would be waiting for Joel. However, they did not prepare the visa for either of the two names and they did not inform Budapest of that critical fact.[6] Both Kasztner and members of the Istanbul delegation confirmed in their testimonies that the emissary's arrival was coordinated in advance with the Istanbul delegation. Yet, they neglected to mention that despite the coordination, the required visa was not prepared. The confirmation telegram received in Budapest from Istanbul read: "Let Joel come. Haim is awaiting him. Barlas."[7] The telegram contained no mention of any difficulty with the envoy's arrival or with obtaining the requested visa for him. In light of the importance of the mission, at least for the Jews in Budapest, it was believed that the Haim mentioned in the telegram was Haim Weizmann (who later became the first president of the state of Israel). It later transpired that the "Haim" referred to Haim Barlas himself who sent the telegram and referred to himself in the third person, calling himself "Haim," and signing as "Barlas." The truth is that neither Haim Weizmann nor any other senior figure of the Jewish leadership could have met Joel simply because they were not informed of his planned arrival to

---

5   On May 2, 1944 according to Braham, 1994, p. 1082, and Rosenfeld, 1955, p. 462. On May 12, according to the verdict of the Supreme Court in the Kasztner-Greenwald Trial.

6   Barlas, 1975, p. 113.

7   Brand, 1960, p. 42.

meet with the Jewish Agency delegation. Apparently, the Istanbul delegation did not find it fit to update the Rescue Committee of the Jewish Agency or the Jewish Agency Executives in Jerusalem of this extremely unusual and critical information. It was Bandi Grosz who came up with a solution to enter Turkey. Using his personal contacts, he managed to arrange for Joel and for himself short stay visas for Istanbul.[8] Joel's immediate deportation, which could have had catastrophic effects, was averted. Such deportation would have probably been perceived by the Germans as an irrefutable proof that no one, not even in the free world, wanted the Jews and that even stopping or pausing the extermination plan would not help them to establish any contacts in the West.

In his book, Ḥaim Barlas alleged that he spoke with Joel at the airport.[9] However, in all existing documentation, including Barlas's book where the claim is made, there is no reference to the content of such conversation, if it happened at all. There is also no mention of any report of the alleged conversation to anyone. Had Barlas met with Joel at the airport and heard details from him about the mission, he would have reported it to someone. It seems, then, that such a meeting never actually happened. Barlas further claimed that the Turks, on his request, approved Joel's stay at a hotel and arrested Grosz. This is also wrong. Barlas confirmed that Joel came to the hotel on his own, and was not escorted there by a representative of the Jewish Agency, as would have been expected had the visa been arranged for Joel by the Jewish Agency. Ze'ev-Wenja Hadari (Pomeranz) rejected Barlas's version and confirmed all the details later provided by Joel, including the fact that the representatives of the Jewish Agency, including himself, were at the airport at the time of Joel's arrival.[10] He also confirmed that it was Grosz—not Barlas or the Jewish Agency people—who made it possible for Joel

---

8   Brand, 1957, pp. 108–109 (Weissberg, 1958, pp. 127–129); Hadari, 1992, p. 199; Brand and Grosz British interrogation files, June–July 1944.

9   Barlas, 1975.

10   Hadari, 1992, p. 199.

to leave the airport using his local personal contacts (or by other methods).

According to Ḥaim Barlas, "the Istanbul airport received an instruction that when the man [the emissary] in the airplane comes, he may go to town without a visa." This argument has no support anywhere. To explain the lack of visa, Barlas added that "the head of the Istanbul airport informed me immediately that he received no instruction to provide two messengers with entry certificates." Barlas's attempt to blame the absence of a visa on the presence of Grosz is not convincing. After all, it was an aircraft charted by the German government for diplomatic missions arriving from Nazi-occupied territories, so, naturally, most of the airplane passengers were Nazi Germans.

Further, Barlas claimed that Joel's short-term visa was only received after he pleaded with the UK and USA ambassadors. Not only do the historical facts show that the stay visa was not received through these ambassadors, but the alleged contact with a British official made no sense since there was no logic to exposing the mission to the British. On the contrary, exposing the mission to the British would have been damaging. The British did not want, under any circumstances, thousands of Jewish survivors heading to Palestine. Barlas's claim that he allegedly arranged for Joel to "briefly enter town without a visa" seems to indicate that he intended to meet the envoy in town or at the airport, and quickly send him back, ending the whole affair. To emphasize the alleged difficulty in obtaining an entry permit for Joel to Turkey, Barlas presented Joel as an "enemy citizen." It seems that Barlas forgot that Turkey at that time was neutral and sympathetic to Germany.

This approach seems puzzling. To this day, no one seriously examined the delegation's conduct and its motivation. The negligence to arrange a visa, following the erroneous and misleading telegram that the emissary was being expected, is critical to understanding the attitude of the Jewish Agency's delegation in Istanbul to Joel's rescue mission. Some historians tend to overlook this episode. Instead, they prefer to focus on the efforts made by the Jewish Agency executives, at a later stage, to convince the British to negotiate the deal. Those attempting to portray the Jewish

Agency positively make a special effort to forget that without Bandi Grosz's involvement, no one would have ever heard of this mission. Should that have happened, the Jewish Agency's senior leaders would not have needed to convince the British to open the doors to Palestine, contrary to their long-standing policy. Moreover, these historians try to put the blame on the messenger who had "limited understanding capability" and "never really understood the powerlessness of the Jewish representatives from Palestine."[11] This is a puzzling statement considering the fact that the Jewish Agency saw it fit to send about fifteen delegates to Istanbul.[12]

Joel's immediate deportation at the airport would have entirely undermined the efforts of the Budapest Rescue Committee. Bandi Grosz, whose personal contacts with Turkish officials prevented the expulsion, was known to the Istanbul delegation. They used his services to transfer information and money to and from Budapest. Kasztner despised Grosz, the uneducated criminal. On his part, Grosz hated the arrogant and intellectual Kasztner. Grosz, who was a courier and agent of every possible secret service agency, has never undermined Jewish interests. Letters and money that have been entrusted with him always made it safely to their destinations. For some reason, from the moment he arrived in Istanbul with Joel and managed to prevent his deportation, he suddenly became perceived as an enemy of the Jewish people and was persecuted by the Zionist leadership as well as by the young State of Israel.

Contrary to Joel's impression, Bandi Grosz was not sent by the Germans to supervise him but rather for an entirely different mission for which Joel's mission and the rescue of Jews was, or could have been, merely a cover. Grosz's mission was to try and find in someone in the West who would be willing to discuss a peace treaty with Himmler's representatives. After Grosz became convinced that neither he nor Joel could succeed in their respective missions, he decided to turn himself over to the British since he

---

11   See Bauer, 2001, p. 172.

12   Porat, 1986, p. 220.

feared his own fate should he come back without success.[13] Bandi Grosz told the British he was a smuggler, but in fact he was a failing businessman who found himself in debt. He volunteered to serve the Hungarians and the Germans to avoid a pending imprisonment for failure to pay his debts and for similar complications. His past with the various secret service agencies had excessively and unjustly tarnished his reputation. With regards to the Jews, there are only two reasons that could have turned the wrath of the Israeli establishment and the researchers who worked on its behalf onto Grosz. First, his presence in Istanbul and his ability to attest to the failing, negligent preparation of the delegation for Joel's visit; and second, the fact that the Jewish Agency probably owed him a lot of money that no one wanted to repay.[14] Kasztner, who was angry at Grosz, among other things for the fact that he was not chosen to go on the mission, took it one step further in his report and blamed Grosz for "giving away the rescue operation to the Gestapo."[15] Hadari (Pomeranz) copied this slander into his book[16] ignoring the fact that the Rescue Committee members had not been arrested by the Gestapo at any stage.

Grosz's connections with German intelligence officers made him aware, at an early stage, of the wish of senior Germans to make contacts with the West. He was the one who proposed to the Germans to use the Rescue Committee for this purpose. From the German perspective, Grosz was the more important envoy and his role was to find a partner in the West for conducting secret negotiations for peace (between the Western countries and Germany). Joel's rescue mission was also important for the Germans as they had great interest in trucks and strategic raw materials in short supply. They were hoping to obtain these through the negotiation for rescuing Jews, but this was, without a doubt, a secondary issue for them.

---

[13]   A previous envoy of Himmler named Langbehn was executed after his mission failed and he was exposed.

[14]   Brand, 1960, p. 186.

[15]   Kasztner's report, 1946, p. 13.

[16]   Hadari, 1992, p. 174.

Barlas's report to Budapest that the envoy was expected in Turkey, without even trying to prepare a visa for him, is perplexing and requires a thorough examination. The effort of some historians to overlook this issue is just as serious and requires an examination of the degree of their loyalty to the historical truth. From the Germans' perspective, Istanbul was not the only possible place to conduct the talks. Switzerland was also acceptable to them, but Turkey was chosen because of Joel, who believed in the Palestine delegation there. From the 1944 British interrogation reports it transpired that the Germans expected potential difficulties in Turkey. They told Grosz in advance that if negotiations would not be possible in Turkey, he (and Joel) must go back and try again in Switzerland and other places. An honest report of the situation in Turkey and knowledge of the difficulties in attaining a visa would have directed the emissaries to Switzerland where a visa was likely to have been arranged (as one was arranged for Kasztner, for the passengers of the Hungarian train, and for the Orthodox passengers of the train from Theresienstadt). The severity of this failure cannot be overrated as it made the rescue efforts in Hungary extremely difficult and damaged the chance for better results. Given that the delegation in Turkey represented the Palestine-based leadership that later became the leadership of the State of Israel, it is also impossible to rule out the possibility that the young State of Israel did its best to prevent the truth from surfacing. In his book, Ehud Avriel claimed that a Turkish Jew by the name of Shimon Brod was the one who prevented Joel's deportation and arranged for him the first approval to leave the airport.[17] This is inaccurate.[18] While Brod arranged for Joel a limited stay visa in Turkey, this was at a later date.[19] This demonstrates that there was no real difficulty in obtaining a visa without British assistance, at least for a limited period.

Barlas, the official representative of the Jewish Agency in Istanbul, had a reputation for mounting difficulties in front of people

[17]   Avriel, 1975, p. 175.

[18]   Hadari, 1992, p. 199.

[19]   Avriel, 1975, p. 181.

who asked for visas, and Joel was no exception. Barlas complained about the large number of unnecessary delegates and envoys that wandered around the place and he was not happy to apply for additional visas. Tuvia Friling described him as a "pedant, loyal officer" and said that even Ben-Gurion had troubles convincing him to prepare a visa when he wanted to send an additional envoy to Istanbul.[20]

When Joel left the airport with Grosz's help and arrived at the headquarters of the Jewish Agency delegation in Istanbul, the delegates expressed much interest but offered no substantial help. Everyone listened with great interest to his reports but no proposals or ideas were made to promote the plan. After a few days during which the delegation made no progress toward advancing the mission or even arranging a visa, a proposal—or possibly, a demand—was raised that Joel should leave the place and go back to Hungary, thereby allowing the Jewish Agency representatives to go back to their daily routine. Apparently, saving Jews seemed like a headache to them since the pressure applied on Joel to go back began nearly upon his arrival in Istanbul.

Joel refused to go back to Budapest without something that may bring some hope to the Jews in Hungary. At some point, Menaḥem Bader, a member of the Istanbul delegation, who was tasked with convincing Joel to return to Hungary, agreed to draft an "interim agreement." According to Joel, this agreement was signed on May 29, 1944, after a few nights of attempts to pressure him into going back empty-handed "of his own free will." Joel considered this agreement as a measure to slow the extermination down and empower Hansi and Kasztner in their negotiations with the Nazis in Budapest.[21] The members of the Palestine delegation saw it just as a tool to pressure Joel into going back to Hungary, thus allowing them to return to business as usual, as Eḥud Avriel said explicitly

---

[20]   Friling, 1998, pp. 376–377.

[21]   In retrospect it is quite clear that Joel's decision was correct. It allowed Hansi and Kasztner to carry on with their pretence and achieve whatever was possible without any outside help.

in his book.[22] Joel expected the agreement to be sent to Budapest as soon as possible whereas the members of the delegation delayed its delivery. The document was received in Budapest after more than one month,[23] on July 7, 1944, an eternity in terms of the period and in light of the fact that twelve thousand people were being sent to liquidation every day.

Ehud Avriel described the events as follows: "It was up to Menachem Bader to convince Brand to return to Budapest. Every night Bader would struggle with him. Brand protested that he could not return empty-handed."[24] In his descriptions, Avriel is quite angry with Joel for his "cowardice"—a man who risked himself on a daily basis for at least two years in caring for refugees and illegal immigrants—for not willing to go back to Budapest without any results and vanish into oblivion like six million other Jews. According to Moshe Sharet's report,[25] Joel believed that his failure would mean the continuation of the extermination in full force. He was of the opinion that the only chance to minimize the damage was by sending telegrams to Budapest alleging the existence of negotiations.

According to Ehud Avriel, the British did not want to allow Joel to stay in neutral Turkey. They probably fully understood the situation and estimated that sending Joel back to Budapest without letting him meet anyone was the best way to ensure the continued extermination, thereby reducing the number of Jews who would want to immigrate to Palestine. This explains the British behavior, but it raises questions about the actions of the Jewish delegation who embraced the British approach without considering its implications. The British, then, preferred that Joel would immediately go back to Hungary. In other words, they estimated that the damage his return would cause to the Jews would be bigger than the damage his arrest would cause. They eventually agreed to let him travel

22   Avriel, 1975, p. 182.

23   Kasztner's report, 1946, p. 74.

24   Avriel, 1975, p. 182.

25   See Appendix 1.

to meet Moshe Sharet in Syria, a territory they controlled at the time, probably only after they realized that Joel was not inclined to voluntarily go back to Budapest without any achievement that could help the Hungarian Jews. By letting him travel to Syria they could arrest him thereby thwarting his mission. Different members of the delegation warned Joel against traveling to a territory under British control fearing that he would be arrested, but none of them proposed a better alternative. The option of helping Joel "disappear" in neutral Turkey or taking another illegal action to avoid the trap was something no one was willing to consider.

Avriel said that he approached his British contacts asking to arrange a stay visa for Joel in Turkey, in vein. According to him, the British perceived Joel as unreliable as Grosz who served various intelligence services as a double agent.[26] This alleged "unreliability" was fostered over the years so much so that Yitzhak Ezuz wrote in his book *Understanding the Holocaust* that "Brand's background casted a heavy shadow on the trustworthiness of his mission".[27] Contrary to Avriel's opinion and Ezuz's statement, both the Jews and the British regarded Joel as trustworthy. In a telegram sent by Sharet on June 15, 1944 he said: "[I] interviewed him [Joel] Sunday six hours, found him one hundred percent reliable, was deeply impressed by his purity, character, spirit, self-sacrifices, factual exactness, soberness."[28] With regard to the British, their own actions and statements demonstrated that they viewed Joel and Grosz very differently and trusted Joel. Specifically, they treated them very differently when they were arrested: Grosz was held as a prisoner while Joel was handled with kid gloves. The only limitation they imposed on him was the prohibition to go back to Budapest. The British interrogation report of Joel ended with a clear statement: "Brand has not been sent to the Middle East with any mission other

---

[26]   Avriel, 1975, pp. 179–180.

[27]   Ezuz, 2015, p. 321.

[28]   Eichmann's trial, t\1177.

than the business-deal of 'blood for goods' which he had come to negotiate."[29]

While on his mission, Joel was able to report on the state of the Hungarian Jewry to the US (Jewish) Ambassador to Turkey,[30] to Moshe Sharet, to the Jewish Agency Executive, to Ḥaim Weizmann, to the British authorities, and to the US War Refugee Board. A review of the report written by Moshe Sharet after he had met Joel, a short time after his arrest by the British in Syria, shows that Joel managed to fully convey the situation. The fact that all of them decided against sharing the information with the general public and alerting global public opinion cannot be considered a failure of the messenger, but rather that of the information recipients who acted as they did. Joel had no control over what was done with the information he provided, certainly not while he was held by the British in Egypt.

To portray Joel as a "problematic" rescue envoy, some researchers attempt to misuse the cautious position of Western intelligence entities towards him and his mission.[31] Actually, most people who had direct contact with him, including the British interrogators, trusted Joel. They obviously did not like the deal he brought and the German political intentions behind it. The Western countries, including Australia,[32] Canada,[33] the United States,[34] and England[35] showed little interest in rescuing Jews during the Holocaust. Given the indifference of the Allies to the lives of Jews

---

29   Joel Brand files in the British Intelligence, SIME/P.7769, p. 36, para. 205.

30   Indirectly as the Turks refused to approve his travel to Ankara.

31   Hadar, 1971; Vago, 1975.

32   Australia did not want Jewish refugees in order not to "import" anti-Semitism which supposedly did not exist there.

33   Irving and Troper, 1983.

34   As proof, the attitude of the American government to the refugees on board of the ship St. Louis and its position on taking in Jewish refugees in general, including at the Bermuda and Évian Conferences.

35   The United Kingdom did everything it could to prevent the possibility that Jewish immigrants would enter Palestine.

at that time, the identity of the envoy could not have had any meaningful impact on the outcome. There was no real chance of full success for the mission. The possibility that the Allies would supply trucks or other goods of any value in exchange for Jews was non-existent.[36] In all likelihood, the members of the Budapest Rescue Committee did not expect real supply of military goods such as trucks, but they certainly hoped to stall for time. They hoped that the Jewish institutes would find a way to leverage the mission to delay or postpone the extermination by pretending to accept the principles of the deal and engaging in endless discussions with the German about logistics and technicalities.

Not a single person in the Jewish delegation in Istanbul was willing, able, or even interested to introduce himself as a party to negotiations with the Germans. The Allies, in particular the USSR, could not as much as conceive the possibility of supplying trucks or conducting direct negotiations with the Nazis. They forbade their citizens to have any contact with the enemy, namely the Germans. This might have been the reason for the cold shoulder Joel received from the Jewish Agency representatives in Istanbul and their desire to get rid of him as soon as possible. The Jewish Agency representatives in Turkey made sure to strictly abide by the law. It did not occur to them to deviate from instructions, even though peoples' lives were on the line. Indeed, the Jewish representatives in Istanbul had no authority to discuss trucks, but nothing should have prevented them from pretending to discuss the trucks, as their peers at the Budapest Rescue Committee (and especially Kasztner, Biss, and Hansi) did.

A valid question is whether it was possible to buy time without the Allies' direct help. Joel was not sent to meet with the Allies—he was sent to meet with the JDC, as per Moshe Sharet's report about his meeting with Joel in Aleppo, Syria. Since the JDC is an American organization, it might have been possible to stall for time simply by waiting, truthfully or fictitiously, for the arrival of

---

[36]   For the Allies' unwillingness to take any real step to help the Jews, see Hadar, 1971.

a JDC representative from the USA. It is difficult to accept the fact that no Jewish entity or individual—not even the representatives of the Jewish Agency in Istanbul—made any serious attempt to exploit the Germans' proposal, not even to stall for time. All the efforts focused on lobbying with foreign entities, mainly British, which, on their part, demonstrated no interest in saving the lives of the Jews.

The Palestinian Jewish rescue committee was not the only Jewish organization represented in Istanbul: a representative of the JDC, Reuben Resnik, was stationed there as well. Upon the request of the American ambassador in Ankara (Laurence Steinhardt), Resnik sent him a report about Joel and his mission. In his report he said: "I had several interviews with Brand and met him briefly." Neither Joel nor Barlas mentioned these interviews. Resnik did not seem too excited about the possibility of rescuing Jews and did not go out of his way to try to promote Joel's mission. On the contrary, his report was very skeptical: "I had the impression that he was not as sincere and straight-forward as other observers thought him to be." Resnick's lack of interest or knowledge on the subject is demonstrated in the fact that he does not mention the issue of advances and the possibility of saving at least a few thousand Jews without giving the Germans anything.[37]

The attitude of the Western powers, including the United States and the United Kingdom, is well documented. Tuvia Friling said:

> Most of the researchers believe that the Allies' reasons for their refusal to blow up Auschwitz and the roads leading to it range from dishonesty to overt lie. . . . [An examination of the details] unhesitatingly leads to the finding that the repetitious refusal was rooted in their indifference to the fate of the Jews who were being murdered in Auschwitz and other places.[38]

Most of the official representatives of countries who acted to save Jews during the Holocaust did it contrary to their governments'

[37] Resnik report, June 4, 1944 (Central Zionist Archive, Jerusalem).

[38] Friling, 1998, pp. 771–772.

explicit instructions, and some paid a heavy personal price for their help. On the other hand, not a single official of Jewish organizations violated government orders in order to save lives. Violating the regulations of the British mandate government and other entities was common among the Zionist activists for illegal immigration by sea or for defense purposes. Similar violation of the law was never considered for the purpose of rescue since it was not viewed by the leadership as directly related to promoting a Jewish state in Palestine.

Western powers had no interest in saving Jews or engaging with the Germans; and the representatives of the Jewish Agency in Turkey did not lift a finger to assist. In such circumstances, no Jewish envoy, as capable as he may have been, could have accomplished the objectives of his mission through them. However, Kasztner, Biss, and Hansi, who stayed in Hungary, took full advantage of the situation to rescue the train passengers, the deportees of Strasshof, a considerable part of the Jews of Budapest, and possibly some of the inmates of the concentration camps. While directly confronting the Nazi monsters, Kasztner made false representations of alleged delays. He stalled by justifying the Jewish world's unwillingness to negotiate due to the continued extermination at full speed. His successful pretense under very difficult conditions underscores what a Jewish personality in the free world, with a bit of motivation, could have achieved.

The Germans believed in the Jews' ability to influence the world, particularly to advance the negotiations. This is evident from a telegram sent from the Reich embassy in Budapest to Berlin on July 22, 1944.[39] In this telegram, the Reich plenipotentiary in Budapest explained that, according to his sources, the talks in Turkey were progressing well. He even justified the publications in the Western media (after Joel's mission was leaked) as intended to conceal the true status of the negotiations from the Soviets. This perception is also evident from Himmler's order to stop the deportation from

---

[39] Eichmann's trial, t37_151.

Hungary. The order followed Becher's optimistic report about the alleged progress of the talks after the crossing to Switzerland of the first three hundred train passengers.

At the time of his meeting with Moshe Sharet, Joel already knew that a quick cruel process of concentrating Jews in ghettos was going on in the Hungarian periphery. Eichmann already informed him of the intention to deport Jews at a rate of twelve thousand people a day without waiting for his return. In his talk with Sharet they also discussed the consequences and implications of returning (or not returning) to Hungary. According to Joel, going back to Hungary with a positive answer might have resulted in successful rescue but he was not certain of that. Failing to return or returning with a negative answer seemed to him at the time as a catastrophe to his family and to the Jews in general. It is a hypothetical question whether Joel would have gone back, even without anything to show for, had he not been arrested by the British. It seems that the arrest by the British was the best outcome. Staying in the free world voluntarily would have been perceived by the Germans as an escape due to failure in the negotiation. Going back without an agreement could have been a disaster. It would have forced Joel to make false pretenses to the Germans of alleged accomplishments and consents. At that stage, after the crisis Joel had experienced following the meeting with the representatives of the Jewish Agency in Turkey, it was doubtful that he could persuasively make such pretenses. The failures of the Jewish Agency representatives in Turkey, who feared to even slightly deviate from the laws and regulations in order to save people, traumatized Joel and he never recovered. Furthermore, without a willing partner in the free Jewish world, such pretenses were doomed for failure. In the absence of any cooperation from the Jewish leadership and any desire of the Allies or even the Jewish organizations to take seriously the rescue of survivors, it seems that Joel's arrest was the best way out, albeit not planned whatsoever.

Kasztner, some of the refugees' leaders, and others have claimed that Joel should have gone back to Hungary at all costs. To some extent, Joel felt that way too. Extremists argued that his failure to go back from his mission resulted in the death of hundreds of thousands of Jews.[40] It is difficult to imagine a more unfounded argument. Joel's return to Budapest empty-handed, whether after two days due to lack of visa or after two weeks of house arrest without meeting any official figure willing to negotiate, could have only worsen the situation of the Hungarian Jews. Many Hungarian Jews were sent to extermination before the time Joel was supposed to go back. Many others were saved by the activity of the Budapest Relief and Rescue Committee. Joel's failure would have thwarted the attempts of the Rescue Committee to make false representations of an alleged progress in the negotiations, thereby preventing the rescue of the survivors.

No positive development could have resulted from Joel's return from Turkey to Hungary without any accomplishment, as the representatives of the Jewish Agency in Istanbul wanted. All those complaining about the fact that Joel did not return avoid a logical analysis of the situation. However, it is understandable that those who were left behind in Budapest, who had no knowledge of the events in Turkey, anticipated Joel's return and truly believed that his return from his mission would make the Hungarian Jewry's situation better.

What Could Have Possibly been Done?

Many have asked what could have possibly been done in the face of the Allies' unwillingness to exchange anything for the lives of Jews. There was no reason at any stage to believe that there was a chance for the supply of trucks. Therefore, there was no connection between the Allies' unwillingness to discuss the supply of trucks and the failure (or thwarting) of Joel's mission.

The two first things the delegation in Istanbul should have done was to prepare a visa for Joel to stay in Turkey, and to inform Budapest the truth about its availability. Regardless of the availability of the visa they should have informed their superiors in Jerusalem, without leaking anything to the British, about the possibility that a Jewish

---

[40]   See, for instance, Biss, 1973, p. 233.

envoy may come from German occupied territory on an important mission. Had a visa been available, they should have invited a senior executive of the Jewish Agency from Palestine, preferably Moshe Sharet, with some kind of bureaucratic excuse not to leak the real reason for the invitation to the British. Since it was clear and known that the British had no interest in saving or evacuating Jewish refugees out of Germany's occupied territories, the basic condition for success was to withhold information from them and keep them in the dark. Unfortunately, the delegation wasted at least a full week without doing anything while the Hungarian Jews were sent to Auschwitz at a rate of twelve thousand a day.

The visa for Joel could have been easily arranged through a local Jew (Shimon Brod) who, indeed, was able to do just that later on, when he was asked to, even at a time when things were more difficult due to British involvement.[41] The representative of the Jewish Agency should have been invited under some bureaucratic pretext, for instance, personal or budgetary difficulties, which were in abundance at the time—in order to conceal from the British that this was a rescue attempt. The telegrams sent from Budapest to Istanbul did not contain any detailed information about the nature of Joel's mission, but the very arrival of a Jewish messenger from the Nazi hell was an extremely unusual event during the Holocaust. It certainly justified an urgent summoning of a senior executive of the Jewish Agency even if not all the details were clear.

Upon the messenger's arrival, a telegram could have been sent to Budapest. It could have been acknowledged that the German proposal was received and brought to the attention of the JDC board members (who were the addressees of the mission in the Germans' eyes). It could have further been argued that the board members were not willing to come to Istanbul to discuss the proposal unless they received a report that the extermination had stopped.

There is no way to know whether such course of action would have delayed the extermination of the Hungarian Jewry, a delay which could have meant the rescue of twelve thousand people each

41   Avriel, 1975, p. 180.

day. Someone should have tried, but no one did. A similar course of action in Budapest did succeed to rescue some people. It is therefore likely that such action from the free world could have produced at least similar—and probably much more substantial—results.

Avoiding any independent Jewish rescue attempt did not appear to be a local failure of the Istanbul delegation. That was the policy of the leadership in Jerusalem. In fact, immediately at the meeting when the leadership received the report from Istanbul on Joel's mission, the leadership decided to inform the British, with the clear knowledge that the British had no interest in saving Jews.[42]

In retrospect, there is no certainty that an intelligent intensive attempt of the Jewish Agency delegation to exhaust the possibilities embedded in Joel's mission without British involvment would have resulted in the rescue of any Jews. But why did they not try?

Many books and researches have been published over the years about Joel's mission, but none provide a reasonable explanation to the telegram sent by the Istanbul rescue delegation, which read: "Let Joel come. Ḥaim is awaiting him," while the delegation neglected to prepare the visa that they knew was vital. Attributing the visa complication to Grosz, who was known as an agent that served many masters, is not convincing. Grosz was the type of passenger to be expected on a German air courier. Furthermore, he was known to the delegation that used his services on previous visits. The attempt to explain the absence of visa by Joel's misspelled name in his passport is also unreasonable because such a minor problem could have been corrected within a short time.

The British were adamant not to help Jews escape from Germany's occupied territories. As such, all the actions taken by the executives of the Jewish Agency, after they shared all the information with the British, were futile and could produce no results. They sent letters to the Allies' leaders and they visited the world's capitals. These activities allowed the Jewish Agency, after the war, to politically hide behind a false presentation to the public that they allegedly made every effort possible.

---

[42]   Porat and Weitz, 2002, p. 261.

Finally, despite the failures and negligence of the Jewish Agency's officials, the messenger, Joel, managed to leave the airport and succeeded to relay his story to the world, including to the US government. It seems that this had direct and meaningful contribution to the rescue of Jews. On June 27, the United States warned the Hungarian government that should the deportations continue, the United States would act decisively. A few days later, on July 2, in the absence of a significant change in the Hungarian attitude, Budapest was attacked by Allied bombers that inflicted heavy damage on the city. Many consider this warning as the main reason behind Horthy's decision, at the beginning of July, to stop the deportations of Jews from Hungary, which led to the rescue of many of the Jews of Budapest.

We tend to assume that the delegation in Turkey was interested in rescuing Jews, but as we shall see later on, this assumption is not proven. The delegation did its best to rescue pioneers, members of Zionist youth movements, but there is no certainty that they were interested in saving just every Jew.

Joel's mission was probably more successful and productive than he had known and believed at the time. His message reached the top leadership of the American War Refugee Board including its representative in Europe—McClelland, its director—Pehle, the Minister in charge—Henry Morgenthau (on June 6, 1944), and President Roosevelt (on June 8, 1944). This information energized their rescue attempts and contributed to saving many Jewish lives. Most of the foreign representatives who met Joel or questioned him in Istanbul and in Cairo viewed him as a reliable person. The less supportive comments were mainly voiced by Jewish representatives. As for Joel's suitability to his mission, it seems that Peretz was right in his predictions: "in Istanbul, Joel's strong words and loud voice would be more influential than Kasztner's diplomatic statements."

15. Pre-State Israel, the Jewish People, and the Holocaust

The Jews around the World: What They Knew and How They Reacted

The Jewish leadership in Palestine and the free world were aware from an early stage of the serious threat posed to the European Jewry following the Nazis' rise to power, but they had severe difficulty in coping with it.

By the end of 1932, Ze'ev Jabotinsky, leader of the minority stream in the Zionist movement, noticed the danger posed to Jews in Germany. In early 1933, after Hitler came to power, he saw Germany as a danger to the entire world. In early 1934, the dominant leader of the Jewish community in Palestine, David Ben-Gurion, stated that Hitler's government was endangering the entire Jewish world.[1] In response, Jabotinsky attempted to organize a rapid mass immigration of Jews, mainly from Eastern Europe, to Palestine, but his initiative failed and the line adopted by the Zionist movement was completely different.

The mainstream of the Zionist movement favored "an orderly, slow exodus that would help them in building up Palestine"[2] as an "idealistic" Jewish homeland for selected people, according to Ḥaim Weizmann, the senior leader of the Zionist movement at that time, as Ben Hecht says in his book *Perfidy*:

> In August 1937 Dr. Weizmann, as leader of World Zionism, addressed a Zionist convention in London. Hitler at the time was sowing their new mission into German souls, the extermination

[1]   Segev, 1991, p. 15.

[2]   Bauer, 1994, p. 8.

of the Jews of Europe. This new factor in "Jewish affairs" did not alter Weizmann's blueprint for a selective Jewish homeland; neither did it move him to urge the six million Jews of Europe to save themselves by coming to Palestine. Dr. Weizmann remained loyal to his "idealistic" concept of the Promised Land—that it was no place to crowd up with Jews.

Of the six million Jews who were in a few years to be exterminated by the Germans, Dr. Weizmann, addressing the four hundred and eighty Zionist delegates, fifteen hundred visitors, two hundred press correspondents from all corners of the earth, and official foreign representatives from a score of nations, had this to say:

"I told the British Royal Commission that the hopes of Europe's six million Jews were centered on emigration. I was asked: 'Can you bring six million Jews to Palestine?' I replied: 'No.' . . . The old ones will pass. They will bear their fate or they will not. They were dust, economic and moral dust in a cruel world. . . . Only a branch shall survive. . . . They had to accept it. . . . If they feel and suffer they will find the way—be'aharit hayamim [when the Messiah comes and all the dead will be revived]—in the fullness of time. . . . I pray that we may preserve our national unity, for it is all we have."[3]

In his speech, Weizmann referred to his testimony in front of the Peel Commission that was established in 1936 to look into the unrest in Palestine at the time. To put things in context, Weizmann probably tried to minimize the impact of Jewish immigration in order not to aggravate the British government. Nevertheless, the cruelty of the words reflected the political division and elitist attitude of the Zionist leadership. The Zionist movement at that time clearly favored the interest of the establishment of a "Jewish homeland," and in fact, a Jewish state in Palestine over the life of the Jews for which the future state was intended.

This attitude of favoring the interests of the future state over the interests of the people for whom the state was intended was clearly demonstrated also by Ben-Gurion, who claimed he would have

---

[3]   Hecht, 1999, p. 19.

preferred to rescue only half of the Jewish chidren from Germany by bringing them to Palestine than rescue all of them by sending them to England.

Ben-Gurion's attitude about the Holocaust and its potential victims represented the attitude of the Jewish leadership in Palestine at that time. Many historians who idolize him object to any comment that questions his care for the potential victims and his alleged incessant efforts to save them. Yet, there is no proof or documentation for any real rescue action initiated by Ben-Gurion. Ben-Gurion acted a lot to increase immigration to Palestine (of "suitable" elements, in his opinion), but this immigration was not a rescue initiative. The motivation for immigration, in Ben-Gurion's eyes, was to promote the Zionist-Israeli interests and possibly the national interests of the entire Jewish people. The purpose of the immigration was certainly not to rescue anyone but rather to empower the Jewish community in Palestine.

It is a common mistake to associate immigration to Palestine with rescue. In Michael Bar-Zohar's book, *Ben-Gurion: The Man Behind the Legend* (1986), there is no mention of any action on the part of Ben-Gurion that may be construed as a rescue attempt or even involvement in rescue-related activity. The same holds true for Tuvia Friling's book, *Arrows in the Dark: David Ben-Gurion, the Yishuv Leadership and Rescue Attempts during the Holocaust* (1998), which attempts to describe, in its two volumes, the alleged rescue efforts of Ben-Gurion and the leadership of the Jewish community in Palestine. These attempts to present immigration to Palestine as rescue operations are not convincing. The leadership activity focused on bringing suitable people to Palestine.

Rescue for the sake of saving lives, as opposed to immigration to Palestine, received very little attention. Rescue actions per se, which are not related to immigration to Palestine, such as Joel's mission, were delegated to the Allies whose interest in saving Jews was negligible. An interesting chapter in Friling's book discussed the attempts to rescue children: there was great enthusiasm to save them in order to bring them to Palestine and raise them on desirable values. The enthusiasm subsided when the hope to bring these children outside the quota of immigration certificates was proven false.

In a thick 2009 book, edited by Dina Porat, *When Disaster comes from Afar: Leading Personalities in the Land of Israel Confront Nazism and the Holocaust, 1933–1948*, various writers describe the attitude of the leaders of that generation to the Holocaust. The general picture it portrays is depressing as it is difficult to find among those leading figures anyone who dedicated significant attention and energy to any rescue attempts. Even Yitzhak Gruenbaum, after accepting the role of the head of the rescue committee established by the Jewish community in Palestine, took it as a partial task and preferred to keep for himself some other responsibilities such as a director in the Jewish Agency. An especially interesting chapter is the chapter dedicated by Friling to Ben-Gurion, titled "Palestinocentrism? David Ben-Gurion and 'Negation of the Diaspora' During the Holocaust." This chapter addresses the negative image of Ben-Gurion as it relates to the Holocaust. Friling attempts to paint a somewhat positive image of Ben-Gurion by listing many things he said and wrote about the European Jews during the Holocaust. Yet even Friling was unable to cite any rescue attempt supported by Ben-Gurion. It seems that Ben-Gurion accepted the situation and settled for verbally expressing his sense of helplessness.[4] A sense of helplessness is neither a policy nor an action. Worse, it does not justify Ben-Gurion's statement about rescuing ten thousand Jewish children from Germany on December 7, 1938: "Had I known that all the Jewish children could be saved from Germany by being transferred to England, whereas only half of them could be saved if transferred to Eretz Israel, I would have chosen the latter."[5] For the many who could had been part of the other half this statement and the corresponding conduct of the leadership are unforgiveable and inexcusable. It seems that the Jewish leadership before and during the Holocaust did not internalize the severity of the situation and they certainly did not foresee the harsh impression that their words would leave on future readers. And thus, it is not surprising that

4   Friling, in Porat, 2009, p. 364.

5   Ibid., p. 362.

when the Holocaust happened, they remained helpless and failed to react properly.

Despite the early understanding (almost a decade before the events themselves) that the Jewish people were facing a Holocaust, when the information about the Holocaust came to the attention of these leaders, they still had difficulty believing it.

Plenty of information about the methodological extermination of European Jews in the territories of the Third Reich reached the free world and Palestine in early 1942, much earlier than the end of that year, as various Israeli sources have claimed. British, Polish, Russian and even Jewish sources, such as Bernard Jacobson (the representative of the Joint Distribution Committee, JDC, in Budapest, who left Hungary after it had declared war on the United States at the end of 1941), reported hundreds of thousands of victims by 1941. A detailed report of the extermination plan devised by Germany[6] was sent by Dr. C. Posner from Geneva and reached the American Jewish leader Stephen Samuel Wise and the Jewish Agency via Istanbul in August and July 1942 respectively, but it was only in November of that year that a committee for the Jews of occupied Europe was established in Palestine and the content of the telegram was brought to the public's attention in the United States.

Despite having plenty of reliable and detailed information in Palestine and in the United States about the extermination by mid-1942, most of the leaders could not grasp the severity of the situation. In her book *Back to That Place*, Hanna Bin Nun described very well the doubts the Jewish leadership in Palestine had with respect to the reports of the events taking place in Germany's occupied territories. Following her departure of Europe at the beginning of 1943, Bin Nun and another European refugee met with David Remez, who managed the General Council of the Zionist Workers Organization in Palestine,[7] to brief him on their experiences and their first-hand knowledge of the events in Europe. Bin Nun tells that at the

---

6   The Riegner telegram (Gerhart Moritz Riegner).

7   The most important Jewish political and economic organization in Israel at the time.

end of the meeting Remez asked her (in Yiddish): "My child, did everything you say really happen? Perhaps you added something from your imagination?"[8]

Another example of the inability to cope with the available but overwhelming information is an article published in Mapai's[9] newspaper *Davar* on March 17, 1942, in which the writer complains about the overrated rumors, in his opinion, of the number of murdered Jews:

> Not to say that the Nazi murders did not hurt, crush, and dismember Jews, but the irresponsible informants continue to add to Jewish destruction. They accept every rumor, they desperately search for sensational numbers, and they hand them to newspapers and their readers in a form and content that is truly blood-curdling. . . .
> Those who disseminate information about tens of thousands of dead and murdered Jews or even a quarter of a million Jews should know that the public no longer takes these numbers to heart due to their exaggeration. . . .
> Slow down, informants and reporters, when you pour Jewish blood into your papers![10]

This was printed after the publication of a JDC report about 240,000 victims and a Russian official report (delivered through American channels) about 100,000 victims in Kiev (Babi Yar), all of this before the end of 1941.

The failure to grasp the reality, internalize the information, and adjust priorities accordingly, took a central stage in Yizhak Ezuz's book, *Understanding the Holocaust*.[11] According to Ezuz, Ben-Gurion realized before others the unprecedented disaster of the Holocaust.

---

8   Bin Nun, 1997, p. 4.

9   A Jewish Social-Democrat Political party. The dominant Jewish political party in Palestine at the time and during the first years of the State of Israel headed by Ben-Gurion.

10   *Davar*, March 17, 1942, p. 2, an article entitled "Something." The author's name is not mentioned.

11   Ezuz, 2015.

Nevertheless, Ben-Gurion did not consider it a reason to deviate from his priorities and policies.

Much more poignant words were written in 1962 by the author and researcher S. B. Beit-Zvi in a letter he wrote to Ben-Gurion:

> After intense research, I conclude that the Zionist movement and the Jewish community in Palestine committed mortal sins to their comrades in Europe. They did not take actions that were required to save them, and they did take actions that severely hindered the rescue possibilities. In fact, rescuing Jews was not put as a goal at all, not even after the scope of the extermination was known and made public.

The author adds an even more acute allegation:

> The cruelty of the Zionist movement to the Jews of Europe extended to exploiting the catastrophe to help its own cause. It publicly and openly planned how to exploit the dire postwar situation of the European Jews to promote the Zionist agenda.[12]

Beit-Zvi concluded that regardless of the emergency situation due to the war in Europe, the Zionist movement declared its own war against any Jew who would escape Europe and find refuge outside of Palestine.[13] An extreme demonstration of this policy was reflected in the campaign of Zionist entities against accepting the Dominican Republic proposal made at the Évian Conference to take in 100,000 Jewish refugees. This option was available throughout the war.

In defense of Ben-Gurion and the local leadership of the Jews in Palestine, it may be argued that they had their own existential issues to deal with. Until the end of 1942 a great fear prevailed from a possible invasion of German troops stationed in North Africa that threatened Egypt and Palestine. In addition to this external threat, there was also a fear that a local war could be initiated by the Arabs in Palestine, backed by the neighboring Arab states against

---

[12]   Beit-Zvi, 1977, p. 7.

[13]   Ibid., p. 8.

the Jewish community at the end of World War II. While these arguments have a basic truth to them, they are not too convincing when one takes into consideration the length of time and number of discussions that were dedicated to internal party politics and power struggles relative to the time spent exploring ways to rescue fellow humans.

An additional consideration that probably guided Ben-Gurion is whether the Jewish community in Palestine would be able to save the European Jews while Britain and other nations refused to take in Jewish refugees. The limited achievements of the Évian Conference in July 1938 and the total failure of the Bermuda Conference in April 1943, where the issue of the Jewish refugees was discussed, demonstrated the indifference of the world in general, and the United States and the United Kingdom in particular, regarding the fate of Jews prior to and during the war.[14] However, there were countries, mainly less popular countries such as Spain and Portugal, that did not refuse to absorb refugees and did not deport Jewish refugees back to Germany's occupied territories.[15] The Jewish leadership in Palestine, including all factions of it, considered immigration to Palestine[16] as the best and maybe only way to rescue Jews and focused all its efforts in this direction. It did not properly consider the fact that Palestine was not the only possible haven and that immigration to Palestine was not the only means of rescue. In fact, options that did not necessarily lead to Palestine were not exhausted—an issue normally concealed.

The poisonous anti-Semitic propaganda disseminated by the Germans and their supporters affected global opinion and, to a great extent, also the Jews in Palestine and around the world. This influence is well reflected in the derogatory references to the dead

14 The Évian Conference is regarded in Israel as a total failure mainly because it has not promoted the immigration to Palestine. See Beit-Zvi, 1977, from p. 159.

15 Fascist Spain did not deport refugees who arrived there during the war and could certainly absorb more refugees than it did. Also see Porat, 1986, p. 206.

16 Subject to "suitable distinction"; see Hartglas's document in Appendix 2 hereunder.

Jews, such as "financial and moral dust,"[17] "soaps" and "lambs to the slaughter." Moreover, the leadership of the Zionist movement in Palestine considered a significant part of European Diaspora Jews a risk to forming a socialist "ideal society" in Palestine.[18] The rescue policy of the Zionist leadership at the time defined a considerable part of this population as a "harmful element."[19] The negative image of the European Jews damaged the sense of solidarity of the local public with the victims.

While many of the Jews in Palestine had relatives in the German occupied territories, the information the general public received about the Holocaust was very limited, especially since the local media did not prioritize this issue. The Hebrew media of the time mainly included a British-controlled radio station and press controlled by various political and public entities. None of these entities found it fit to make the Holocaust a main concern. However, despite the limited information, it seems that the Jewish public in Palestine and around the globe was not indifferent to the events and was willing to assist the European Jews, and it seemed that this willingness was greater than that of the local leaders. Internal discussions among leaders in Palestine demonstrated that there was no difficulty in raising public donations to assist Jews from occupied territories. Yet, the leadership deliberately avoided announcing a special fundraiser for rescue needs so as not to reduce the revenue from other fundraisers that were more important to the Palestine leaders. The use made by the Jewish leadership during the Holocaust to realize its financial and political interests is amply documented: suffice it to indicate Morgenstern's essay about the Rescue Committee of the Jewish Agency and its actions in 1943–1945.[20]

The leaders of the Jewish communities in the free world also had difficulty coping with the reality of the Holocaust. They

---

[17]   This statement is attributed to Ḥaim Weizmann; see: Hecht, 1999, p. 20.

[18]   Ezuz, 2015, p. 390.

[19]   Morgenstern, 1971, p. 73.

[20]   Ibid.

feared—somewhat justly—that the war would become a "Jewish war," as the Nazi propaganda tried to present it, which would increase anti-Semitism in their localities. As a result, they limited or refrained from applying any pressure on their governments to take meaningful actions. For example, they largely refrained from advocating for increasing the number of immigration certificates to their own countries for Jewish refugees which could have reduced the dimension of the Holocaust. The free world leaders of that time were not free of anti-Semitism, neither themselves nor the public they represented. To increase the hostility and reluctance of the general public in the West to take in Jewish refugees, they defined refugees as "enemy citizens," thereby representing and labeling them as a threat to the security of their own country.

The inability to grasp the unperceivable reality coupled with a dose of anti-Semitism also affected the actions of aid institutions, charity organizations, and churches in the Western world, such as the International Red Cross and the Vatican. Jewish aid organizations also failed to realize how grave the situation was. The JDC representative in Switzerland, Saly Mayer, stated in response to an aid request from Slovakia Jews that "This is the way of East-European Jews—to exaggerate horror stories in order to extort money from Western Jewish philanthropists."[21]

Jewish Rescue Policy

As the war raged in Europe and Jews were murdered by the millions, the secretariat of the Rescue Committee established by the Jewish community in Palestine, drafted guidelines for a rescue policy. This Jewish Rescue Committee supposedly represented all the Jewish factions in Palestine; however, the document was classified as confidential, intended for Zionists' eyes only. It

---

[21] Hadari, 1992, p. 122. A similar comment about the same person is also included in Hansi's memoires. Ronen attributes to that person a comment on a report of a refugee from Będzin from where he escaped in 1940: "Some crazy immigrant from East Europe told [me] horror stories" (Ronen, 2011, p. 244).

was drafted most probably by Apolinary Hartglas, the political secretary of the Rescue Committee and later the first Director General of the Ministry of the Interior for the State of Israel. The fact that Gruenbaum, who was the head of the committee, appointed Hartglas, the head of the secretariat, to be the first Director General of the Israeli Interior Ministry, when Gruenbaum himself accepted the role of Interior Minister, indicates the good relationship between the two people and the high likelihood that the document drafted by the secretariat was acceptable to the head of the committee, Gruenbaum. The document written in the spring of 1943 acknowledged that approximately seven million Jews were expected to be destroyed in Europe. This number included the total number of Jews who until the war lived in areas under German occupation or under German influence such as Hungary in the spring of 1943.

Because of its importance, the full text of the document is present as Appendix 2. Here are some points that seem particularly important. First, about the number of Jews needed (probably in Palestine), the document says: "we need to save 50,000 who would be beneficial in the building of the country and revival of the nation." It may be disturbing to find that the rescue efforts were due to a seemingly small number of immigrants needed at the time in Palestine but that number was a very large number in terms of the period and approached about ten percent of the Jewish population in Palestine at that time.

Second, the document explains that a selection process was required to determine the preferred people to rescue—those who, in the opinion of the decision makers, were suitable to build the country. To clarify this point, the document brings an example:

> The immigration of adults (Jews) from Teheran[22] provides an example of what troubling results immigration without suitable distinction may lead to. Besides *halutzim* and Zionist activists,

---

[22]   A group of 1,230 Jewish refugees, among them 860 children, who arrived in Palestine mainly from Poland via Russia and Iran in February 1943.

many people who have nothing to do with Zionism arrive, people who are tainted with total national demoralization.

The reason for the dissatisfaction of the leadership regarding the immigrants was the unwillingness of many newcomers to remain in the status of agricultural workers in *kibbutzim*. Later, after the establishment of the state, many of the immigrants from the Islamic countries were also treated in the same way and forced to accept similar jobs and status.

Further, the document presupposes that rescue options were extremely limited, thus eliminating the need for thinking and trying other options that may allow for more significant achievements: "For lack of any other option, the work of the Rescue Committee is narrowed down to small-scale actions, namely to save [single] Jews and small groups only." And thus: "we cannot dream about saving more than twelve thousand or a few tens of thousands of Jews." This approach may explain the cold shoulder that Joel received from the rescue delegation in Istanbul when he arrived there during his mission.

A large part of the Jewish people, and in fact most of those supposed to be victims, were defined in the document as a harmful element, which eliminated the need to save them:

> Had we had the means to save both kinds, there is no doubt that we should have accepted things as they are, but unfortunately we do not have sufficient means to save the good elements, and therefore, for the lack of any other option, we are forced to relinquish saving the harmful element.

"Harmful elements" were politically undesired people, as in the case of Lichtenstein and Armée Juive (the French Jewish Army) that will be discussed later on.

The researcher Aryeh Morgenstern, who brought this document to the public attention in *Yalqut Moreshet*,[23] summarizes his impression from the document as follows:

---

23   Morgenstern, 1971.

The conclusions of the memo for outlining the policy of the Rescue Committee are that if the rescue actions would lead to extremely small results in numerical terms, we should at least produce a long-term political benefit from them from a Zionist point of view: the actions of the Rescue Committee will prove to the entire world that the only country that wants to receive the surviving Jews is the Land of Israel, and that the only public in the entire world wishing to absorb these Jews is the Jewish population in Palestine. Another conclusion is that the actions of the Rescue Committee will prove to the world and to the Jewish people in general that it is the Jewish Agency that initiated, operated and acted to save the Jews in Europe. The actions of the Rescue Committee would also result in the Jews, who would be saved from the slaughter during or after the war, recognizing that the Zionist movement and Jewish population in Palestine made the biggest efforts to rescue them. As a result, Zionism would be acknowledged as the only entity that Jews could turn to. Israel would be recognized as the only destination to the masses of Jews who have been deported from Europe or rescued from the slaughter.[24]

Not all factions in Palestine were in complete agreement with the selection policy proposed by the document. However, their main consideration was not humanitarian but rather a concern that an Arab majority would be formed in Palestine. This is what Prof. Joshua Supraski, leader of the General Zionists in Palestine,[25] said on this issue: "If we do not rescue and we remain a handful of half a million Jews here—then [the Arabs] will be the landlords here. . . . It is also from a Zionist point of view that we need to spend a large portion of the budget to save anyone who can be saved."[26]

Again, reasons other than pure humanitarian aid guided opinions, efforts, and budgets.

To raise money from non-Zionist Jewish entities abroad, such as the JDC, the Rescue Committee officially declared that it would

---

[24]   Ibid., p. 73; also see p. 74 about the Zionist leadership's struggle to gain a positive image.

[25]   A non-socialist Jewish political party in Palestine at the time.

[26]   Segev, 1991, p. 89.

help all Jews, without bias. Morgenstern wrote as follows about complying with these declarations:

> When I asked Zissu [who was one of the leaders of the Zionist movement in Romania] why instructions to include Filderman [who was the leader of the competing, larger, non-Zionist Jewish Party] were not complied with, he answered: "No! We shall not include him. We shall not have him. We shall not save them. We shall save our own people." And when I asked him: "The others are also Jews," he said: "Yes. They are Jews. But this is a global quarrel. Eternal quarrel. And we shall prevail."[27]

In the two decades preceding the foundation of the State of Israel, including during the Holocaust, the Zionist leadership and its representatives clearly separated between *halutzim* (pioneers) and other immigrants to Palestine. This followed the spirit of Ben-Gurion, who proclaimed in the Eighteenth Zionist Congress in 1933 that "The Land of Israel needs *halutzim*, not 'just any' immigrants. The difference between them is simple: the immigrants come to take from the state, the *halutzim* come to give to the state. Therefore, *halutzim* should have first priority for immigration."[28] This cemented a political distinction between "positive" and "negative" elements. In pre-state Israel, the distinction between the types of candidates for immigration was mainly based on cultural and political background. After the foundation of the State of Israel, the ethnic factor became more pronounced (although it did exist in Zionism from its early stage). Jews from Middle Eastern and North African countries were considered culturally inferior.[29] This strong preference to save "suitable" Jews was reflected, for instance, in the following description, probably from early 1943:

> Later in the meeting Ben-Gurion sharpened his guidance for the management team [of the Jewish Agency] as far as rescue activity

---

27   Morgenstern, 1971, p. 75.

28   Kadosh, 1991.

29   Picard, 1999.

is concerned. With respect to "rescue, meaning taking Jews out and transferring them to Palestine," there is no question "that the Agency assumes the children's travel expenses." However, Ben-Gurion distinguished between two types of "helping Jews in their place of living": the management team will support veteran Zionists and send them passports, but as for "programs to prevent persecution using bribe"—by that he meant the Transnistria Plan and probably also the Slovakia Plan—"the Agency cannot provide money."[30]

Meaning, according to Ben-Gurion, there was money for issues that promoted state-related interests but not for preventing the murder of "just any" Jew. For that purpose, lobbying would suffice, which is consistent with the behavior Joel encountered when he met the members of the Jewish rescue committee in Istanbul when he arrived there during his mission.

In her book, Dina Porat tells about the Jewish Agency's messenger, Lichtenstein, who met with the representatives of the Armée Juive (the French Jewish Army). The resistance representatives asked the messenger for financial support in order to accelerate the smuggling of Jews out of occupied France into Spain. Lichtenstein declined to help them, both due to lack of means and because he considered them "dangerous to Palestine, candidates for the Irgun."[31] The Irgun (or Etzel) was the political predecessor to today's Likud Party, the archenemies of Mapai, today's Labor party. Porat adds that Lichtenstein left for Portugal for the purpose of "sorting refugees in Spain and Portugal who are suitable to bring to Palestine." In regards to rescue paths, Lichtenstein said explicitly: "These were not within the realm of my mission." To be fair to his superiors, he added an interesting comment: "However, they did not oppose that . . . but without involving any financial expenses."[32] It is not very comforting to know that he was not explicitly prohibited from rescuing Jews. Another blunt example of

---

[30]   Friling, 1998, p. 791.

[31]   Porat, 1986, p. 206.

[32]   Ibid.

the leadership's indifference is found in Eliyahu Dobkin's words about the rescue possibilities via Spain. When the options were brought to his attention and to the attention of the Jewish Agency, he said: "We did not pay any attention to it [to the French Jewish Army]" and "We did not think that any work could be done from there."[33] By "work" he meant immigration to Palestine.

In 1975, Ḥaim Barlas, the head of the Rescue delegation in Istanbul, published his book *Rescue in Times of Holocaust*. In the book, the author described his extensive activity at the time to promote immigration to Palestine. There is hardly anything in his book regarding rescue attempts that were not connected to immigration to Palestine.

In 1992, ten years before his death, Prof. Hadari, the number two figure in the delegation, published his book *Against All Odds* (the Hebrew title is *Istanbul Junction*), which includes harsh criticism of his own actions and the actions of his colleagues there, mainly of what they had not done. Already in the introduction, Hadari tells about forty-two years of misgivings that preceded the writings of the book whose aim was, according to Hadari, to "summarize the little action" taken during the war. This is how he described the course of action of the Jewish Agency envoys in Turkey:

> When I came to Istanbul, I immediately felt that my main role was to build the illusion that we came to save all the people we were in touch with. How could it be that in Palestine, and among the Jews of the free world, no one grasped the severity of what was going on already during the first days of the war? Were there rescue possibilities? There was no doubt about it: until 1942 it was possible to rescue more than in 1942 and onwards, but also from 1942 there were opportunities to rescue Jews.[34]

As for the passivity of the Jewish leadership in Palestine and in the world, he said:

---

[33]   Ibid., p. 207.

[34]   Hadari, 1992, p. 10.

The concurrence of the Jewish leaders in Palestine and in the United States with the point of view expressed by Roosevelt is puzzling and amazing: "The Jews will be rescued following the victory of the Allies" and therefore there is no need or ability to initiate rescue operations to emigrate from the occupied countries already from the first days of the war.[35]

The passive approach mentioned here is not the subjective impression of a single envoy but the policy of the Head of the Rescue Committee of the Jewish Agency, Yitzhak Gruenbaum who did not believe in the rescue and refused to allocate resources from National Funds for it.[36]

Prioritizing immigration to Palestine over saving the lives was not exclusively advocated by the leadership. In a book published by the Ghetto Fighters' House organization in memory of Zvi Goldfarb (*On the Verge of the End*, 1980), the authors wrote as follows on behalf of Goldfarb: "The *halutz* movement believed that as many Jews as possible should be saved for the sake of the Land of Israel".[37] It seems that saving Jews required justification, in this case in the form of Israeli interests—an astonishing disrespect to human life. It was not human life that was valuable—it was the contribution to the interests of some elitist ideal. It is worth noting that this poor phrasing was printed in 1980, thirty-five years after the Holocaust. The leaders of world Jewry, like their counterparts in Palestine, did not go out of their way to help European Jews and examples of this are plentiful.

Earlier we mentioned Saly Meyer's refusal to promise to the Germans that sometime in the future they would receive some compensation for the release of Jews and his arrogant response that a Swiss citizen does not promise what he cannot keep. It seems that his pride was more important to him than people's lives.

---

[35]   Ibid.

[36]   Morgenstern, 1971, p. 70. Ronen, 2011, pp. 242–243. See also Yad Vashem's website: https://www.yadvashem.org/odot_pdf/Microsoft%20Word%20-%20 1038.pdf

[37]   Goldfarb, 1980, p. 101.

More disturbing is the behavior of the Jewish leadership in the United States that, for most of the Holocaust, refrained from mobilizing public opinion to assist European Jewry. When the Bergson Group entered the space left by institutionalized leadership, they did their best to narrow their steps and limit their influence. When, under the influence of the Bergson Group, the Americans decided to form the War Refugee Board, the institutionalized Jewish leadership, headed by Stephen Wise, tried to prevent its establishment because encouraging immigration to Palestine and, in fact, opening the country's gates for Jewish immigration was not included in the board's mandate.

Part IV

DECEPTION

16. The Struggle for the Narrative

Right after the war, a struggle broke out among the rescue activists for their place in the political establishment and in history. The ongoing bickering between Kasztner, Saly Mayer,[1] and Moshe Krausz escalated as each of them blamed the others of not adequately supporting his own respective rescue efforts. These old quarrels were compounded by additional disputes with the paratroopers, the representatives of the Jewish Agency, and with the Brands.

The Jewish Public in Palestine/Israel and Its Post-War Leadership

The Jewish leadership, in Palestine and in the free world, did very little in terms of rescue during the Holocaust and the public did not show any interest in it soon after the war. This situation was definitely comfortable for the leadership of that time. The leadership was not interested in exposing the fact that ordinary people did more than it had, and were successful at that. The existence of survivors who successfully negotiated the rescue of people also endangered the leadership's public relations campaign to educate the public that armed struggle alongside immigration to Palestine were the only possible path to rescue. This situation resulted in a cold and even hostile reception in Palestine to the few who tried and succeeded.

Yoel Palgi offered a good description of the state of affairs right after the Holocaust in the epilogue to the later edition of his book, which was printed in 1977. He pointed at many of the key factors that

---

[1]   Saly Mayer, for example, took credit for saving the train passengers "while risking his life." Prof. Y. Bauer regards him as one of the Jewish heroes of the Holocaust, while others emphatically disagree See Braham, 1994, p. 1103.

guided the attitude of the public and triggered the Kasztner affair, the trial, its unfortunate outcome, and the murder that followed it:[2]

> Everyone wanted me to tell what happened there, but what I said about the horrifying fate of the Jews who were abandoned by man and God, was not what they wanted to hear. They only wanted one story: about the few who fought like lions in the name of Eretz Israel. Wherever I went the following question was thrown in my face: why did the Jews not rebel? Why did they go like lambs to the slaughter? I suddenly realized that we are ashamed of those who were tortured, shot and burnt. Public opinion was formed that the Holocaust victims who died were human dust. We unknowingly accepted the Nazis' view that the Jews were nothing but sub-human. "Soaps." But we excluded ourselves[3] from this definition. History bitterly mocks us: it is we who put the six million on trial.
>
> Those whose fate enabled them to look at the Holocaust from a safe distance assumed the right to judge and superficiality divide all the Jews into two: the masses who were led as lambs to the slaughter, and the few—the heroes. And some divided the Jews to righteous or traitors, as they believed that it was impossible for such catastrophe to occur without traitors on the inside. Those who have not experienced the inferno themselves, seek heroic stories in the light of which to educate generations to come. They held onto the glorifying heroic deeds of the few and failed to realize the mute heroism of the masses of Jews who were hurled into the slaughter without any way out. They were exterminated without fighting but nevertheless kept their humanity throughout that hell until their very last breath. I withdrew into myself feeling in my heart that I returned from a different planet, and that those who sent me there and the society to which I returned would never completely understand. They will not understand because they were not there. And those who survived the killing fields by blind fate are perhaps doomed to eternal solitude. We all use the same words but their meaning is entirely different.

---

[2]   Palgi (1977 edition), pp. 243–246.

[3]   Ourselves—meaning the Jews of Palestine who are supposedly the very antithesis to the Jews of the Diaspora.

While on my way home I met Moshe Sharet in Cairo. In the conversation with him I demanded that the Haganah [a Jewish illegal paramilitary organization in the British Mandate of Palestine] should investigate the events that have occurred in Budapest and that Kasztner would be sentenced by the Haganah, and until then would be disqualified from any public position. My demand was indeed granted. A position at the World Jewish Congress, which was designated for him, was not given to him. The trial was conducted during the first postwar Zionist Congress that convened in Basel in December 1946. I could hardly recognize Kasztner. He was a shadow of his former self. Nothing was left of his self-confidence. In his defense, Kasztner told the Haganah judges the entire affair of the Rescue Committee in Budapest and tried to prove that the motives for all his actions were pure. If he made a mistake—he said—God would be his judge, but he protests against villainizing him. The judges were convinced that Kasztner's purpose was one: to rescue Jews, and that he acted at the best of his understanding and out of loyalty to this purpose. However, they refrained from judging his each and every step. They found that those who hadn't experienced hell themselves could not judge those who acted under those horrible circumstances. I found it difficult to accept the judgment. Wounds that I thought had healed were once again opened and bleeding. I started having nightmares again. The images of my parents and sister Lutzi haunted me day and night asking for revenge. I lived in a kind of a private hell. Both when I was awake and when I was dreaming, I was tormented with a question I could not utter: why, why were they not put on the rescue train? Why was their right to live any less than those who lived? 388 Jews from my town had been rescued on the train. Why weren't they among the survivors? Some of those who prepared the list— including Kasztner—were friends of me and my sister, people we went to school and to the youth movement with. Why did they not save Lutzi, my parents, and why did they have to die? But someone had to die instead of them had they been on the list. The more I was angry with those who could save and did not save, the more I became guilty for being alive. I was guilty for not being able to forgo the sense of revenge against those who were my friends and betrayed me. We may indeed never know according to what considerations the survivors were chosen, and it is doubtful that any research conducted in this regard will get to the bottom of those considerations. But what can one do when one must determine who shall live and who shall die? And should one leave 1200 additional Jews to their fate only to spare from himself the tortures of making a decision? I started having consuming doubts: maybe it was my wish for revenge for the loss of my parents and sister that motivated me to sue Kasztner. At the congress I saw quite a few leaders who left their communities to their horrible fate and found refuge for themselves across the border—and they are now well respected. I could not but ask myself: is the one who stayed out until the very end albeit having an opportunity to save himself—worse?

I have mulled this over a lot and eventually accepted the judges' conclusions and considered them a leveled, responsible conclusion to this horrible affair, which must be concluded so that one may be able to continue living. I also considered it my duty to help Kasztner immigrate to and settle in Israel. I believed that this was the end of the affair, but fate wanted otherwise.

Malchiel Gruenwald, an old Jew who emigrated from Hungary and resided in Jerusalem, used to distribute a private pamphlet with insults and defamatory words against public figures, to whom he, Gruenwald, wished harm. In 1953 he blamed Kasztner of collaborating with the Nazis in that deal entitled "Blood for Goods", deliberately concealing from the Jews of Hungary the fate awaiting them, saving his relatives and some leaders in the train of the privileged, and thwarting broad rescue actions. The Attorney General of Israel filed a defamation lawsuit against Gruenwald.

Gruenwald's attorney, Shmuel Tamir, managed to turn the trial against Gruenwald into a trial against Kasztner. Moreover, he managed to make it into a political trial against Ben-Gurion, Moshe Sharet, and the people of the Mossad Le'Aliyah[4] (Institution for Immigration). He blamed them for being servants of the British and for preventing widespread rescue actions of Jews which allegedly could have been carried out if it were not for the relationship between the heads of the Jewish Agency, the British mandate, and the Nazis, who were all connected by Kasztner. I protected Kasztner, and as retaliation Tamir accused me too for cooperating with the Gestapo "in order to save your life", as he said, "and this is why Peretz died there and Hannah died there."

---

[4]   This was the *Mossad Le'Aliyah Bet* (Institution for Immigration B), which dealt with illegal immigration.

At the trial [in 1955], the judge, Benjamin Halevi, mainly sided with the arguments of Gruenwald and Tamir and found that "Kasztner sold his soul to the devil." Such a dramatic statement, reflective of the German culture, still loudly echoes in our world. In the meantime, the echoes of the shots that pierced the heart of Kasztner, who was killed by hot-tempered men, have long been forgotten. In addition, not many remember that the Supreme Court entirely overturned judge Halevi's judgment.

This unfortunate affair, which divided the nation into two groups and indeed led to a political crisis, embodies the sick, broken soul the Holocaust has left to the Jewish people. This was nearly a frenzy run to national destruction.

Would it have been better to conclude this book without reminding that which has been forgotten? Perhaps. However, I could not do that. We have not made a contract with history, so who would vouch for us that a Holocaust would not happen again? The very reason for the existence of the State of Israel is perhaps its ability to save Jews and prevent another Holocaust. We, however, are still trapped in a catch-22 as we still follow this rule: if you go and don't return—you shall be a hero. If you go and return—you shall be judged. If you sit idle and do nothing— you shall be the judge. This nation will, however, will continue to exist if there will always be people who say: who will go if not me? And they will go—knowing that if they return, they might be judged by those who did not go.

The lack of interest in the victims and in the attempts to rescue them was clearly demonstrated in Ben-Gurion's attitude to the issue, as is expressed in Tom Segev's book *The Seventh Million*. When asked about understanding the meaning of the Holocaust, Ben-Gurion response was: "What is to be understood here, they are dead and that's that."[5] This indifference to the fate of the victims is reflected also in the fact that in Israel, there is no Holocaust Memorial Day, and instead there is a "Holocaust and Heroism Remembrance Day." For years, the attitude about the memory of the Holocaust

---

[5]   Segev, 1991, p. 405.

was to emphasize the ethos of the "fighting Jew" while the "lambs to the slaughter" were left in the shade.

In 1953 Israel established "The Holocaust Martyrs' and Heroes' Remembrance Authority" — Yad Vashem. The authority was charged with commemorating the six million Jews who were murdered by the Nazis and Nazi collaborators; the Jewish communities of Europe that were destroyed; the heroism of the soldiers, underground fighters, partisans, and prisoners of the Ghettos; and the Righteous Among the Nations.

Jews who saved Jews are not mentioned.

The Attitude toward Jewish Rescuers of Jews

In the atmosphere prevailing after the war in Palestine/Israel, Jews who saved Jews were not accepted warmly. Kasztner's initial situation was especially problematic. The public campaign against him, initiated by Palgi, made things worse for him. And the members of the JPU, who did not like him at all, certainly did not help. The reception that awaited Kasztner when he arrived in Switzerland at the end of the war was tepid. He did everything he could to stand out as a Jew-saver during the war and did his best to minimize the part of others. This behavior turned him into the main addressee for all the frustrations of the survivors, relatives of victims, and others. The fact that some Jews were saved put all those involved in rescue operations, especially Kasztner, in a predicament, for several reasons.

First, many Jews who lived outside of Germany's occupied territories had relatives who did not survive. Many of them did not forgive that their relatives were not chosen to be among the survivors. Next, the survivors themselves, and mainly the passengers of the "train of the privileged," had relatives and friends who did not survive. To enhance their own image, some of them opted to deny that they had been warned and knew what was happening, but failed to warn their friends, relatives and communities. This was especially true for survivors from Cluj but also other places.

In general, people who owe their life to someone feel that the debt is too big. There is no way to repay it. It is an awkward feeling.

Hansi often made efforts to refrain from accidental meetings with people she had assisted after she noticed their unease at her presence.[6] Hansi described it as follows:

> My experience in Budapest, Switzerland and Israel taught me what I must expect .... Those who were rescued by us will never forgive us because we have not saved their loved ones. The debt of gratitude will weigh them down. No one can bear such debt. Their instincts will always guide them to minimize the debt in their mind, so to allow them to live a normal life. They will trivialize and justify it: it was their job to rescue, so they did it; or: look at the good life they live today, who knows how much money they earned from these rescue actions.[7]

In addition, the public was led to believe, by its leadership and by its failed rescue representatives, that it was completely impossible to rescue the victims. Hence if someone nevertheless did the impossible, they must have done it using some unacceptable means. The very contact with the Nazis may certainly be considered "unacceptable means" in the eyes of those who prefer dead heroes over living, breathing, flesh-and-blood people.

According to Hansi, and even according to Palgi himself, Palgi contributed significantly to the hostile attitude of the Jewish Agency to Kasztner and to the Rescue Committee. He attempted to cast on them the blame for the failure of the mission he and his friends, Hannah Szenes and Peretz Goldstein, assumed. As it relates to this, Hansi said:

> In Basel we felt for the first time the cold shoulders around us. In a conversation with Palgi I found out that we were accused

---

6   In 2008, after Anna Porter's book about Kasztner train was published, the author got a phone call from two brothers from Australia, whose mother was among the train survivors and who was included on the train by Hansi herself. According to them, their mother lived in Tel Aviv for many years and was familiar with Hansi's address but never tried to contact her. One of her daughters-in-law tried to convince her to contact Hansi, and the survivor made one attempt, heard that the line was busy, hung up, and could not be convinced to make another attempt. Maybe it is not an unusual reaction.

7   Brand, 1960, p. 116.

of negatively affecting the paratroopers' fate. I told Palgi that I wished to hear explicit allegations and have the opportunity to address them. At his proposal, I went ten times to see Shaul Meirov at his hotel, but I was never accepted for a discussion. I realized that they wanted fog to exist as they were concerned of what they would see after it lifted. When I passed through Marseille, Wenja Pomeranz (Prof. Hadari) approached me and introduced himself as a delegate of the Agency in Turkey who was in contact with me. In our conversation he asked what Rezső (Kasztner) was doing. I told him that he was going to immigrate to Israel. His reaction was: "Is he not scared?" I asked Mr. Pomeranz as to the nature of his question and he evadingly explained that this was nothing but a slip of the tongue. That "slip of the tongue" was not a good sign for the future.[8]

When Hansi wrote this (1960), she did not know that it was already in Basel that Kasztner had pointed an accusing finger at her with respect to the paratroopers' affair, as part of a deal he made with the Jewish Agency.

---

[8]   Brand, 1960, p. 106.

17. THE KASZTNER AFFAIR

As the reception that awaited Kasztner at the end of the war was not warm, the political future he was trying to build for himself was vague. The most severe threat for his future were the accusations made by Palgi against him. There is no doubt that securing his political future was a central consideration for him at that time. Not only the content and style of his report were affected by it, but also the tight timetable under which it was written. Kasztner rushed to finish the report so that it could be used to clear his name and present his personal achievements before the Twenty-Second Zionist Congress that was about to convene in Basel at the end of 1946. The time pressure manifested in technical errors (mainly in dates) and in problematic statements that found their way into the report.[1]

Kasztner's Report

In 1946, in the days leading to the Twenty-Second Zionist Congress in Basel, Kasztner wrote a long document titled: "Der Bericht des jüdischen Rettungskomitees aus Budapest 1942–1945" (The Report of the Jewish Rescue Committee from Budapest 1942–1945), known as "Kasztner's report."[2] When Kasztner wrote his report about the activities of the Budapest Rescue Committee, his main goal was to please the leaders of the Jewish Agency. He realized that the best way to secure his political future was to support the agency's stance

---

[1]   For example, about the need of keeping confidentiality (see Kasztner's report, 1946, p. 46).

[2]   In some cases also "Kasztner's book."

and help their efforts to conceal their indifference and lack of rescue action.

The report, as Kasztner wrote it, was severely criticized by Joel and Hansi and other rescue activists in Hungary.[3] In the Brands' book Joel said that, by writing the report, Kasztner sold his soul in an attempt to appease and appeal to the grace of the Jewish leadership by concealing their negligence and lack of action from the public.[4] This is particularly evident in the way Kasztner tried to explain the reasons for the failure of Joel's mission. At the time of writing the report, Kasztner was aware of the rift between Joel and the representatives of the Jewish Agency, and made sure to side with the Jewish Agency. Moreover, Kasztner positioned his testimony, which covered the history of the Budapest Rescue Committee, as the Committee's report. In Hansi's testimony to Yad Vashem, she explicitly testified that the report did not reflect the Committee's story, but rather was Kasztner's personal account.

Regarding Kasztner's testimony, Braham said that it was "detailing his achievements, in a controversial and understandably self-serving report."[5] The other members of the Rescue Committee are hardly mentioned there.

For some reason Kasztner opted to show a draft of the report to Joel, although he was not one of his close friends.[6] The draft was acceptable to Joel, but he was extremely surprised to read the final report, which was apparently substantially different from the draft. What had happened in the meantime? Kasztner probably presented the draft to other people, particularly cronies of the leadership, who advised him that a fair representation of the events in general and Joel's mission in particular, would not be in his best interest. Kasztner understood that a fair report would damage some of the delegation members in Istanbul as well as their superiors, which could turn the wrath of the leadership on him. Kasztner was

---

[3]   Brand, 1960, pp. 103–105.

[4]   Ibid., pp. 167–168.

[5]   Braham, 1994, p. 1103.

[6]   Brand, 1960, p. 104.

ambitious, but more than that, he was a politician. Therefore, he decided to sacrifice the truth in favor of his political future.[7] He opted to deliberately present Joel's mission in a distorted fashion that would match the needs of the people who controlled his political future. Sacrificing friends, and in particular, Joel, whom Kasztner envied and looked up to, was a small price for him to pay in order to advance his career. Sacrificing the truth has never been a problem for Kasztner. There is no better proof to that than the contradicting affidavits he gave after the war to Nazi war criminals: he was quick to turn Nazi murderers into Jews' saviors.[8] Regardless of Kasztner's many proven and documented lies,[9] historians associated with Yad Vashem, the official Holocaust memorial of the State of Israel, are careful to downplay this, as Kasztner followed the party line. On the other hand, the same sources, such as Yehuda Bauer's book *Jews for Sale*, are quick to label Joel, who deviated from the party line, as a liar, without having a shred of proof for these allegations.

The following essential points are missing from Kasztner's report. First, he neglected to mention Joel's part in the formation of the Rescue Committee and his role in activities that preceded its official foundation. In general, he made every effort to undermine Joel's share and contributions. He also played down Hansi's role and important contributions to the rescue actions.

Furthermore, there is no reference in the report to the fact that the delegation members in Istanbul informed the rescue committee in Budapest that they were allegedly ready for the arrival of the envoy, knowing full well that they had not arranged a visa for him.[10] Had early information been received in Budapest that a visa was unavailable in Turkey, the envoy would have been sent to another

---

[7]   Ibid., p. 124. This was said by Hansi who highly regarded Kasztner, was close to him more than anyone else, and was the only one, other than his family, who visited him after his injury.

[8]   Ishoni-Beri, *Yalkut Moreshet*, No. 59, April 1995, pp. 86–87.

[9]   See the Attorney General's remark about Kasztner later in the chapter "Kasztner''s Trial" in this book.

[10] Barlas, 1975, p. 113.

destination, such as Spain or Switzerland. This omission allowed Kasztner and others to point a blaming finger at the messenger while protecting the image of the delegation.

There is also no reference in the report to the pressure applied by the Istanbul delegation on Joel to return to Hungary empty-handed.[11] That would have derailed any opportunity to pretend to the Germans that negotiations were progressing.

Likewise, the report does not mention the fact that the Istanbul delegation coordinated all its actions with the British, which were likely to oppose any deal aiming to save Jews. The British feared that a large number of survivors would increase the pressure to open the gates to Palestine for Jews to enter. Both Avriel and Barlas confirmed that they transferred the information to the British. The delegates' failure to understand the risk, implications, and consequences of exposing the rescue attempt to British at such an early stage, raises many doubts as to the skills and intentions of these delegates.

Kasztner also accused Joel of failing to inform the world about the hardships of the Hungarian Jewry. He did not mention that Joel actually passed on the information to Moshe Sharet and other senior officials, who failed to complete the mission.

Next, Kasztner refrained from mentioning the German promise for a "prepayment," even though he was fully aware of it. The existence of a proposed prepayment is accepted by most historians — the disagreements are only about its size. Kasztner did not mention it since he knew that the mere existence of a prepayment was embarrassing for the Jewish Agency. Kasztner's knowledge of the "prepayment" and to its size is evident from page 188 of his report where he addresses the missed opportunity to save 100,000 Jews from the gas chambers.

Moreover, Kasztner neglected to describe the delay by the Istanbul delegation in sending the "interim agreement" that was desperately needed in Budapest to demonstrate some progress in the negotiations. Since the "interim agreement" promised payments, the Istanbul delegation probably requested the approval

---

[11]   Avriel, 1975, p. 182.

of the British authorities, which resulted in a significant delay. By the time it arrived in Budapest it was practically useless.

Finally, in order to please the senior leaders of the Jewish Agency, Kasztner explicitly blamed Joel for failing the mission. This narrative allowed the management of the Jewish Agency not only to conceal its own failures, but also to taint the historical perspective per its needs and preferences.

Kasztner lied everywhere where the paratroopers' affair was mentioned. He lied in his report where he said that he was arrested and that he accompanied Hansi to meet with Goldstein. He lied in his letter where he blamed Hansi for having turned Goldstein in. He lied in the trial Palgi organized against him where he falsely accused Hansi, while neglecting to mention his discussions with the Hungarian police agents when she and the others were arrested.

In addition to all that, Kasztner refrained from mentioning in his report the leaders who were explicitly warned about the imminent danger and rescued themselves without warning those around them.[12] Specifically, he neglected to mention the details of his talks with the leaders of the Cluj community during his visit there prior to the extermination of the ghetto. This was the first nail Kasztner put in his own coffin.

The report was received sympathetically by the establishment of those days. The establishment embraced Kasztner and within a short time he became a candidate for the Israeli parliament. At the end of December 1946, after the report had been filed, Palgi officially withdrew his complaint against Kasztner. The document summarizing the withdrawal of Palgi's complaint also contained an implied threat to Hansi, which was probably intended to warn her against exposing the truth.[13] In the body of the document, it is indicated that the Jewish Agency representatives "had to express our opinion whether Rezső's and Hansi's behavior was—in practical terms—appropriate or inappropriate." As for Kasztner, they concluded that "there is no material here for any blame."

---

[12]   Brand, 1960, pp. 123–124.

[13]   Haganah Archive, File 14/524; Haganah Archive, Basel, December 26, 1946.

Concerning Hansi, they deliberately left the topic hanging and wrote: "We were not tasked with investigating Hansi's behavior. . . . We cannot express an opinion on this." The document confirms what Hansi wrote in 1960 without knowing about the existence of this document—to the effect that the Jewish Agency representatives deliberately evaded from investigating the subject.[14] What Hansi did not know at the time was that the one behind the conspiracy was Kasztner. Throwing accusations and deliberately refraining from investigating the facts could only serve one purpose—preventing criticism of Kasztner's report, thereby concealing the responsibility of the Jewish Agency representatives in Istanbul to the failure of Joel's mission.

To Ḥaim

We heard Yoel's report and Rezső's reply. After both of them answered our questions, we have no further questions.

Neither in the summary nor during the investigation have we heard anything from Yoel that could be construed as a personal fault of Rezső.

Therefore, we had to provide our opinion as to whether the behavior of Rezső and Hansi was—in practical terms—appropriate or inappropriate.

This is a most difficult task. The circumstances were extremely complicated. An opinion in this matter can only be made with complete knowledge of all the circumstances and the twists and turns of those days; and we cannot assume such judgment.

It may be that the message to the authorities of the arrival of Yoel and Peretz—after Yoel had disappeared and detectives were following him—was given too soon. The message was given within the first ten–twelve hours after Yoel disappeared and there was a place to believe that it was possible to wait. Twelve hours later, Yoel contacted Rezső but this was following the message to the authorities. Yoel himself agreed that the notification to the authorities was appropriate, but he too believed that this was

---

[14]   Brand, 1960, p. 106.

done hastily. There may have been a <u>mistake</u> here but there is no material for accusations.

We were not tasked with investigating Hansi's behavior. Thus, we did not ask for the details of her conversation with Peretz, and without that we cannot express an opinion on <u>this</u> portion of the affair. Rezső informed that he only found out about Hansi's approaching Peretz after Peretz had turned himself in because it was only then that he saw Hansi.[15]

This affair is part of the rescue attempts that involved various forms of contact and cooperation with the Nazis. These activities had unfathomable aspects that we refrain from delving into, without any allegations having been voiced before us.

Signed

Moshe A.
Israel G.[16]

Basel 24.12.46
6-D

Kasztner's acquittal from allegations that he extradited the paratroopers to the Hungarian and German secret services. The document also sends an implied threat to Hansi as if she was responsible to the extradition of Peretz Goldstein.

Joel and Hansi were extremely offended by the final doctored report, and they were not the only ones. Other rescue activists were also offended, including Biss[17] and Peretz Révész.[18] From Kasztner's perspective, this was the least of his problems. The senior leaders of the Jewish Agency had personal interests in preventing the truth

---

[15]   Either this or the description of the event in his report must be false because they contradict each other. Kasztner's report, 1946, p. 72, claims that he went with Hansi to see Goldstein.

[16]   Israel Galili was the Chief of Staff of the Haganah at the time. He later became an Israeli politician, government minister and member of Knesset.

[17]   According to Joel and Hansi (Brand, 1960, p. 104), Biss too was offended, but in his book (Biss, 1973) he directs his entire wrath against Joel only, probably since Kasztner was no longer alive then. Biss harshly criticizes Kasztner who did not lift a finger for Biss's release, as he was requested and indeed could have done.

[18]   Brand, 1960, pp. 104–105.

from ever coming out. While misleading and lying in the report helped Kasztner advance himself in 1946, the fear that the report would be amended at some stage hovered over the senior leaders of the Jewish Agency thereby risking Kasztner himself.

Kasztner's Mission to Nuremberg

On February 17, 1948, a few months before the foundation of the State of Israel, Kasztner was sent, with the funding of the Jewish Agency's Finance Department, to Nuremberg—where many Nazis who were waiting for their trial were imprisoned. No documentation has been furnished to explain why Kasztner was sent abroad with the Jewish Agency's funding, at a substantial cost. If the purpose was to testify against war criminals, there was no reason to hide anything associated with this trip, including the report that Kasztner wrote following his journey.[19] The Jewish Agency could not have financed Kasztner's trip to testify in favor of SS officers, what he actualy did, even if they helped him to rescue Jews at the end of the war. Spending money on such a task was inconceivable then and it is just as unthinkable today, even in the presence of modern Germany and its part in the modern world. The copy of the check slip proves unequivocally that Kasztner's trip to Nuremberg was funded by the Jewish Agency—100 Palestinian pounds were paid to Kasztner for his expenses on his trip.[20]

The only reasonable justification for such a trip is to collect a substantial contribution—in money or weapons—to the power of the young state against the anticipated invasion of the armies of the Arab states. Many Nazis had valuable information about where money and weapons were hidden.[21] Kasztner was not the

---

[19]   This was partially exposed during Kasztner trial and had a major effect on its results.

[20]   100 Palestine pounds were about the same as 100 British pounds at the time.

[21]   The money may have also been forged British money produced by the Germans in good quality and large quantity. It seems that such money also made its way to the JPU in Budapest through van Harten (see Révész, 2001, p. 241).

The slip proves unequivocally that the Jewish Agency paid for Kasztner's trip to Nuremberg—100 Palestinian pounds were paid to Kasztner for his expenses on the trip.

only Jewish representative who helped former SS officers at that time. As far as the Jewish Agency was concerned, there were circumstances under which this was certainly acceptable,[22] and the first and vital condition to the acceptability of these actions was confidentiality. The fear that Kasztner would someday expose all the details associated with this trip to Nuremberg, which to date have not been fully disclosed, was a constant threat to his senders, and therefore yet another real threat to Kasztner himself.[23] In the Brands' book, Joel mentioned sketchy relationships between Nazis and Israeli messengers right after the war.[24] A document filed in the Haganah Archive (File 14/514) shows that Joel warned against this behavior back in 1946 in a letter sent to the Jewish Agency on August 30, 1946, which includes details about the help provided by the Agency's messengers to Nazis in Europe. The first recipient of the document was Golda Meir, the future prime minister of Israel:

[22]   Brand, 1960, pp. 96–97.

[23]   For further details regarding the State's effort to conceal Kasztner's testimony for Becher, see Brand, 1960, pp. 118–119.

[24]   Ibid., p. 96.

Tel Aviv, 30.8.46

Typed 6.9.46

To

Golda, Zeev, Gideon, Zvi.

Dear comrades,
As the memos I submitted on April 5, 46, May 6, 46 and June 2, 46 have apparently not gained any attention, I will try once again to mention several facts together with my comments.

1. Several hundred—perhaps more—of the most senior and rich Nazis and Volksbund people in Hungary (a political party representing the Germans in Hungary) were circumcised— some in hospitals in Budapest. They also blurred the SS symbols that were tattooed on their skins, thereby preparing themselves, with the help of our Beriḥa Movement,[25] to escape Hungary.

2. These options were enabled by Zeltzer from Mukachevo, who received large amounts of money from them for this service. Zeltzer is very senior in the Beriḥa Movement. Our comrade, delegate Jonah, used his help, without knowing anything about the foregoing, since Zeltzer could provide cheap train cars and other vehicles for escape purposes.

3. Important Nazi agents who used to work at the "Jewish Department" and at the German military intelligence service exploited, in Vienna, the escape for "commercial purposes", and these are the names of some of them: Rudolph Scholz, Jozsi Winninger Fernell, Dr. Schmidt, etc. etc. Our comrade, delegate Asher, without knowing their past, used their help because they could buy and sell currency at better prices and could also provide cars and the like for cheap.

4. After I told comrades Gideon and Asher of this matter, this was looked into, and they were told that these Nazis now supposedly work for the British against the Americans. (If there is any truth to that I do not understand why these Nazis are so eager to be involved in our escape matters).

[25]   The underground organized effort that helped Jewish Holocaust survivors escape post-World War II Europe to British Mandate Palestine in violation of the White Paper of 1939.

5. Important elements in Bratislava, Geneva, Zurich, and Paris are trying to get close to our comrades.

6. Our Beriḥa Movement is exploited to a great degree by smugglers, black-market people, and the like.

7. Many of our camps and refugee centers lack strict control on those who come and go and this is how these places easily become centers for black-market businesses, prostitution, and possibly espionage and smuggling Nazis across various borders.

In the meantime, I will refrain from submitting a detailed plan, but I wish to emphasize the necessity of organizing an efficient intelligence service to examine the people who surround our delegated, as well as other entities.

Such kind of action may enhance our political positions and strengthen our struggle for immigration.

Obviously, the above is merely an overview of the facts. Details and further explanations can only be provided orally.

Farewell,

Joel

5.A

In the absence of any other reliable information, it is likely that this was the kind of dealings for which Kasztner was sent to Nuremberg.

Kasztner's Trial[26]

This trial, which initially appeared as a routine libel trial, became one of the most important in the legal and general history of the State of Israel. In this trial, for the first time, the Israeli public learned about the efforts made in Hungary to save Jews and the question aroused in all its seriousness how much support, or alternatively, disruptive, was the Israeli leadership to these efforts.

---

[26]   This is the common name by which this trial is known, but the right name is The Attorney-General of the Government of Israel v. Malchiel Gruenwald.

30.8.46, תא"א
6.9.46, הודפס,

אל:
ולדת, זאב, גדעון, צבי .

חברים יקרים,

חירות ןהתזכירים שהגשתי ב-6.4.46, 6.5.46, ו-2.6.46 לא
זכו, כנראה, לתשומת לב, אנסח שוב לציין מספר עובדות, ולצרף
הערותי בזדן.

1./ כמה מאות – אולי אף יותר – ראשי ופעשידי הנאצים ואנשי
המולקסבונד בהנגריה בפולו – בהלקם בבית החולים
כבודפשט – וכן ששטשו את ספלי הס"ס שחיו טבועים בערום בקעקע, וכך
הכשירו עצמם, בעזרת ארגון הבריחה שלנו, לצאת את הונגריה.

2./ אפשרירת לכך ניתנר לנאצים תללו בין הסאר ע"י אחד זאלצר
ספולבקאץ', שקבל מחם עבור שרותו זה סכומי כסף גדולים.
מעמדו של זאלצר זה בתוך ארגון הבריחה בנונגריה היה חשוב
ביותר.

חברנו, השליח יונה, בעזר אצל בן, מבלי דעת מאומה על הנאל,
חירות וזאלצר ידע לחמציא בזול קרונות-רכבת וכלי רכב אחרים במכיל
הבריחה.

3./ סוכנים נאצים חשובים, מלבבים, שהיו עובדים בי"מחלקה הידודית"
ובשרות הרגול של הצבא הגרמני בצלו אתה, בן יצא את הבריחה
ל"עסקי ספחר", ואלה שמות אחדים מהם: .Dr. Schmidle, Ferenc..
Josx Winninger-, Rudolf Scholz וכו'. חברנו השליח אשר, מבלי
לדעת עברם של תללו, בעזר בהם כי הם ידער לקנות ולמכור ואלותו
במחיריב סובים יותר, וכך ידעו לספק סכוריות וכדומה בזול.

4./ לאחר ספרתי על ענין זה לח"מ גדעון ואשר חקרו בדבר, והוגד
לחם כי הנאצים הללו עובדים עתה כביכול למען חברישים נגד האמריקאים.
(אם יש אמת בדבר איני מבין על שום מה נאצים אלה לחוטים כ"כ אחרי
עבודה בעניני הבריחה שלגו).

5./ בברטיסלבח, ג'בבה, ציריך, ופאריס
מגסים אלמנשים חשודים לחתקרב אל חברינו.

6./ מפעל חבריחה שלגו פגוצל במדה רבה ע"י מבריחים, אנשי שוק-
שחור וכיוצ"ב.

7./ הרבה מחנות שלנו ומרכזי-פליטים – חסרה בהם בקורת קפדנית
על בכסים ויוצאים, וכן תופפיט פקומות אלה בנקל אצב לפרברזים
לעסקי שוק-סאחור, זנות, ויתכן גם רגול ותהברחת נאצים מעבר לגבולות.

לפי שעה אמנע מלהגיש תכנית מפורשת, אך ברצוני להדגיש את
ההכרח בארגון שרות אינטליג'נס יעיל כדי לבחון אנשים המקיפפים את
שליחים שלנו, וגורמים אחרים.

פעולה מעין זו עלולה לחגביר את עמדותיינו הפריגינות, ולחזק
את מאבקנו על עליה.

מובן מאליו שהדברים הנ"ל אינם אלא סקירה בלבד של העו בדות,
ותערכתן: פרטים ותסברה נוספת אשר למסור רק בעל פה.

שלום רב,
יואל.

א.5

The original Hebrew version of Joel's complaint about activists who collaborated with Nazis

In the early 1950s Malchiel Gruenwald, a hotel owner in Jerusalem and an amateur journalist, decided to devote his remaining years to journalism, but no one was about to employ a seventy-two-year-old man who wrote no Hebrew. Gruenwald therefore began self-publishing a more-or-less weekly three-page mimeographed pamphlet, which he would have translated from German into Hebrew before distributing up to 1,000 copies, all free of charge. Titled *Michtavim el Ḥaveray beMizraḥi* ("Letters to my Friends in Mizraḥi," a religious Zionist political party), the pamphlets consisted of attacks on leaders who were corrupt, on religious officials who, in his opinion, were not worthy of their posts, on greedy public officials, and on people in authority positions. Gruenwald's targets included various leaders of religious groups, including Mizraḥi, and ministers and members of the Knesset and other politicians from all parties, in particular those from the ruling Mapai party.

In August 1952, Malchiel Gruenwald used his pamphlet to attack Kasztner, who was then the spokesperson for the Israeli Ministry of Commerce, accusing him of being a Nazi collaborator. The Minister of Commerce, Dov Yoseph, decided that this should not go unanswered and that Kasztner's name should be cleared so that he would be able to serve in his office. Criminal defamation charges were filed by the state against Gruenwald. The trial was held between January and October 1954 at the District Court of Jerusalem before Judge Benjamin Halevi. The judgment was rendered on June 22, 1955, acquitting Gruenwald on most counts of the indictment. In effect, it convicted Kasztner.

During the court's proceedings, the question whether Kasztner testified in favor of war criminals came up. Kasztner had many doubts how to handle this issue. On one hand, he could truthfully provide valid reasons for the testimonies he had given. On the other hand, the prosecutor representing the State (thus representing Kasztner), Amnon Tel, demanded him to deny it. In the evening prior to giving the crucial testimony, Hansi recommended to Kasztner—in the presence of one of her neighbors—to tell the truth and not to deny having provided the testimonies. The next day, however, probably due to his counsel's pressure, Kasztner denied having testified in favor of war criminals. Shortly after this testimony, the prosecutor on behalf of the State filed with the court a document in which he confirmed that Kasztner had indeed testified in favor of SS Colonel Kurt Becher.[27] Tamir, the lawyer who represented the defendant Gruenwald, found this document. At that moment, Kasztner's moral destruction was completed.

Another issue that damaged Kasztner's reputation severely was his visit to the Cluj ghetto. Many witnesses from among the ghetto survivors accused him and his associates on the ghetto leadership of spreading reassuring rumors that discouraged the escape of people who could do so. The survivors believed that the ghetto leadership did so to secure their place on the train of the privileged.

Kasztner was not the only one who was asked by the prosecution, which in this case was the State Attorney's office, representing the State of Israel, to lie. In a recording found at Yad Vashem, Peretz Révész testified that the prosecutor on behalf of the State demanded that he, too, should lie at the same trial, but he refused.[28] Clearly, the officials of the State of Israel valued the leaderhip's agenda more than they valued the law or the truth.

Kasztner's behavior during the trial was so poor that the Attorney General, who personally defended him in the appeal to the Supreme Court, on Gruenwald's acquittal (and Kasztner's actual conviction) had to admit that: "The District Court was right in its criticism of slaps, inaccuracies and even lies" in Kasztner's testimony[29]. Kasztner made a series of other mistakes in conducting his case. He trusted too much the State Attorney, who was obviously more concerned with protecting the Israeli State than protecting Kasztner. As a result, Tel, the lawyer who represented him on behalf of the State of Israel, presented to the court the damning documents that proved that Kasztner testified in favor of Nazis while demanding that Kasztner deny it. Another serious mistake of Kasztner and the State was their attempt to conceal and downplay the importance of Joel's

---

[27]   Brand, 1960, pp. 118–119.

[28]   Minute 76 in the recording "Peretz and Hansi 1" (in Yad Vashem).

[29]   Weitz, 1995, p. 321

mission to Istanbul. Originally, "the train of the privilaged" was supposed to be a German gesture to support Joel's mission. Given the position Kasztner and the State took, the train was perceived as an attempt to rescue the prominents on the expense of the public. This mistake resulted in a decisive District Court ruling that "Kasztner sold his soul to the devil." Kasztner and his attorney also poorly selected their witnesses. As a result, the people who were summoned to testify in his favor, with his recommendation, were office holders who denied, in the course of their testimony, that they had been warned in the past of the implications of gathering Jews in ghettos and of the deportations. They testified that they had escaped or joined the train "by accident" without warning the general public. People like the Brands or Springman were not included on the list of witnesses that Kasztner recommended to summon.

Judge Halevi's harsh and unjust judgment—"Kasztner sold his soul to the devil"—was a direct outcome of the mistakes made by Kasztner and the state attorney that represented him during the trial. The expression "sold his soul to the devil" is not a legal expression and has no place in a court decision, even in light of the bad impression Kasztner made. But there was no going back. This judgment sparked a public uproar and malicious incitement against Kasztner. It tainted the public view of many rescue activists who risked their own lives to save others, only because they were close to Kasztner. Hansi, who selflessly risked her own and her children's lives for years, was hurt the most.

The incitement, especially by anti-Mapai parties (Mapai was the ruling party at the time), was directed at Kasztner, probably out of the belief—that proved wrong—that tarnishing the man would help tarnishing the party. Mapai's opponents were probably afraid to attack the Jewish Agency leaders and its representatives in Istanbul directly for their negligent handling of Joel's mission, and for not exhausting the possibilities embedded in rescue opportunities. Most of the political parties in Israel feared that if the conduct of the Jewish Agency's Rescue Committee and its delegation in Istanbul were to be examined, they all would be hurt since all the parties were represented there.

Some of the rescue activists in Budapest tried to help Kasztner despite their personal feelings about him, but it was too late. Given the wild incitements, the State assigned bodyguards to protect Kasztner, but after a while they were removed at the instruction of the Israeli Secret Service. A few days later, on March 4, 1957, Kasztner was shot outside his home in Tel Aviv. He lied in the hospital for eleven days until he died of his wounds on March 15. Hansi visited him in the hospital.[30]

Kasztner's killers were caught quickly and very soon serious suspicions surfaced that the Israeli Secret Service was involved in the murder. In his book, *Quilt*, Kasztner's killer, Ze'ev Eckstein, confirmed that for reasons he was unwilling to explain, he received preferential treatment in prison. This treatment was unique given the severe offence of which he was convicted (murder) and the severe verdict (life imprisonment) he was handed.[31] Hansi described surprisingly tight relationships between the Secret Service and those who were involved in the murder.[32] She raised a series of questions as to the prior information the Secret Service had and their failure to proactively prevent the murder given the information they had. Other questions, just as puzzling, are found in Prof. Yechiam Weitz's book, *The Man who was Murdered Twice*. Weitz describes how in November 1962 the Director of the Israeli Secret Service, Isser Harel, asked Ben-Gurion to pardon the killers after they served a fraction of their life imprisonment sentence. In February 1963 Ben-Gurion called Kasztner's family to examine how the family members would accept the pardon, and in May 1963, following Ben-Gurion's intervention, all the killers were pardoned and released from prison. This chain of events strengthens the belief

---

[30]   Weitz, 1995, 326, opines that Hansi was the only person outside of his family who was permitted to visit the wounded Kasztner, and that too occurred only once.

[31]   In Gaylen Ross's film *Killing Kasztner*, a GR Films Inc. Production, 2008, Eckstein claimed that his shot missed Kasztner because of the darkness, and an additional shoot from some unknown person actually killed Kasztner

[32]   Brand, 1960, pp. 206–208.

that even if the Secret Service did not actually commit the murder, it intentionally did not prevent it.

This part of history has not come off the public agenda. The questions raised by Hansi and others remained unanswered, despite all the attempts to bury them. In an article in *HaAretz* dated January 11, 2015, after confidentiality restriction was lifted from some relevant government documents, Ofer Aderet wrote:

> Reviewing the protocol [of government meeting dated March 11, 1957] only deepens the mystery surrounding one of the stormy affairs in the history of Israel and may strengthen those who believe in the involvement of Israel Security Agency in the murder of one of the most controversial figures in the history of the State of Israel. Fifty-eight years after the murder, the protocol raises some tough questions, such as why the Director of the Security Service, Isser Harel [formerly Halperin] asked to pardon the killers before they served their sentence; how was the murder not prevented despite of the fact that the Israeli Security Agency knew in advance of the intention of assassination that was committed by an informer of the organization? And why was the killer not sentence prior to the murder when he distributed defamatory pamphlets regarding the affair?[33]

Later, in February 15, 2020, another article by Ofer Aderet in the Israeli daily *HaAretz* asked: "What Is Shin Bet Hiding About Killing of Israeli Accused of 'Selling His Soul' to the Nazis?" The subtitle said: "High Court gives security service sixty days to justify keeping files sealed in case of Israel (Rudolf) Kasztner, who was shot dead outside his Tel Aviv home in 1957." Because of the Coronavirus crisis the case will most probably be postponed for a long time.

To conclude the affair of Kasztner's trial, it should be mentioned that after his murder, in January 1958, the Supreme Court overturned the ruling of the District Court by a majority vote. The judges acquitted Kasztner from the charge of assistance to commit murder, but they reiterated that he testified in favor of Nazis. This judgment,

---

[33]   Ofer Aderet, "The Protocols Expose: The Israel Security Agency Knew of the Killer's Intention to Assassin Kasztner," *HaAretz*, January 11, 2015, http://haaretz.co.il/news/law/.premium-1.2534456.

which cleared Kasztner from the heavy accusations against him, has never made much public noise.

Following the decision of the District Court and prior to the appeal before the Supreme Court, another trial was held. It was a trial directly against Kasztner on the charge of perjury at the District Court (in regards to the testimony in favor of SS Officer Kurt Becher). Kasztner was acquitted in this trial, mainly for technical reasons, and thanks to the status of Becher (who was not prosecuted or convicted as a war criminal due to Kasztner's testimony).[34] It was Kasztner's luck that the other testimonies he had given in favor of convicted war criminals were not known at that time.[35]

[34]   Weitz, 1995, pp. 300–309.

[35]   Bauer, 2001, p. 259; Ishoni-Beri, 1995.

18. Rewriting the History

In the spring of 1946 when Hansi and Joel met after almost two years of separation, one of the first issues discussed was the future of the family. Joel, despite his disappointment with the Jewish leadership, continued to believe in Zionism and wanted his family to come to Palestine. Hansi at this point was already disillusioned with all the ideologies, including Zionism, so she opposed this idea. Hansi wanted to stay and live in Europe or the United States. She was the first to realize, even before immigrating to Palestine, that Jews who saved other Jews would not be welcomed in the Jewish state. She agreed to come to Palestine as a result of Joel's pressure and the hope that, despite her concerns and many doubts, Israel would be the best place for her children.

This is how Joel describes Hansi's objection to the immigration to Palestine:

> Joel, don't you have eyes to see? In Israel we would be *persona non grata*. We were eye witnesses to the bankruptcy of the leadership of the Zionist institutes. No one will let us talk there. We will encounter the biggest difficulties.
>
> We cannot forget that much Jewish blood was spilled as a result of what our leadership did. We cannot forget and it does not matter if we are veteran Zionists. Our place is not in the Land of Israel.[1]

As we shall see, things developed just as Hansi predicted.

[1]   Brand, 1960, p. 91.

The Early Years: The Holocaust
and Its Victims Are Not on the Public Agenda

In the immediate aftermath of the Holocaust, the Jewish public in Palestine was busy strengthening its power in anticipation of the upcoming struggle for the future of the country. The public yearned for heroic stories of partisans and ghetto fighters and the interest in Holocaust victims was limited. No public attention was given at that time to the fate of those who were perceived as "soaps" and "lambs to the slaughter" and thus their lives was not valued. This situation was convenient for the leadership and the public, none of whom went out of their way in real time to assist the victims.

When the authorities initiated the Kasztner trial, they believed that the trial would end quickly, either with the conviction or with the acquittal of the defendant, and the subject will disappear from the public agenda. Until the Kasztner trial, which was held in the early fifties of the twentieth century, the public in Israel and in the world knew nothing of the rescue attempts made in Hungary during World War II. The leadership believed that the trial would be focused on Kasztner's activities; they were not prepared for the option that their own activities during the Holocaust would be scrutinized or that future examination would ensue to clarify how the leaders and representatives of the future Jewish State functioned regarding the rescue attempts of the European Jews in general and of Hungary Jews in particular.

Joel's Mission Exposure and Its Implications

Up until the Kasztner trial, a conspiracy of silence had surrounded the rescue attempts in Hungary and Joel's mission in particular. The prosecution (namely, Kasztner and the State) did everything to prevent Joel's testimony and the disclosure of his mission, in order not to expose the failures of the Jewish Agency and its representatives in Istanbul. Joel, who was a successful merchant in Hungary, had spent most of his years in Israel unemployed. At that time, Israel ran like a communist country: employment was largely controlled by the ruling party. At the beginning of the trial Joel was penniless and in desperate need of job. When the concern arose that he might be invited to testify, a job with a shipping company was offered to him, apparently to remove him from the country and prevent his testimony. Somehow, the defense counsel, Shmuel Tamir, got a hint about Joel's mission, and this changed the course of the trial and the history.

Joel was summoned only when it became clear that if the State would not summon him, the defense will. Tamir, who realized the explosive potential of the testimony, feared for Joel's life, probably justly enough, and demanded for guards to be assigned to him, which was indeed the case. This demand seemed puzzling at the time, and Joel and Hansi did not take it seriously. Similarly, they did not take seriously the threat on Kasztner's life either. They allowed their son to go on rides in his car for full days when he drove to visit activists of the Budapest JPU, who were spread in various *kibbutzim* across the country, to solicit their support during his trial. In retrospect, it is difficult to rule out the possibility that a guard—or to be precise, the demand for a guard—saved Joel from a similar fate to that of Kasztner.

As part of Joel's discussions with Tamir in preparation for the trial, Joel presented a letter written to him by Ḥaim Weizmann, the most important Zionist leader at the time and the first President of the State of Israel, in which he noted that due to travels and other engagements he would only be able to meet Joel a few weeks later. On the evening of the testimony, the Brands' house was mysteriously broken into and some documents, including this one, were stolen. The documents were the only objects stolen from the apartment that contained nothing valuable. During the trial, an attempt was made to file a photocopy of the document, which was in possession of Tamir, but the prosecution firmly objected to that and demanded that only original documents should be introduced.[2]

After the trial, endless attempts were made to keep Joel silent and prevent him from publishing his book (the first one, from 1957). There was even a conspiracy to declare that he was insane and

---

[2]   Hecht, 1999, pp. 228, 229, 280.

have him involuntarily committed.[3] It was only the fear of Hansi's severe reaction that prevented the perpetrators from realizing their plan.

In both the Kasztner and Eichmann trials, the State did its best to prevent the Brands from testifying in court. It was clear to the leaders of the State that public awareness about the thwarting of Joel's mission would be frowned upon by their constituents. In the end, they realized that the subject was impossible to hide, so the Brands were eventually included in the list of witnesses. The State's efforts to prevent uncomfortable testimonies can be learned from an article published in the daily newspaper *Israel HaYom* (*Israel Today*) on September 24, 2008, titled: "Another Myth is Shattered." According to the article, during the preparations for the Eichmann trial, Ben-Gurion appointed a special envoy to ensure that none of the witnesses in the trial had an ideological background that might cause them to attack Mapai. The article explained that this step was the result of what happened in the Kasztner trial, in which some of the witnesses accused the Jewish Agency and Mapai that they had abandoned the Hungarian Jewry during the Holocaust.

The Eichmann trial marked a change in the attitude of the Israeli establishment to Joel Brand and his mission. Until then, everything was done to make him and his mission forgotten. This included the attempts to prevent the publishing of his 1957 book. Once these attempts failed following the Kasztner trial, the publication of his book, and especially after the Eichmann trial, new methods were needed to protect the image of the leaders and to conceal their failure.

Exposing the Jewish leadership's rescue failures during the Holocaust, and especially with regard to the negotiations with the Germans, shocked the public, especially those who experienced the horrors of the Holocaust. One of them, Naphtali Lavie, a journalist, Holocaust survivor from Buchenwald, and brother of the former Israeli chief rabbi, Rabbi Israel Meir Lau, followed the Eichmann trial. He was shocked by the rescue failures of the Zionist leadership

---

[3]   Brand, 1960, p. 179.

during the Holocaust. At the end of the trial he wrote three articles in which he severely criticized the rescue failures of the Zionist leadership. Lavie decided not to publish these articles at the time due to the fear of creating an atmosphere of self-blaming, but fifty years after the trial, he chose to publish them in the Israeli daily *HaAretz* on April 8, 2011.[4] Lavie was particularly shocked by the behavior of the Joint representative in Switzerland, Saly Mayer, who, in Lavie's opinion, cared about Jewish lives less than the Germans. It is interesting to note that the said behavior did not prevent an Israeli historian from portraying Saly Mayer as a rescuer of Jews like Weissmandl, Brand, and Kasztner.[5]

A series of issues that arose from the testimonies of Joel and Hansi in the Kasztner and Eichmann trials disturbed the leaders and cast a heavy shadow on their judgment and behavior during the Holocaust. It was shown that the Jewish leaders blatantly disregarded the importance of the arrival of a Jewish envoy from the occupied territories, expressed in the absence of any preparation for his reception and the false report, as if they were waiting for his coming, when in fact they did not prepare a visa for him. Moreover, there was no effort to present alleged progress in negotiations on the German proposal. This is expressed in the prolonged and unexplained delay in sending the "interim agreement" to Hungary. And more importantly, the leadership made no effort to try to save at least those who might have been saved in the framework of the advance payment offered by the Germans.

In order to conceal these failures, historians affiliated with the establishment have embarked on an orchestrated offensive. Their goals were the following:

- to play down the importance of Joel's mission explaining that the German proposal was not serious and had no chance;[6]

---

4   https://www.haaretz.co.il/misc/1.1171040.

5   Bauer, 1994, p. 259.

6   In Isaac Noy's program on Network B of the Israeli radio, "They Let Them Die" in proximity of the Holocaust Day of 2009, Prof. Aronson said that the

- to delete, as far as possible, the name Brand from the history of the rescue attempts during the Holocaust;
- to impair his credibility and present him as an untrustworthy and unreliable person;
- to attribute the achievements of the Brands to others and the disadvantages of the others to the Brands, regardless of and even contrary to the factual truth.

negotiations of Kasztner and others with Eichmann could not rescue more then the 1700 train passengers: See also Friedländer 2007, pp. 581–584.

19. Deception Techniques

Most of the disturbing facts mentioned in this book in general, and in this chapter in particular, were brought to the attention of Yad Vashem but received no response. In one case, on May 15, 2018, a senior historian from Yad Vashem referred me to Prof. Bauer saying "Prof. Bauer is Yad Vashem."

Yad Vashem's approach in presenting the character and activity of Hansi and Joel matches that of Prof. Bauer, so one may consider attributing the false and misleading descriptions as if they were made by Yad Vashem.

Because of this statement, I chose to concentrate on problematic points in Bauer's publications, although there are similar flaws in some other works by Israeli historians, many of whom were his students.

Real-Time Documents

Real-time documents do not necessarily represent factual truth. Their content reveals only what the writer wanted others to know. They refrain, as far as they can, from mentioning inconvenient facts. They suffer from the same limitations that the document writers themselves suffer and this includes personal and political interests, possible effect on other issues, and human mistakes.

Unfortunately, historians are not always aware of the issues mentioned here and are not always aware of the complex considerations that can be faced by document writers, so they may overstate the value of the existing documents and not show sufficient sensitivity to possibly distorted or missing data that should have been found in documents but are not there.

Non-German Documents

Very few governments and people can take pride in their activities during the Holocaust regarding the Jewish issue, hence the interest of many parties to present a distorted picture of reality. The following examples are just a minimal selection.

In November 1943, following the pressure of the "Bergson Group,"[1] a congressional hearing was summoned to elaborate on the situation of European Jews and the American activities for them. As part of this, the State Department representative, Breckinridge Long, testified about his office's activities for the persecuted Jews. His testimony in the congressional hearing was accepted so well that he himself decided to reveal it to the public, which did on December 10, 1943. According to this testimony, the United States accepted 580,000 refugees since 1933. This number, of course, has no basis.[2]

The British records refrain from mentioning the real reasons for the British objection to any activity that could have helped the victims of the Holocaust. One can always find excuses or secondary reasons in the documents. No one wanted to admit that the overriding reason was always preventing the possibility of strengthening the Jewish community in Palestine.

The same holds for the British and American reasons for not destroying the extermination facilities in Auschwitz and the railways leading there. Many historians doubt whether the reasons mentioned in the documentation were genuine.

Resnik's report from June 4, 1944 claims that he had several interviews with Joel in Istanbul but the important issue of advanced payment was not mentioned at all.

Kasztner's report, which is close to real time, claimed that it was not the bribery that stop the deportations from Slovakia.[3] He also refrained from mentioning his negotiations with the Germans

---

[1]   A Jewish rescue activist (his real name is Hillel Kook), whose activities to save European Jews have been strongly opposed by the Zionist establishment in the United States and Israel. See Erbelding, 2018, p. 37.

[2]   Ibid., pp. 44–45.

[3]   Kasztner's report, 1946, p. IV.

for the "goods for blood" deal as the reason for preventing the extermination of the Jews of Budapest in August 1944. Any other argument might have hurt the Zionist leadership and hence, his future political career. There is no way to know what Kasztner really thought when he wrote his report. His character, his later behavior, and some controversial phrases in his report do not allow us to rule out the possibility that his report was tinted with non-relevant considerations. In his book,[4] Joel mentioned the difficult question of finding a place willing to accept large number of Jews in case of a deal with the Germans. This crucial issue must have been known to any rescue activist, but it is not mentioned in Kasztner's report (except for a hint in the last page).

Israeli documentation refrained from mentioning how the "Blood for Goods" deal was supposed to be carried out, and especially not the fact that at first the Germans were supposed to release a hundred thousand Jews and only then receive trucks. Barlas's book confirms the method presented in Brand's books and testimonies on how the deal was supposed to be carried. For some reason, the Israeli record does not report what Joel said to the Jewish Agency delegation in Istanbul. Such report must have existed, but for some reason this document is not available. It is impossible to rule out the possibility that these documents were intentionally hidden or destroyed so as not to reveal inconvenient details.

Israeli documentation abounds in rescue operations of the Israeli leadership and Ben-Gurion. Thousands of pages were written about these actions. A brief examination of the documents dealing with these alleged rescue operations indicates that they were intended for the purpose of bringing suitable immigrants, not necessarily legally, to Palestine. The documentation provides no examples of the Israeli leadership rescuing Jews indiscriminately; their efforts were always backed by Zionist political agenda.

The first success in saving a substantial number of Jews during the Holocaust was the meeting of Joel Brand's brother-in-law with the Hungarian Minister of the Interior in August 1941, which spared

---

[4]   Brand, 1960, p. 67.

the lives of tens of thousands of Jews.[5] This event had been wiped out, almost totally, from documented history in Israel.

In general, Israeli Holocaust documentation tends to prefer indoctrination and myth over factual truth.[6] The control of the past by political parties means that Israeli Holocaust literature, in significant part, is useless.[7] An example of the Israeli tendency to amend history in favor of the politicians can be found in Palgi's book. In the first edition of the book, in 1946, he gives a detailed description of the promise to enable the families to emigrate to Palestine before the arrival of the parachutes. In later editions, this promise has disappeared.[8]

German Documents

The reliability of German documents with regard to their treatment of Jews is particularly problematic, and this is because of the Germans' attempts to hide from the whole world, including the Germans themselves, the information about their true intentions regarding the Jews. Another reason is the desire of many Germans involved in exterminating European Jews not to leave incriminating information about themselves. Especially problematic are documents discussing rescue deals with Jews. These deals were not always fully backed up by all ranks in Germany up to Hitler himself. Here the Germans face a double problem, both to hide their share in and the awareness of the extermination of the Jews, but also not to be perceived as rescuing Jews, or worse, traitors who released Jews for bribes.

Historians who find it difficult to deal with the lack of action from the Jewish leadership in Palestine and the free world also find it easy to present the rescue attempts of the few who tried as unserious and impractical. In cases when these attempts led to practical positive results, many efforts are made to attribute

---

5   Braham, 1994, pp. 205, 213.

6   Ronen, 2011, p. 272

7   Bei-Zvi, 1977, p. 17

8   Palgi, 1946, p.; 17

these achievements to political entities. The Germans' dedication to concealing their dealings with the Jews often plays into these historians' hands.

The first known serious attempt to substantially decrease the number of Holocaust victims was made in Slovakia by the working group that operated there headed by ultra-Orthodox Rabbi Ḥaim Michael Dov Weissmandl and Zionist activist Gisele (Gisi) Fleischmann. After the working group paid the Germans a ransom of fifty thousand dollars,[9] the deportations from Slovakia were halted and extermination there stopped for two years. Extermination resumed after an anti-Nazi uprising erupted in Slovakia in which many Jews took part. There is full correlation between the payment dates and the halting of the extermination. The deportations were renewed when a payment was delayed, and they were stopped once again when the required payment had arrived. Despite the clear correlation, some historians attribute the halting of the deportation to pressures and demands of political entities. They base the claim on contemporary documents that show that such demand indeed existed. These historians ignore the methodical German effort to conceal the stops and delays in the extermination process originating from deals with the Jews. The ransom paid to the Germans in Slovakia was not a personal initiative of local German officers. A long time after that deal, Eichmann's entire headquarter was aware of it, clearly showing that the deal was conducted under the approval and knowledge of their superiors. It is doubtful that the Germans would have met the terms of the deal had they had won the war. But the conditions on the ground meant that every delay in the extermination equated to a rescue. Historians also tend to discount Himmler's need to protect himself with an adequate "cover story" for the event that such a deal would be exposed and he would be forced to explain himself to Hitler.

Among the first to claim that it was not the money that stopped the extermination in Slovakia was Kasztner, in 1946. Kasztner wrote

---

9   It is quite possible that ten thousand dollars of the mentioned amount were taken by the Jewish mediator (a corrupted Jew named Karol Hochberg).

his report to not only glorify his accomplishments, but also to exempt the Jewish leadership in Palestine from any potential allegations about its failures during the Holocaust. The most prominent failures were the Slovakian deal and Joel's mission. About three thousand Slovakian Jews were sent to extermination since no Jewish entity outside the occupied territories, including the JDC and the rescue delegation of the Jewish Agency in Istanbul, was willing to help the Slovakian Jewry to raise a sum of twenty-five thousand dollars.

Himmler's order to stop all deportations from Hungary was received in August 1944, immediately after the first three hundred train survivors crossed the border. Wisliceny, one of Eichmann's assistants, claimed that the order was given in order not to upset the Hungarians and trigger them into leaving the alliance with Germany, as Romania did at the same time. Wisliceny's statement notwithstanding, Himmler simply could not afford himself to explain the real reason. It seems that Wisliceny's unlikely explanation was the most available excuse at that moment.

The Swiss protested before the German Ministry of Foreign Affairs against the transfer of the first group of the "train of the privileged" to Switzerland without any coordination or visas, and requested explanations. The German Ministry of Foreign Affairs, whose degree of awareness of the entire subject was unclear, approached the security authorities, namely Himmler's SS, requesting explanations.[10] The answer to the Ministry of Foreign Affairs was provided by Himmler's people orally only, and this is how the event is described in the protocol of Eichmann's trial:

> **Mr. Bach:** In the meantime, the first transfer arrived in the Bergen-Belsen train, from Bergen-Belsen to Switzerland, those 318 Jews we heard about. In the next document, our No. 449, there is an entry by Wagner [from the German Ministry of Foreign Affairs] dated September 16, 1944. He reports of a request by the Swiss Legation informing that on August 22, 318 Jews arrived in Basel, most of whom with a Hungarian citizenship, without the required documents. The Swiss wish to know where these Jews

---

10   Eichmann's trial, session 61, p. 915.

came from and who they were, and request that in the future the Swiss government should be provided with details before sending such transfers. From the end of the report it is clear that Wagner now requests an explanation from the Reich Main Security Office.

Presiding Judge: This will be marked P/1231.

Mr. Bach: Our next document is No. 450, which was submitted to the Defendant and was marked P/37 (154). Here Wagner refers to the same previous document saying that the Reich Main Security Office informed von Thadden that those 318 Hungarian Jews are part of a transfer for obtaining vital goods for the military effort of the SS, and for the benefit of the SS. The details of the deal are not known in Berlin as the discussions between the Reichsführer and the proxy for the deal, Obersturmbannführer Eichmann, were made directly and orally only. Per the instruction of the Security Police, nothing has been put in writing in this matter. For the same reason, they said, the Ministry of Foreign Affairs can receive the answer orally only. And it suggests at the end, in connection with the Swiss memorandum, to refrain from providing any answer for the time being. And if Switzerland raises the problem again, an answer should be given to them after an adequate period of time, orally, that the investigations in the matter yielded no results.[11]

This document is interesting in some additional aspects that are worth analysis. From Becher's optimistic report about the discussions in Switzerland we know that Berlin was informed about the discussions. We know also that Berlin knew that Becher was handling the discussions and not Eichmann whose name was mentioned in order to become the scapegoat for Himmler and Becher in case of problems. This document clarifies the sweeping German policy of avoiding the production of written documentation on deals with Jews.

Because of this policy, the written communication regarding the "Jews on ice" deal was vague. The written notice of transfer of

---

[11]   It should be noticed that Himmler shifts responsibility for the topic onto Eichmann and refrains from mentioning Becher.

forced laborers to Vienna includes an unusual order to the effect that also those unfit for work should be kept alive, at least temporarily. The document itself includes no explanation for this unusual order but rather only a reference to receive oral explanations.

The German effort to not leave any documentation of rescue deals with Jews is also evident in the Auschwitz extermination halt in October 1944. The camp commander Höss had to travel to Hungary to receive oral clarifications in November of that year. This is how the event is described in the protocol of Eichmann's trial.[12]

In his own trial, Höss says on p. 105 the following on the subject of stopping the operation of the gas chambers:

> It so happened that when the order came that Jews should not be exterminated any more, I was sent by Obergruppenführer Pohl to the Reich Main Security Office to meet with Gruppenführer Müller, Chief of the Gestapo, who was then also acting for Kaltenbrunner, to learn from him why this order had been given. Müller could not give me any information and referred me to Eichmann who was negotiating with Becher in Switzerland and in Turkey. I was therefore sent to Budapest so that I can determine over there whether the extermination of Jews was stopped only temporarily and would be renewed at a later stage, and also so that I could learn there about the reasons for the order to stop the extermination.

He then talks about the negotiation and adds:

> The Jews insisted that despite the promise to stop the extermination, it was still continuing, and they claimed that they would only begin concrete negotiations when they see that the extermination actions were halted. This is why an order was given to stop the extermination of the Jews.

The systematic effort not to leave any written documentation is yet again evident. In addition, this provides an unequivocal corroboration for the substantial achievement of the Budapest Rescue Committee.

---

[12]   Eichmann's trial, session 72, pp. 1102–1103 in the protocol.

Downplaying the Importance of the Rescue Attempts

The Israeli public, in the period immediately after the Holocaust until the trial of Kasztner, was not really interested in the Holocaust and its victims, as we learned from the description of Yoel Palgi, discussed earlier. No special efforts were needed in this atmosphere to keep rescue attempts (or the lack of them) from the public eyes. It was only after Joel's mission was made public during the Kasztner trial that questions began to be asked. The initial answer was that the mission did not matter because the Germans did not intend to release Jews anyway.

Prof. Aronson has stated that it was impossible to save more than the passengers of the "train of the privileged," whose rescue he usually attributes to Kasztner only. This is because he says Himmler did not intend to allow Jews to be saved. Friedländer downplays the importance of Joel's mission by saying: "To this day, it is hard to believe that the astute and savvy Kasztner had high hopes for the success of Joel's mission."[13]

For years, the public was led to believe that negotiations with the Nazis never had any chance of success since they never intended to keep their promises. This misconception is losing ground due to recent research. For instance, the Research Institute of The United States *Holocaust Memorial Museum in Washington* showed that in 1944 Himmler was looking for ways to establish contact with the West, and in particular with the United States.[14] Since Himmler believed his own Nazi propaganda, it is certainly likely that he truly believed that the route to the American governance went through the Jews. His actions related to Joel's mission support this theory. Becher's optimistic report about alleged progress in the negotiation and the chance to get critical strategic raw material for Germany is just another example.

---

[13]   Friedländer, 2010, p. 584 (Heb).

[14]   Zoltán and Gábor, 2013.

Eliminating the Brands from the History

In her testimony to Yad Vashem in 1995, Hansi told a fascinating story: shortly after returning safely from the deportation of 1941, her sister's husband met with the Hungarian Minister of the Interior. After the meeting which was arranged by Joel, with the assistance of Springman[15] and Jewish entities in Hungary, the deportations halted. While Joel was involved in organizing the visit, he probably did not participate in it himself.

In his book Randolph Braham describes the deportation of "alien" Jews, its planned scope, and Joel and Hansi's contribution to stopping it, at least temporarily. The book tells the story of a survivor named Lajos Stern, Joel Brand's brother-in law, who was brought to the Hungarian Minister of the Interior through a Jewish welfare organization. Stern told the minister about the mass murders and atrocities of the deportation. The Minister of the Interior, who, according to Braham, was a decent man and was probably the only minister who opposed the deportation, instructed to immediately stop the deportations. The minister probably had prior information about the atrocities of the deportation and Stern's visit merely corroborated this information. According to the book, in addition to halting the deportations, the minister instructed to recall seven trains that were already on their way to the border, including two trains that were already waiting at the border itself. This probably occurred on August 8, 1941[16], approximately three weeks before the systematic murder of those who had already been deported, mainly on August 27 and 28. The break in the deportation did not save those already deported but it at least prevented additional victims.

In his book, Braham described how productive this visit between Hansi's brother-in-law and the Hungarian Minister of the Interior was:[17]

---

[15]   According to Braham, 1994, p. 808, Brand and Springman had good contacts with Hungarian officials.

[16]   See, Eisen and Stark, 2015, p. 10, about the deportation of the alien Jews in the summer of 1941.

[17]   See, Braham, 1994, pp. 213 and 808, as well as the earlier edition of 1981. The date of the meeting is not mentioned there.

One of the survivors by the name of Lajos Stern, Joel Brand's brother-in-law, accompanied a delegation of MIPI members led by György Polgár, which informed Keresztes-Fischer about the details of the Kamenets-Podolsk massacres. The Minister of the Interior was visibly shocked and declared that he had enough of this and ordered Pásztóy to halt all further deportations. In fact, Pásztóy was compelled to recall seven trains en route to the border, two of which had already reached Kőrösmező, the border crossing point.

In 1973, Yad Vashem published a reprint of that chapter from Braham's research with a small but indicative change. Instead of "Lajos Stern, Joel Brand's brother-in-law," they wrote just "Stern."[18]

This visit was probably not the only reason for stopping the deportation. While the overzealous Hungarians were enthusiastic to deport Jews, it was the Germans who tried to stop the deportation since they had no idea what to do with the deportees. As stated above, the decision to halt the deportation was probably made on August 8, 1941, but according to Braham, until August 10, 1941, some fourteen thousand people had been deported at a rate of one thousand people per day. Braham also revealed that additional four thousand people were deported by the end of that month, the time when the operation was completed.[19] So it seems that the decision made by the responsible minister to stop the deportation was made without the government's full support. Thus, anti-Semites, who were sufficiently persistent, managed to find ways to bypass this decision and continue with the deportation for a short time.[20]

The details provided by Braham suggest that this meeting, which is conspicuously missing from research and history books in Israel, was, in fact, the most successful rescue operation in the beginning of the Holocaust. It largely thwarted a plan aimed at deporting tens of thousands of Jews. It did not save the twenty

---

[18] *Yad Vashem Studies*, No. 9, 1973, p. 143.

[19] Braham, 1994, p. 211.

[20] As Adolf Eichmann did in time, when he continued with the deportations while also following Horthy's decision to stop them.

thousand people who were already deported, but it directly saved the passengers of the seven trains who were either on their way to the border or at the border crossing itself. Braham maintains that the total number of detained Jews already arrested by that time and intended for deportation was thirty to thirty-five thousand.[21] Clearly, the successful operation lifted, if only temporarily, the immediate danger hovering over the many thousands of Jews who were already arrested, who were on their way to be arrested, and many others who were not yet arrested.

The halting of the deportation of the "alien" Jews is mentioned also in Bauer's book *Jews for Sale*. The text is similar to the text of Braham, but the Brands' name is also omitted here.[22]

The main characters associated with the Budapest Rescue Committee were Kasztner, Brand, and Springman. In order not to connect the rescue activities with the Budapest Rescue Committee, with which Joel's name is closely linked, Bauer writes that the rescues were performed by the "Kasztner-Komoly committee."[23]

In the six volumes (in Hebrew version) of the *Encyclopedia of the Holocaust*, published by Yad Vashem in 1990, there is no trace of Hansi's decisive contribution to the rescue attempts in Hungary. She is only mentioned there as the wife of Joel.

In 2004 Yad Vashem published Prof. Gideon Greif's book *I Am My Brother's Savior: Jews Save Jews during the Holocaust*. The Brands are not mentioned there. When asked a question, Greif replied that he had no room left for them.

Kasztner's Unborn Children

In his works, Prof. Bauer has a notable tendency to portray negative traits of others as if they are Joel's traits, and to attribute activities and achievements of Joel (in fact, Joel and Hansi) to others.

---

[21]   Braham, 1994, p. 205.

[22]   Bauer, 2001, p. 148.

[23]   Bauer, 2001, pp. 207, 208, 210 and more. In the English version, the Hebrew word *Va'ada* ("committee") is used, Bauer, 1994, p. 158.

The following example illustrates this topic. In Bauer's book *Jews for Sale* (1994), page 198 (among others) says:

> The Nazi agreement to have the train leave Budapest could be another trick; the passengers could debark at Auschwitz, just as all the others had. The gamble was a tremendous one, and to convince others that it was worth the try, Kasztner put his own family in the train. As Hansi Brand said in her testimony at the Eichmann trial in Jerusalem: "If he [Kasztner] put his own children [on the train], perhaps these people really will be brought to a neutral country. That made me calm, because I hoped that these people, whom we persuaded with such difficulty to get on the train, would be brought to freedom despite everything.[3]

The superscript number "3" at the end directs the reader to a note saying: "Hansi Brand testimony, Eichmann trial (*Book of Testimonies*, vol. 2, p. 914)."

Hebrew readers who decide to check the *Book of Testimonies* will find that the page number is incorrect and that the mentioned topic appears on page 919, but its contents are substantially different from what is written in Bauer's book.

English readers can read the full protocol of the Eichmann trial, including the full content of Hansi's testimony on the internet site of the Nizkor Project (http://www.nizkor.com/). The relevant topic is mentioned in the fourth section of session 58, part of it is attached here.

Q. Do you remember a particular request you made with regard to your two children?

A. Yes, of course.

Q. Please tell the Court about it.

A. I have to leave out what is in fact a rather important period. Things had reached a stage where we were seriously engaged in setting up the group of six hundred, and obviously it would have been easier and quieter for me to remain in Budapest, if I had been sure that my two children were safe. So I went to Eichmann and asked him to authorize my two children to leave on this transport. I came up against extremely marked, pronounced resistance.

May I add something else? Eichmann told me very abruptly that it was quite out of the question. At that time I took it very hard, but when I left, I thought it over, and it struck me: My goodness, it must be something really serious, if he is so decidedly against the children going along; so perhaps it is actually true that these people will be reaching a neutral foreign country. And so, even though I took it very much to heart, it nevertheless comforted me somewhat to think that people whom we had tried to help to board this train would really reach freedom.

Q. Perhaps you would tell the Court something of the problems, and talk about your task in trying to persuade people to take the train.

A. People did not believe us—they did not seriously believe that the transport would really reach a neutral foreign country. After everything that had happened and all the rumors for years, it had never happened that Jews reached a neutral foreign country. It had never happened. At that time it was not widely known that the entire Weiss family was already safe in Portugal. That was not general knowledge in Budapest. People were very skeptical, very mistrustful. Even the refugees, who were already living illegally, said no, we will remain in our bunkers, we will not go to Columbus, because we do not see any guarantee that it really is true that people will reach a neutral foreign country. They were simply afraid.

Q. And you actually wanted your children to leave on this train?

Presiding Judge: That is quite clear already from what she has said, and Eichmann did not agree.

Witness Hansi Brand: Today I am sure it sounds quite improbable, but nevertheless I brought my children to the camp, so that it would become known that the Brand children were also going along, so that people would gain confidence; if Mrs. Brand was putting her children in it, after all, she would not sacrifice her own children.

Presiding Judge: Mrs. Brand, this is very important, but please allow Mr. Bach to tell you what is important to us in these proceedings, and what is not.

State Attorney Bach: Mrs. Brand, I would like you to explain the following to the Court. Given what everyone knew, including yourself, did you believe that this train would leave for a neutral country?

Presiding Judge: She has already spoken about that, Mr. Bach, she said before that, because Eichmann told her it was "out of the question to send your children," she believed that the whole thing was serious.

State Attorney Bach: What I wanted to ask her was whether there was any other reason why she thought this.

Presiding Judge: I do not consider any of this to be important. It is important, as I have said, but we shall never get to the end.

State Attorney Bach: Perhaps just this question, if the witness can reply to it.

Witness Hansi Brand: I would never have asked for permission to send my children with the transport, if I had not known first that my husband was abroad. In other words, this gave me the feeling of security—the fact that he had been sent to negotiate—because then he obviously would not want to liquidate us before the end of these negotiations.

As one can see, Kasztner is not mentioned here at all. Another point is that Kasztner couldn't get his kids on the train because he didn't have kids at that time. The fact that Kasztner did not have children who could be held hostage is one of the reasons that disqualified Kasztner, from the Germans point of view, from being sent to Istanbul instead of Joel.

It seems that the real reason for this discrepancy is the author's continuous efforts to conceal Hansi's significant role in the negotiations with Eichmann. Hansi's involvement in all the rescue attempts in Budapest, including these negotiations is mentioned in Braham's book[24] but not by Bauer.

Damaging Joel's Reputation and Trustworthiness

The Yad Vashem page dedicated to Joel Brand presents his mission as follows: "The first contact with the SS was conducted by Freudiger, followed by Kasztner. Nevertheless, it was B., who was summoned

---

24   Braham, 1994, pp. 1071, 1088 and more.

to Adolf Eichmann on April 25, 1944, and to him the Nazis' bid for a 'blood for trucks' deal was offered." This presentation is far from being accurate. Joel took part in the first contact of members of the Budapest Rescue Committee with the SS. This is mentioned clearly in Kasztner's report.[25] At that meeting, the SS representative thought that Kasztner was Brand's secretary.[26] Later on, Yad Vashem adds: "The real reason why Brand was chosen for the mission is a mystery." This presentation comes clearly to make the reader understand that Joel was a poor choice.

On a radio broadcast on January 9, 2016, Prof. Shlomo Aronson presented Joel as "an ally of a Gestapo Agent [Laufer]." He later added that Joel was "the assistant to that Gestapo agent." In the same broadcast, apparently without his intention, Aronson also added the following interesting comment: "The Kasztner train was a (German) tribute to Brand."

When Andreas Biss writes in his 1975 book *A Million Jews to Save*[27] that he came to correct the misrepresentation of the facts in Brand's book, one should be suspicious of his critical remarks about Joel and rather trust his positive comments. Similarly, but on the contrary, when he writes about Kasztner that "the honesty of the author [Kasztner] is not in question,"[28] one should be suspicious regarding his positive remarks about Kasztner and rather trust his critical ones. Despite the above, Prof. Bauer and many of his followers ignore these comments by Biss and act just the opposite.

Without prejudice to Biss's rights as a Jewish rescuer (including helping to rescue the author himself), it should be remembered that his book is saturated with errors (like many other sources), and therefore his claims must be verified through other independent sources.

---

[25]   Kasztner's report, 1946. p. 24.

[26]   Brand, 1960, p. 33.

[27]   Biss, 1975, p. 34.

[28]   Ibid., p. 33.

Biss claims that Joel was a Hungarian citizen and therefore his aid to refugees did not endanger his life.[29] Joel lost his Hungarian citizenship following the Treaty of Trianon (1920) and never got it back. A lot of other mistakes can be found in the book. The most extreme case is the detailed description of the delay of weeks, which Hansi caused to Kasztner's meeting with Eichmann. According to Biss, this delay cost a lot of Jewish lives[30]. In reality, this has never happened and Kasztner, according to his own report, admits that he met Eichmann days after Joel's departure.

Based on Biss as a sole source, Bauer claims that Joel was "known to drink."[31] No other independent source ever verified this. Joel's British interrogations report does not mention such tendencies. No doubt that the British, who hated the deal brought by Joel (but not Joel in person), would have been delighted to mention such a tendency, if it existed, to undermine Joel's credibility. In a recording from 1998, Hansi said that she considered to sue M. Lerner for showing Joel drunk in his play *Kasztner*. According to her, this never happened and she never saw Joel drunk. More than that, the reports about Joel's time in Istanbul do not mention the problem of drinking even though Joel was in an extreme mental strain at that time. On June 15, 1944, in a telegram sent by Sharet,[32] he stated: "[I, Sharet] interviewed him [Joel] Sunday six hours, found him one hundred percent reliable, was deeply impressed by his purity, character, spirit, self-sacrifices, factual exactness, soberness."[33] Drinking is not mentioned.

Bauer recounted how Joel saved Jews from the deportation of 1941 with the help of his alleged "friend," the Hungarian agent Krem, for money.[34] This allegation has no foundation anywhere. In the same

---

[29] Ibid., p. 42.

[30] Ibid., p. 49.

[31] Bauer, 1994, p. 152.

[32] The second prime minister of Israel.

[33] Eichman's trial, t\1177.

[34] Bauer, 1994, p. 152.

page Bauer wrote: "He [Brand] joined Kasztner and Springman" in the Rescue Committee prior to its formal establishment in 1943. The truth is that Kastzner was invited by Springman to join Brand and Springman,[35] and in the first period Kasztner was the least active of the three.[36] Bauer says that "He [Brand] was not the stuff that pioneers are made," while Kasztner was a Zionist. Bauer forgets that Kasztner could have immigrated to Palestine but preferred to become a "professional Zionist"[37] in Europe and conducted his preferred bohemian lifestyle there.[38]

Incorrect and misleading descriptions of this kind are common in the writings of some Israeli historians, either because they try to protect the image of the leaders of the Holocaust era, or because they are simply repeating things they learned from their teachers without bothering to verify them.[39] It is impossible to present them all.

Since things are as they are, we will focus on the question of lies, and especially with regard to the issue of the prepayment offered by Eichmann in the framework of the "Blood for Goods" deal.

Who Is Misleading?

In his book *Jews for Sale* and in some of his other works, Prof. Bauer states more than once that Joel was a liar. A comprehensive examination of Joel's testimonies and books shows that they are saturated with errors (like most Holocaust survivors' memories). These errors had nothing to do with lies. When Joel wrote in his

[35]   Revesz, 2001, p. 75. Springman testimony to Asher Cohen, p. 4 (GFH); Brand, 1960, p. 22.

[36]   Cohen, 1984, p. 66.

[37]   Ibid., p. 52.

[38]   Braham, 1994, p. 1071; Revesz, 2001, p. 154; Brand, 1960, p. 23.

[39]   Like Dr. Aryeh Barney's speech; Photographed reconstruction of a speech given at the "Flower and Candle for Israel Kasztner" ceremony, Holocaust Remembrance Day, 2015, https://www.youtube.com/watch?v=mKBS13ZJHRA. See also Ezuz, 2015, p. 321: "Brand's background cast a heavy shadow on the credibility of his mission."

book (1957) that he met Eichmann for the first time in April 25, 1944, while to his British interrogators in 1944 he said "mid-April," he is not lying, he is erring. Unfortunately, such errors are used by Israeli historians like Bauer "to prove" that Joel was, indeed, a liar.

The first to express his mistrust at Joel was the Joint representative in Istanbul, Reuben Resnik, who, like the members of the Jewish delegation there, apparently did not go out of his way to help rescue Hungarian Jews. His reason: "I had the impression that he was not as sincere and straight forward as other observers thought him to be. He had ready and direct answers for all questions."[40] Later on, when Joel's answers became more ambiguous, the reason changed and the ambiguity become the reason to mark him as liar. This ambiguity plays a major role in the discussions about the German proposed "downpayment" and hence, needs explanation.

There is broad agreement among historians on the scope of the proposed deal (a million Jews for ten thousand trucks) and on the fact that some downpayment was proposed by the Germans. There is no agreement on the size of the downpayment, or the "first payment," or, simply put, the number of Jews the Germans would have released following the Jews' agreement to their proposal.

The original proposal was heard by only one Jewish representative, Joel Brand, in the presence of a few Nazis, including Eichmann and probably Becher. Both Joel and Eichmann published their versions on the scope of the deal and the down payment. Despite the importance of the subject, Becher, who was questioned during the Eichmann trial in Germany about his activities in Hungary, was not asked at all about this issue.

Shortly after, Joel, Hansi, and Kasztner must have heard the details from Eichmann, and the agency's representatives in Istanbul heard it from Joel.

The first documented source mentioning the downpayment is the minutes of the Jewish Agency's management meeting on May 24 where a messenger sent from Istanbul informed the leadership

40   Resnik's report, June 4, 1944, p. 4 (Central Zionist Archive, Jerusalem).

about Joel's arrival and his mission. The downpayment mentioned there is 10,000 people[41]

The second documented source mentioning the downpayment is a telegram from the British High Commissioner in Jerusalem that reported to his government, based on a report by senior Jewish Agency officials (Sharet and Ben-Gurion) about Joel's mission and a possible down payment of five to ten thousand. The document also mentioned that the full scope of the deal discussed the release of a million Jews.[42]

The following two sources are the letter from the Joint's representative Resnik on June 4 and Sharet's summary of his meeting with Joel in Syria on June 11, 1944. Resnik did not mention any downpayment. Sharet mentioned a downpayment of about the same amount as the High Commissioner in Jerusalem. The document did not mention an exact number but only a frame of five to ten thousand. Both documents mentioned that the full scope of the deal discussed the release of "all the Jews," which was almost the same as a million.

A few weeks later, on June 22, Hirschman[43] met Joel in Cairo. His summary mentioned larger numbers that could reach up to fifty thousand. An important point in this document is that the author's impression is that he won Joel's trust.

During June 1944 Joel was interrogated by the British. The following facts are mentioned in that interrogation's report.

- The basic price is one truck for 100 Jews (par. 92).
- There is a downpayment in the form of a ship in Constanţa (a port in Romania) to Palestine (that became later "the train of the privileged") (par. 102).
- There is a second downpayment in the form of the German's willingness "to make the first move." "If Brand returned with an affirmative or telegraphed to

---

[41] Porat and Weitz, 2002, p. 259.

[42] Barlas, 1975, pp. 115, 116.

[43] A representative of President Roosevelt and the WRB.

that effect, then he [Eichmann] would put the first batch of deported Jews over the frontier" (par. 100).

- The total volume of the transaction can be understood from the number of trucks mentioned — 10,000 (par. 144).

There is a clear difference between the two types of downpayments mentioned; one is to "Constanța," the other is to "the frontier." The data is as vague as possible, just as Joel explained later on.

Later, during his testimony at the Eichmann trial, Joel was required to explain the gap between the numbers he mentioned close to the events and the number of 100,000, which is mentioned later, in his books and testimonies, as the proposed downpayment. Joel tried to explain that he was scared but the judges seemed to have trouble understanding what Joel was afraid of. The judges found it difficult to understand that Joel feared that a large downpayment would increase the British opposition to the deal and lower the chance of rescuing Jews.

The first person to hear about the German offer from Joel in Istanbul was the head of the Jewish delegation there — Ḥaim Barlas. In his book, published in Hebrew in 1975, he described the German proposal as following:[44]

> The Germans will receive 10,000 trucks and large quantities of coffee, tea, cocoa, and soap, and in return, the Nazis will agree to stop the Jewish extermination and send the Jews (100,000 people, and even more), to Spain or Portugal, and not to Palestine. If the proposal is accepted, they are ready to release a first group of 5,000–10,000 Jews as "downpayment" for further discussion that will take place later.

The number of 1,000,000 (for 10,000 trucks) is not mentioned here, but both the 100,000 and the few thousands are. The number 1,000,000 is mentioned in the report of the High Commissioner to London, which was based on Barlas's report. The High Commissioner did not mention the number 100,000.

---

44   Barlas, 1975, p. 114.

The data available suggest that a downpayment of a few thousands was mentioned. In Hungary it was called "demonstration of good intentions" and Prof. Aronson in a radio talk called it "a [German] gesture [or tribute] to Joel."[45] This was the train of the privileged that started with 600 and ended with about 1,700 rescued Jews. This downpayment was intended to convince the Jews and the West that the Germans were serious, and that there was a basis for negotiations. This downpayment is mentioned in par. 102 in the British interogation report. Moreover, there was a second downpayment based on how the deal was to be executed. According to Joel, Eichmann told him:

> If you return from Constantinople and tell me that the offer has been accepted, I will close Auschwitz and bring ten percent of the promised million to the frontier. You can take a hundred thousand Jews away, and afterwards bring me one thousand trucks.

This down payment is mentioned in par. 100 in the British interogation report. This was the 100,000 mentioned by Barlas, Joel, Hansi, Kasztner, and Eichmann.

Both groups, the few thousand (to Palestine via Romania) and the hundred thousand (to the Spanish border) were supposed to be freed before any truck was given to the Germans and hence may be regarded as downpayment. The 100,000 was not mentioned in the report of the High Commissioner most probably because it was not included in the report he received (orally) from the Jewish Agency leadership (Ben-Gurion and Sharet). The written report Barlas sent to Jerusalem (if he actually sent a report) was not presented to the High Commissioner.

There could have been two reasons for omitting the second down payment from the report to the High Commissioner. One possibility is that the agency's management, like Joel, was concerned that if a large number of Jews could be saved before any compensation to the Germans, it would alarm the British and increase their

---

45   Prof. Aronson on Moshe Timor's program, "Personal Friday," Israel Radio B, January 1, 2016.

opposition to the whole issue, just as Joel tried to explain in his testimony in the Eichmann trial. Another possibility is that the agency's management was not interested in rescuing those 100,000 Jews because, unlike the smaller group, they were not supposed to go to Palestine. According to Beit Zvi, the Zionist leadership at that time resisted and even acted to prevent any rescue attempt that did not lead the survivors to Palestine.[46]

This lack of consistency between the various numbers presented by Joel as a downpayment is one of Bauer's main claims to "prove" that Joel was a liar. To substantiate his position, he even refers to Eichmann's interview with the Dutch Nazi journalist Willem Sassen who interviewed Eichmann before his capture by the Israeli Secret Service. This is what Bauer wrote:[47]

> Eichmann offered to blow up Auschwitz and free the first "ten, twenty, fifty thousand Jews" after receiving information from Istanbul that agreement had been reached in principle, or so Brand put it in his June 22 interview with the U.S. emissary Ira Hirschmann (see below). In Brand's postwar book and in the Kasztner trial in 1954, this offer became a promise to free 100,000 Jews. Eichmann also added that the trucks should be properly winterized and that they would not be used against the West. Eichmann himself—in the interview that he granted to the Dutch journalist Stassen prior to his capture by the Israelis-said that the "basic objective of Reichsfuhrer Himmler [was] to arrange if possible for a million Jews to go free in exchange for 10,000 winterized trucks, with trailers, for use against the Russians on the Eastern Front. . . . I said at the time, "[W]hen the winterized trucks with trailers are here the liquidation in Auschwitz will be stopped."

What Sassen really wrote is:

> Suppose Brand had come back and told me, "Obersturmbannführer, the matter is settled. Five or ten thousand trucks are on their way. Give me a half million or a million Jews. You promised me that if I brought you a positive report, you'd send 100,000 Jews to

---

[46] Bet-Zvi, 1977, pp. 107–298 (nearly two hundred pages devoted to this topic).

[47] Bauer, 1994, p. 164. The name is written there "Stassen."

a neutral country as a deposit." Then it would have been easy for us to ship the Jews off.

If the deal had succeeded, I believe I could have arranged to ship the first 20,000 Jews in two days via Romania to Palestine or even via France to Spain.[48]

Eichmann reiterated the same answer in his trial[49] when he explained the idea behind the ten percent and the number of 100,000 just as Joel said. Eichmann did not confirm that he promised to blow up the extermination facilities in Auschwitz.

Eichmann and Sassen cannot be considered reliable sources, and they are mentioned here just because Prof. Bauer used them.

Hansi also confirmed hearing the number 100,000 from Eichmann in Budapest.[50] Even Kasztner, in the last page of his report, mentioned the fact that an option to save 100,000 Jews from the gas chambers was wasted.

There is no doubt that Kasztner never expected the delivery of a thousand trucks to the Germans. When he wrote in 1946 that 100,000 Jews could have been saved from the gas chambers,[51] he was referring to the "advance payment" that Joel mentioned. To save these 100,000 Jews, it would have been enough to find a country willing to accept them. No one in Israel was interested in the truth about the downpayment. Just as the State refrained from finding out about the size of the advance offered by the Germans at the time of Becher's interrogation during the Eichmann trial, it made sure not to delve into this point with Kasztner during his trial, too. The defense, for its part, refrained from elaborating this point because it would have derailed its efforts to portray Kasztner as a collaborator with the Nazis, and thus it remained open for manipulations.

This issue of the downpayment is just an example. Bauer's book is saturated with similar distortions concerning Joel, most of them without any factual basis.

---

[48] Sassen, 1960, p. 19, survivorbb.rapeutation.com/viewtopic.php?f=60&t=3863.

[49] Eichmann's trial, sessions 86, 106.

[50] Eichmann's trial, session 59.

[51] The original German: "man könne 100,000 Juden vor der Vergasung retten."

20. THE BRANDS AFFAIR

The Jewish leadership in Palestine, and later in Israel, has gone out of its way to cultivate a myth of physical, military heroism. A side effect of this myth is a negative image for the seemingly weak and worthless Diaspora Jew. Israeli literature and historiography admire underground fighters, ghetto fighters, and partisans without looking into the details and without showing the full nature of the events.

The family cohesion of the Jews facilitated the extermination process. Healthy young people could have in many cases fleed and saved themselves, but the vast majority refrained from abandoning their family, even though in the reality of the Holocaust this was probably the right thing to do. The minority who left their family often did so because they belonged to an organized youth group. Many of them are considered partisans, ghetto fighters, and even rescuers of the Jews. But no one has ever dared to examine and present the moral and emotional implications of abandoning family and neighbors. Did those young people who abandoned their family and their relatives really act out of altruistic considerations when they helped others in foreign places instead of helping their family and their neighbors?

An unusual case of presenting this difficult moral problem can be found in Beit-Zvi's book. At the opening of the book it is stated: "Dedicated to the daughter of the butcher of Tykocin [a small town in Poland] and to the fate of her two children, see page 384." This is what is written there:

> Aviezer Burstein, present at the time of the murder of the seventy young men who were caught in a bunker of the Bialystok Fighters Organization, says:
> "Of all the [murdered] group members, only one was known to me. It was a weaver by profession, the Tykocin butcher's son-

in-law. I saw his wife, the butcher's daughter, on Sunday—the first day of the deportation—as she walks with her two babies on her arms. She was looking for her husband, who left her alone with her babies at such a terrible time, and wept bitterly. I could not understand at the time, how a husband could leave his wife alone with two babies, one of them, three-month-old, in her lap.

The weaver from Tykocin went out to defend fame of the Jewish people.[1]

Rescue for its own sake, purely for humanitarian reasons, not for the sake of promoting political, ideological or personal interests, at no point during the Holocaust, played a significant role in the considerations of Jewish and Zionist leaders in Israel and in the free world. Rescue of "just" Jews was not regarded as an act to be boasted about. Even the mere mention of such activities may harm the image of the leadership that did not move a finger to save "just" Jews.

The need for ideological justification for rescuing Jews penetrated deeply into the minds of people. Even people known today in Israel as Jewish rescuers need the explanation "for the sake of the Land of Israel" to justify why they valued the lives of "just" Jews.

The Israeli establishment's lack of sympathy for Jews who rescued Jews during the Holocaust is reflected in the definition of Yad Vashem's mission:

There is hereby established in Jerusalem a Memorial Authority, Yad Vashem, to commemorate:

1. the six million members of the Jewish people who died a martyrs' death at the hands of the Nazis and their collaborators;

2. the Jewish families, who were wiped out by the oppressors;

3. the communities, synagogues, movements, and organizations, and the public, cultural educational, religious, and benevolent institutions, which were destroyed in a heinous attempt to erase the name and culture of Israel;

4. the fortitude of Jews who gave their lives for their people;

---

[1]   Beit-Zvi, 1977, p. 384.

5. the heroism of Jewish servicemen, and of underground fighters in towns, villages, and forests, who staked their lives in the battle against the Nazi oppressors and their collaborators;

6. the heroic stand of the besieged and fighters of the ghettoes, who rose and kindled the flame of revolt to save the honour of their people;

7. the sublime, persistent struggle of the masses of the House of Israel, on the threshold of destruction, for their human dignity and Jewish culture;

8. the unceasing efforts of the besieged to reach Eretz Israel in spite of all obstacles, and the devotion and heroism of their brothers who went forth to liberate and rescue the survivors;

9. the high-minded Gentiles who risked their lives to save Jews.[2]

Jews who risked their lives to save Jews are not mentioned.

The hostility of the Israeli establishment towards Jews who rescued Jews is also reflected in the way Prof. Bauer presents them in his book: "The Jewish heroes were no knights in shining armor. Weissmandel was a fanatic, ultraorthodox opponent of Zionism; Brand was an adventurer, a drinker, and a person whose devotion to the truth was not the most prominent mark of his character . . ." and so on.[3] I doubt whether anyone in Israel would have imagined portraying Gentiles who rescued Jews in such a way.

For years, Yad Vashem (including a radio broadcast with the author's participation)[4] has argued that the number of Jews rescuing Jews is so large that justice cannot be done to everyone. In practice, their numbers are negligible, and so Yad Vashem has been trying for years to find definitions that would enable Jews to be defined as Jewish rescuers, even when they do not meet the definitions required of Gentiles. In Bauer's book discussed earlier, he mentioned people like Saly Mayer, Menachem Bader, and Wenja Pomeranz as heroes who saved Jews. None of them come even

---

2   See Yad Vashem's webpage, https://www.yadvashem.org/about/yad-vashem-law.html.

3   Bauer, 1994, p. 259.

4   Voice of Israel Network A, Nov 29, 2016, "Memorial to the Holocaust",

close to the requirements stated by Yad Vashem for non-Jews. Yad Vashem has tried for years to find ways to portray politicians, and office holders on their behalf, as heros and rescuers of Jews, even though they never helped Jews at their own personal risk. At the same time, Yad Vashem is careful to make sure that these definitions will enable it to continue to ignore the true Jewish rescuers who meet all the criteria required of Gentiles.

The Budapest Relief and Rescue Committee was the only group that was founded, under life-threatening circumstances, outside the German occupation areas, to save foreign Jews. They were concentrated in young Zionist but they helped others as well and even tried to save the entire Jewish population in Hungary. When these people emigrated to Israel, just as Hansi had anticipated immediately after the war, the reception they received in Israel was extremely cold. Jewish leadership in Israel refused to forgive them for their attempts to save "just" Jews in general and Hungarian Jews in particular.[5]

The conformist Kasztner had no difficulty adjusting his reports to what seemed to him as the leadership's expectations and very quickly the same leadership accepted him. Because of unknown reasons, Kasztner gave a series of affidavits for Nazis involved in the murder of thousands of Jews and portrayed them as Jews rescuers. Some of these affidavits were given on behalf of the Jewish Agency and with its financial support. To please the senior leadership, he went one step too far and when the State Attorney's Office asked him to lie and deny the affidavits, he, as usual, behaved as expected and lied. This lie sealed his fate. The same leadership, for which he lied, had walked away from him after the exposure of his lies as if he was a leper. The leadership refrained from preventing his murder even though many believed that the leadership could have easily prevented it. From the moment that Kasztner died, the same

[5]   Yitzhak Gruenbaum, Head of the Rescue Committee of the Jewish Agency, agreed to keep the negotiations with the Nazis as part of Joel's mission only under the condition that the first thousand survivors who would be allowed out of the German Reich territories would be Jews from Poland and not from Hungary (Porat and Weitz, 2002, p. 259).

leadership that abandoned him began its efforts to make him a saint. The reason for the change was, that from the time of his death, his lies could be used to protect the leadership against the accusation of abandoning the Diaspora Jews and specially to conceal their indifference to the rescue option brought by Joel.

Unlike Kasztner, the Brands, who stood up for their truth as they saw it, were a threat to the image of the leadership and that threat had to be eliminated in any possible way.

After all the plans to have Joel and his mission removed from the pages of history have failed—including denying his livelihood, threats of physical elimination, and an attempt to commit him to a psychiatric ward against his will—the solution was finally found: to smear his reputation. The task was not easy since until Joel's departure from Budapest, in May 1944, he was the most respected and popular person with the refugees and the leadership of the Budapest JPU. He and Hansi are mentioned with great admiration in all the memoires of these people. More then that, when the rescue committee of the Jewish Agency in Jerusalem looked for a trustworthy person in Budapest, their choice was Joel.[6] Historians who were close to and graced by the establishment were enlisted to the task. They copied and embellished every offensive remark someone ever directed at Joel, without bothering to examine its truthfulness, and spun a fictional smear campaign. They directed their fury at Joel, blaming him for the failures of the leaders of the Jewish community in Palestine just prior to the foundation of Israel and in its first years. In their writings, they incorporated every offensive and degrading expression they could think of, in order to taint his reputation and good standing.

All these techniques were used knowingly and deliberately[7] by Israeli historians and by Yad Vashem. The Brands summed up their feelings of how the rescue efforts were presented to the public by the Israeli historians in their 1960 book, in the following words:

---

[6]   Porat and Weitz, 2002, p. 392.

[7]   Prof. Aronson justified this behavior saying: "Joel attacked Ben-Gurion," on April 8, 2013.

I understood the satanic game the fate was playing here. Those who did not make the history of the rescue—wrote it. Those who made the history of the rescue—good or bad—were the victims of the writers, if they have survived.

How do I know this? I read the written texts about the rescue operations and saw how a mysterious hand touched things—it added a little here and deleted a little there, scraped and repaired, moved the emphasis from the important to the unimportant, added colors and decorations.

How did it happen that those who wrote the history of rescue had to humiliate those who dealt with it? The reason is quite simple: whoever experienced the actions in person might protest against their retrospect description. He might ask for permission of speech and say quietly: "Sorry, gentlemen, this is not the way it happened." Therefore, one must convince the living witness that he should better shake his head and keep silent—or he should be made suspicious and marked as an unreliable witness.[8]

What the Brands wrote here was almost the same as what Palgi wrote later: "If you go and don't return—you shall be a hero. If you go and return—you shall be judged. If you sit idle and do nothing—you shall be the judge.[9]

A well-known and appreciated Israeli poet, writer, and journalist, Ḥaim Guri, who covered the Eichmann trial and specifically Joel's testimony, discussed Joel's testimony in his book *The Seal of Memory*. As an introduction to the passage about Joel, Guri quoted from Nathan Alterman's poem "Archimedes's Point," in which the poet describes the beginning of a slow, quiet, gradual process of the collapse of civilizations:

> *It starts with a reasoned explanation without an end*
> *Who is worthy of saving and who is not worthwhile,*
> *It starts with those from whom*
> *On the Day of Judgment, some of the blood will be demanded.*

[8]   Brand, 1960, p. 20.

[9]   Palgi, 1977, p. 246.

On Joel himself, Ḥaim Guri wrote as follows:

> We are dealing with the testimony of Joel Brand. If this man were a Christian, he would have become St. Brand. But Joel Brand is a Hungarian Jew, a broken man whose hands are shaking while lighting a cigarette.[10]

The Brands passed away long ago, but Israeli Historians and Yad Vashem continue their efforts to conceal the Brands' extensive activities to save Jews, damage their reputation, and defame them.

[10]   Guri, 1962, p. 83.

Epilogue

At the beginning of October 1944 Joel was released from his arrest in Egypt, where he had been held for about four months, and was taken to Jerusalem. At the beginning of 1946 Hansi left Hungary legally, with the approval of the authorities of the communist regime, on her way to a seminar about the care for people with disabilities. My brother and I, the children, stayed in Budapest as hostages, this time held by the communists to ensure Hansi's return. At the end of March or beginning of April 1946, we were smuggled from Hungary to Czechoslovakia,[1] which was then a free country relative to other countries in the Communist Block. The British consul in Prague registered me and my brother in Joel's Palestinian travel document, and we continued with him to Palestine through Switzerland and France. In Palestine we joined kibbutz Giv'at Ḥaim while Joel tried to build himself in Tel Aviv. Hansi was delayed in Switzerland for about a year until she received an immigration certificate. She arrived in Palestine in January 1947 and joined us at the kibbutz.

After returning from Istanbul, Joel, my father, became a different person. He was haunted by nightmares for not having succeeded to fulfill the mission he took upon himself—rescuing the Hungarian Jewry. He slowly came to the agonizing realization that his party, friends and some of the people he considered partners to the rescue efforts, abandoned him and the Hungarian Jews in general. Unlike Kasztner, Joel was not willing to retroactively adjust his perception of reality to match the administration's agenda. Therefore, he was banished, ostracized, and denied any chance for livelihood.

Hansi wanted at first to stay in Europe. She was the first to realize, even before immigrating to Palestine, that Jews who saved

---

[1]   Revesz, 2001, p. 296.

Hansi with her children
after the war,
Budapest, 1945.

other Jews would not be welcomed in the Jewish state. She agreed to come to Palestine as a result of Joel's pressure and the hope that, despite her concerns and many doubts, Israel would be the best place for us, her children. She quickly realized that the Israeli establishment was too strong for her to take on, and that any attempt to face it and expose the truth was doomed to failure. Therefore, for

The united Brand family in Palestine (still under British mandate), 1947.

the rest of her life she underplayed everything related to her activity during the Holocaust.[2]

My brother Michael had a similar personality to my father, Joel. He always fit in and found his place in every group he found himself in. I, on the other hand, could not find my place at the kibbutz, and the first significant thing I did in my life, when I was about six years old, was to force the family to leave the kibbutz. The fact that I was separated from my brother there may have contributed to that, but the real problems were different. Everything I knew was completely different from what the kibbutz children knew, and my experiences from the war period were perceived at the kibbutz as hallucinations of a troubled boy who needed psychiatric care. My mother, Hansi, immediately understood that everything I said was true and accurate, but unreasonable and inacceptable to the kibbutz members. Teachers and caretakers pressured me "to understand" that I was making things up that did not happen—that was too much for me. Just as problematic for me was the unbearable pressure to behave and think "like everyone else," as was common in the socialistic kibbutz. My childhood was so different than anyone else's that it was not possible for me to fit in. I refused to adjust to the kibbutz pressure to conform and they refused to accept the individual I had become as a result of my unique childhood.

And so, my father purchased a one and a half-room apartment for us in Yad Eliyahu neighborhood in Tel Aviv. At first, my mother taught people with disabilities (occupational therapy) at the Tel Aviv Municipality's Welfare Department, and from 1959 she worked as a caretaker at Ma'on HaYeled, a religious orphanage.

My father, Joel, died of a heart attack in 1964 after testifying in Germany in the trial of two of Eichmann's senior assistants in Hungary, Hunsche and Krumey.[3] I was present at that trial which made me question whether Germany had changed at all after

---

[2]   Segev, 1991, pp. 405–410.

[3]   Krumey was one of the Nazis who got a supporting affidavit from Kasztner. Kasztner was acquitted of the trial filed against him on charges of giving testimony in favor of Nazi criminals, among other things because of the fact that this affidavit and others were not known at the time.

the war. Joel died of a deadly combination of diabetes, angina pectoris, and heartbreak. A few historians did not find all of these sufficient and decided to add to the list cirrhosis, which supposedly originated from heavy drinking. The fact that no one has ever seen my father drunk and that he had never suffered from cirrhosis has not troubled the history makers in Israel.

My brother Michael, nicknamed Miki, who was two years my senior, was an anchor of stability for me during the war. The circumstances of our life forced us to grow up much sooner than we should have otherwise, and the presence of a big brother made things much easier for me. In the kibbutz, in 1946, we were separated. This had a considerable weight on my uncompromising wish to leave the place. In 1972, before he turned thirty-four, my brother became ill with a malignant disease of which he suffered indescribably. The doctors misled my mother and me—they did not inform us until the very last moment that this was an incurable malignant disease. At the same time, they refused to give him morphine to ease his pain as they didn't want him to "become addicted."

Hansi, my mother, continued working at the orphanage until her death in 2000 and dedicated her free time to helping others in need. Every Sunday (the first workday of the week in Israel) she appeared at a soldiers' pick-up bus station and handed them sandwiches and beverages. On her last day, when I was traveling abroad on business, my eldest son, Joel, arrived in Israel with Hansi's first two great-grandchildren. Immediately upon landing they called Hansi to schedule a visit, but she postponed the visit because she had promised to take a handicapped person hospitalized in a nursing home for an outing. At night, when she returned, she sat down on her bed and never got up again.

After my mother's death, I thoroughly and to the best of my ability went through the material left at home. There, I found the recording in which she talked, among other things, about the fact that the family's contribution to the early stopping of the deportation of Jews with no citizenship from Hungary in 1941 was documented in Prof. Braham's research data. In the recording, Yad Vashem investigators firmly denied this detail since in the publication of the same research by Yad Vashem, the reference to

Memorial plaques in Budapest to Holocaust victims and members of the Rescue
Committee. Joel and Hansi are mentioned in both plaques. In Israel, they have
no mention.

the Brands' contribution was omitted. Such blatant falsification of
history resembles techniques from the days of Stalin, who erased
his opponents from pictures and encyclopedias in Russia. This was
all the motivation I needed to write this book.

Hansi—the woman with the courage of an "Aryan," as the
Germans described her; the "heart of the consortium," according
to the senior leaders of the Jewish Pioneers Underground (JPU); the
woman who had no relatives on the train of the priviledged; the
woman without whom the entire rescue operation would not have
realized—was erased from history. Joel was persecuted and his
name smeared until the very last day of his life. Actually, the efforts
of the establishment to smear his name have never stopped, even
after his death. He is still being persecuted for his efforts to rescue
Jews, simply due to the administration's fear of exposing the failures
of its contemporary leadership. These defamations are designed to
tarnish Jew savers whose deeds and successes, albeit partial, are
conclusive evidence for the leadership's failures. Such slander is
still being voiced quite often. This is how Israeli historians actually
follow Goebbels's (the Nazi minister of propaganda) theory that
a lie repeated often enough becomes the accepted truth.

Memorial plaques in Budapest.

Appendices

Appendix 1: Sharet's Report[1]

From Joel Brand's report, June 11 1944, Aleppo.

M.S.:[2] I informed Joel that I already heard the story twice from other people, but I wished to hear a report of the chain of events directly from Joel himself.

Joel said that even before the Germans entered Hungary, the Zionist group that was active in Hungary had contacts with a group of Germans that belonged to a military institute, through Dr. Schmidt, Jozi, and Seclacek. There were also contacts with Hungarian military institutes through Bandi (Andor George or Bandi Grosz).

About one week before the invasion it became known that the Germans would invade over the next few days. Contact was immediately sought with the SS group headed by von Wisliceny, known as "Willy," who previously helped the Slovakian Jews by postponing the deportation of the remaining Slovakian Jews in exchange for large amounts of money. Joel and his associates tried to reach Willy through Dr. Schmidt [Willy is Himmler's crony, some say, his brother-in-law]. The meetings with Schmidt included talks about improving the situation of the Polish refugees and about a promise not to renew the deportations from Slovakia. However,

---

[1] Eichmans trial, t\1176.

[2] M.S. is Moshe Sharet (Shertok), head of the Jewish Agency political department and later the first Minister of Foreign Affairs and the second prime minister of the State of Israel

when the question of the Hungarian Jews was raised, there was no reaction on the part of Schmidt.

On the invasion date of Hungary, Joel was arrested—the Germans entered Budapest at 6 am on March 19 and at 9 am that day they came to arrest him. He was officially informed that the arrest was intended for his own good so that he would not be harmed by Hungarian or German institutes of the Gestapo. He found out that the arrest was performed by Schmidt's group, probably in order to prevent Joel from contacting other Nazi authorities. He was not taken to prison but rather stayed at the army's offices. At the time of his arrest he already found out that Willy had been assigned to Budapest and Eichmann assumed the handling of the Hungarian Jewry. He was released on the third day and immediately started seeking contact with Willy. Jozi and Schmidt first refused to liaise between Joel and Willy, probably as they wanted to pocket the main part of the payment associated with negotiations for ease of conditions. After Joel had promised Jozi and Schmidt an amount of 20,000 dollars for Willy, in addition to 4,000-dollars brokerage fee, a meeting with Willy was guaranteed. The following people attended that meeting: Jozi, Willy, and an SS Sturmführer unknown to Joel. On behalf of the Jews: Joel and Kasztner. Before the beginning of the negotiation, an amount of 200,000 dollars was promised for the negotiation itself. The large part of the amount (6,500,000 pengő) had been paid. In the negotiation, Joel and Kasztner presented the following demands:

A) securing the life (of the Hungarian Jews), namely no extermination;
B) no deportations;
C) no establishment of ghettos and concentration camps;
D) permission to immigrate to Palestine and elsewhere.

The issue was, first and foremost, the attitude to the Hungarian Jews. In exchange for fulfilling the four aforesaid demands, the Jewish delegation proposed a payment of 2,000,000 dollars (this is the amount that was requested at the time by Willy in exchange for halting the deportations from Slovakia).[3] Willy's reply[4] was that such a meager amount was out of the question because the number of Jews in Slovakia, which amounted at the time to less than 10,000,[5] could not be compared to the number of the Hungarian Jews, which he estimated at 1,200,000.[6] Besides, the negotiation should not only be conducted with respect of the Hungarian Jews, but rather with respect of all of the Balkans' Jews, whose number was estimated by Willy at two million.[7]

As for the demands, his reply was as follows: as for Bullet A—he was willing to promise that no extermination shall take place as the German method was not to kill Jews but rather to use them as forced laborers. As for Bullet B—he commented that the deportation was exclusively up to the Germans who were not interested in it at the time. However, he added a comment that it was impossible to promise that there would be no victims at all. The number of victims may be in the range of 10-15,000. As for Bullet C—he said that he was willing to promise that there would be no general gathering in ghettos and concentration camps, but that the Jews of villages and small towns would be transferred to larger cities, which would involve the creating of some concentration camps. He also commented that the limitations on travels and wearing a yellow badge cannot be prevented. As for Bullet D—he answered that the Germans were not interested in the immigration of a few hundred selected people, but rather in a massive immigration of hundreds of thousands; and requested a plan for a mass immigration. Joel

[3]   This was the requirement for halting the deportation in general, known as the Europe plan.

[4]   All the data Willy provides here are incorrect (compare next three notes).

[5]   In reality, about 20,000 Jews remained in Slovakia, and for the prevention of their extermination, Germans received a sum of 50,000 dollars. Of this sum, it is reasonable to assume that the Jewish mediator Hochberg took 20%, or 10,000 dollars.

[6]   In reality, less than a million.

[7]   A significant part of the Balkan Jewry was exterminated earlier by Willy himself. Willy was one of the Nazis whom Kasztner testified in favor of after the war.

and Kasztner said, that based on their knowledge, the Agency had 30,000 immigration certificates for heads of families intended to support the immigration of 150–160,000 people to Palestine [they multiplied the 30,000 by five heads per family]. At that meeting, Joel and Kasztner commented that 750 people could be immediately taken out to Romania as, to the best of their knowledge, a ship was waiting at Constanţa ready to transfer the immigrants to Turkey.

In the second meeting that was held several days later, Willy informed that they were willing to grant a permit for 750 people to exit, but he explained that the immigrants would have to first go through German territory in order to turn them—according to his expression—from Hungarian goods to German goods. The plan was to transport that group using a boat on the Danube. To make them "German goods," the ship would first sail to Vienna or Slovakia, and from there it will continue to Romania. Willy explained that the candidates for immigration would be concentrated in a camp in Budapest and 750 immigrants would be selected from the camp.

At that time, extremely cruel deportation of Jews from the villages began and they were sent to concentration camps. In addition, in the larger cities the Jews were concentrated in ghettos. The concentration was executed in a wilder, crueler way than the concentration of Jews in ghettos in Poland. The representatives of the Jews immediately approached Willy protesting against this based on the answer he had given at the time: that there would be no concentrations. His answer was that the Hungarians were responsible for the cruelty rather than the Germans. At that time, one of the active members, Moshe Schweiger, was arrested. Joel demanded to release him. Willy promised he would be released, but Joel did not know whether the promise was kept.[8]

At the beginning, the contact with Willy was handled through Schmidt. One day Schmidt informed Joel that he must wait at 10 am

---

[8]   The promise was not kept but he survived the war, probably because of special orders in his case.

at the corner of one of the streets, and from that place he would be taken to Eichmann. At exactly 10 am a car bearing a police number came and took Joel, and brought him to Eichmann's office. This was about mid-April. In addition to Eichmann, a man in civilian clothing and a secretary were present. Eichmann said: "You know who I am. I solved the question of the Jews in Europe. I solved the question of the Jews in Poland. I executed the deportations. Before coming here, I first tried to find whether you still have something to negotiate with. I approach you as a representative of the JDC, to make a deal with you. The deal is blood for goods. I am willing to give you all the Jews. You probably want first of all the young Jews, the men who can have children and the women who can give birth." Joel's answer was that it was not up to him to seal the fate of such or other Jews. Eichmann insisted: "What do you chose? Goods or blood?" Joel answered: "If not all our property has been confiscated, we are willing to give you all the goods and all the property that we have." Eichmann: "Think carefully about what I am interested in and you will realize that it is not your goods that I'm interested in." Joel: "If I understand you correctly, then I must go abroad to solve this matter." Eichmann answered: "As far as I am concerned, a permit will be given to you and you must contact the suitable institutes."

After this talk, a meeting was held with Schmidt who informed that he would not agree, under any circumstances, to the travel of any Jew abroad. In that talk with Schmidt, the financial issue was readdressed and Schmidt repeated what he had said, that the amount of 2,000,000 dollars was out of the question. The topic of the exit of 750 people was raised again, and it was agreed to pay 10,000,000 pengő for the exit permit. In addition to that, Schmidt demanded that twenty seats would be allocated for him to sell. A few days after the talk with Schmidt, Joel's comrades found out that the authorities' attitude to Schmidt had worsened, and that he was accused of embezzlement from Jewish property. This was considered a serious offense. The negotiation between the Jewish delegation and the SS representatives [Gestapo] was conducted since then without Schmidt's liaising. After a while they found out about the arrest of Schmidt and Jozi [Jozi's correct name is

Winniger]; who also used the name Duft. Joel assumes that Schmidt and Joel[9] were hung.

In further talks with the SS the following people attended: Shrader [Joel commented that this was not the man's correct name but he was threatened not to reveal his real name], Klages, and Krumey. Joel described the later, Krumey, as a kind, hospitable farmer who tried to be helpful and made the impression of an honest person. Joel mentioned that when Krumey escorted him to the Vienna Airport, he commented that the overseas institutes might take the entire plan more seriously once they learn that Eichmann included Krumey, Klages, and Shrader in the negotiations. Krumey once again emphasized his humane attitude. He tried to imply that his attitude to the Jewish question was quite the opposite of Eichmann's who was notorious for his cruelty.

From all the talks, it became clear that even if an agreement was reached regarding a massive immigration, immigration to Palestine through the Balkans was out of the question for the following reasons.

A) The SS people assumed that the Turks would not permit the passage of a large number of Jews.

B) The Germans were not willing to upset the Arabs by too large a Jewish immigration.

C) They were not willing to support the foundation of a too strong Jewish community in Israel. They said: "If you build a large force in Palestine, then at some point we shall have a conflict with you once again."

D) To allow the evacuation, the Germans needed to turn the Jews into German goods. To that end, the Jews should be first gathered in Germany, and should not be taken directly out of the Balkans where they would leave as Hungarians, Romanians, and Bulgarians.

E) The SS people truly believed that Judaism was cancerous. They therefore wished to spread them among the Allies

---

9   The source says "Joel," probably by mistake.

in order to infect their enemies rather than let them
concentrate in Palestine, where they would become
a consolidated force, which would strengthen the Jews
and would not weaken other nations.

To the question of M.S. whether Joel assumed that the Germans
would take the plan seriously, he answered: A) he believed that
they were genuinely interested in the goods; B) however, their
intention might have been for the Allies to take this gesture into
consideration during negotiations for peace.

Joel explained that their intention might have been specifically
for the following purposes: 1) more lenient treatment for certain
people, such as Krumey, Klages, and Shrader; 2) more lenient
treatment for Eichmann's group; 3) or possibly that this would
be credited to Germany as a whole. The SS people might assume
that: there were eight million Jews in Germany and the occupied
countries, six million were killed. They have two more million left.
They might be willing to give away these two million so that in
exchange the world would forget the murder of the six million. Like
a thief caught stealing a hundred liras. He proposes twenty liras to
the man who catches him so that he would keep silent about the
eighty.

During the negotiations, the Jews also raised the issue of
the inmates at the Theresienstadt, Reichenau, and Birkenau
concentration camps. The SS replied that if the plan was carried out,
all the Jews who were located in Germany and in its occupied and
controlled territories in all of Europe could be evacuated.

The following countries were mentioned as destinations: Spain,
North Africa west of Tunisia, America, and so forth. As for Palestine,
Eichmann commented that if one or two ships received a special
instruction or order from a British or American warship to sail to
the shores of Palestine for military reasons, no one would consider
this a big disaster, but normally the flow of immigration should not
to be directed to Palestine. As for the entry visas to the destination
countries, Eichmann emphasized that the Jews must organize this
aspect (he assumed that the Jews, who, in his mind, controlled the
entire world and whose orders were obeyed by all the American

senators, would not encounter any difficulties obtaining these entry visas).

Joel commented that during the negotiation he often had the feeling that he was presented with a diabolical plan behind which there might be a justification towards the world for a fast extermination of the remaining Jews in Europe.

The talks also touched upon the issue of transportation. Eichmann emphasized that the Germans assumed the task of supplying the required number of cars to concentrate the Jews of the Balkans in transit camps in Germany (in order to make them "German goods") and later on transported them from Germany through France to Spain or Portugal.

The "commercial" part of the negotiation was conducted mainly with Klages and Shrader. Eichmann, on his part, only suggested that the Jews would provide trucks in exchange for securing the immigration plan. He did not go into details but only mentioned in one of the talks the number of 10,000 trucks. Eichmann explained that he needed these trucks for the civil SS whose trucks were all out of order. He wished to obtain new trucks from the military SS, but to do so he needed to provide them with new trucks which he wanted to receive from the Allies in exchange for the Jews. Eichmann made this proposal after he had returned from a trip to Germany and commented that while he was absent from Budapest, he visited Berlin and Berchtesgaden and received the consent of the highest authorities to such plan. He mentioned all that without going into details.

Some of the talks were attended by generals who ranked higher than those who conducted the talks (Krumey, Klages, and Shrader). In one of the talks, a civilian, whose name was unfamiliar to Joel, mentioned that other than trucks they needed 200 zentner of tea, 200 zentner of chocolate, 800 zentner of coffee, and 2 million pieces of soap.

On the Jewish side, in some of the talks Kasztner and Joel were present but in most of them only Joel was present.

Later in the negotiation they discussed practical issues related to the deportations, creation of ghettos, and so forth, especially with Krumey; and commercial issues—with Klages and Shrader, who constantly emphasized that they wanted to make a straight, clean business.

M.S. asked firstly whether the Nazis really meant the exchange of goods or rather the exchange of cash, and secondly, whether they meant material considerations or perhaps there was an entirely different hidden meaning.

Joel answered that while money had great value for them, it should be assumed that there was political motiviation behind the negotiations. Joel emphasized that he had such an impression already during the negotiations in Budapest and this opinion had been reinforced after he found out about Bandi's special mission. However, it was clear to Joel that they needed goods. Other than trucks, he received a list of spare parts of various machines. They also mentioned in the negotiation money in foreign currency: dollars, pounds sterling, and sakuda. In one of the talks a proposal was mentioned to exchange civilian detainees. Eichmann informed that if they reached a principled agreement with the Jewish institutes abroad (they said: the JDC), he was willing to make the first move and immediately send the first group, a few thousands[10], for no consideration. The next groups would always[11] leave in exchange for the goods when they arrive.

To the question if children in particular were discussed, Joel answered that after he had answered Eichmann at the first meeting that he was unwilling to abandon any kind of Jew, Eichmann told him: "You can have all the Jews, but we cannot assume that you have so much money that you can evacuate all of them

---

[10]   Since the British were present, Joel did not specifically indicate the size of the human advance concerned. Despite the great importance of this issue, M.S. did not request further clarifications.

[11]   There is a clear reference to the performance method mentioned by Joel in his book and confirmed by Eichmann in his testimony. Bauer tries to claim that only "several thousand people" were concerned but he does not mention the fact that under his own assertions, assuming rounds of 5,000 people (50 trucks) and assuming that each round lasts at least one week, the entire deal might have required 200 weeks, which are approximately 4 years, an entirely unreasonable time. Hence, the basis for Bauer's assertions is doubtful in the best-case scenario and entirely far-fetched in the reasonable-case scenario.

immediately. This is why I will give you first those who are unfit for work. Those who are fit for work will work and live under good conditions. They will even receive the extra food given to laborers in hard works." Eichmann emphasized that, in the meantime, the children and women should be fed, and this would cost money, so the negotiations should be expedited.

In the last talk with Eichmann, Joel asked if he was willing to stop the deportations during the negotiation. Eichmann's answer was: "on the contrary, the deportations will begin immediately, with full effect." He quoted a number of twelve thousand per day. This would serve, in his opinion, as pressure to lead the negotiation to positive results. Joel claimed that there was no reason to apply pressure as they knew that five years of liquidation had not convinced the world to make any concessions to Germany. As such, he argued that they better take a more moderate approach. Krumey answered that he was willing to promise that no one would be killed in a deportation until Joel's return from overseas. The deportees would write letters to those who stay. After initial information would be received about real chances for an agreement with the Jewish institutes abroad, the deportations would stop and the Jews would be transported to transit camps in Germany where immigrants would be selected.

When Joel came to complain to the SS people about the harsh measures taken in regards to confiscating property and the continuation of the cruel deportations from small towns, he was answered that these actions were performed by the Hungarian authorities and the Germans were not happy with them. In Joel's opinion, there was a certain degree of honesty in this reply. Since the Germans' invasion, disagreements have arisen between the Hungarians and the Germans with respect to benefitting from confiscated Jewish property. The Hungarians were quick to confiscate property in order to immediately appropriate it to themselves, before the Germans penetrated into the economic life in Hungary and benefited themselves from the destruction of the Jews.

At the end of the talks, it was established that one of the Jewish leaders must go abroad. After consultation with the Jewish Committee, Joel informed that he was willing to go. The Germans gave him the choice of leaving to Switzerland or Istanbul. He chose Istanbul assuming that he would be able to contact the institutes in Jerusalem from there. He thought that immediately upon arriving in Istanbul he would be able to introduce the proposal to the top institutes in Jerusalem, and possibly also to conduct the negotiations with the Allies' institutes.

M.S.: "What happens if you return with a positive answer? What happens if you return with a negative answer? What happens if you do not return at all?"

Joel: "At first, I believed that if I returned with a positive answer, I would bring salvation. Today, after I became aware of Bandi's mission, I am not sure of that. If I return with a negative answer— total liquidation would begin immediately. It is conceivable that my family and the families of my friends would not be exterminated immediately, in order to leave another option for negotiations. If I do not return at all—they would kill immediately all my friends and there is a 99-percent certainty that my family members would be among the first to be killed. I am not saying 100 percent because it is very possible that they would keep my family alive as hostages and would showcase them as the victims of that bastard Brand who had abandoned them and schemingly managed to save himself. There is no doubt that general liquidation of the Jews of the Balkans would begin. If it was possible to set a meeting in one of the neutral countries with a representative of Eichmann's group, it might have been possible for me not to return."

To the question whether Eichmann's group could allow massive emmigration without the consent of the highest institutes in Germany, Joel answered that the Security Service (Sicherheitsdienst), headed by the Reich Main Security Office (Reichssicherheitshauptamt), was a powerful entity that could act contrary to the directions of some high authorities such as the Ministry of Foreign Affairs, but it should be assumed that this would require the authorization of Himmler and possibly of Hitler himself.

M.S. asked Joel to relate everything he knew about the Bandi affair.

Joel: "The name of the man is Andor George or Bandi Grosz. He is a Jew who worked for the Hungarian espionage service. He was associated with a high-profile group from the Hungarian military headquarters and often traveled to Istanbul on their behalf, where he met Hatch and Bágyoni (Hatch was appointed a few months ago as military attaché of the Hungarian legation in Istanbul). After the Germans' invasion, Bandi made some attempts to help his contacts in Istanbul to stay there, rather than return to Hungary. Despite his efforts, they returned and were arrested. Bandi himself was also arrested, and probably during his arrest he formed contacts with the circles of Klages and Shrader (not Eichmann). After he had been released, Schmidt and Jozi were arrested. Bandi probably led to their arrest."

When the topic of Joel's travel came up, Bandi proposed himself as an escort. Joel was asked by Eichmann whether he insisted that Bandi escort him. Joel answered that he did not demand that but he found it convenient that Bandi, who was familiar with the travel conditions to and in Istanbul would join him.[12] Later on, Bandi angrily asked Joel (or at least pretended to be angry) why he did not forcefully insist on him as an escort. The fact that Bandi knew of the talk Eichmann had with Joel was suspicious. Bandi explained to Joel that without him, he would encounter many difficulties on the way, at which point, Joel requested Eichmann that Bandi would join him. It seemed that Klages and Shrader were interested in Bandi's travel. On the other hand, Eichmann and Krumey pretended that they did not care one way or the other. In reply to a question of M.S., Joel confirmed the assumption that there might have been an ulterior motive to manipulate things such that Bandi would go as a result of Joel's request and not because of someone's order, so as to conceal the real purpose of his trip. Joel emphasized that since the proposal of including Bandi came up, he had the feeling that other than the role of supervising Joel, Bandi also assumed another role. He figured so after he saw that Bandi had had many talks with Klages and Shrader, without Joel's presence. When Joel was summoned to a meeting with Krumey to schedule the trip to Vienna, he found Bandi in the coffeehouse they chose as the meeting

---

[12]   It was probably a good decision. Without Grosz, Joel would have been sent back almost immediately by the Turks to Germany.

place. After Joel left the meeting place, Bandi was left there alone with Klages and Shrader. When they left in Krumey's car, Bandi took out four sheets typed with a typewriter and told Joel that these were his instructions and that he must memorize them as he could not take them abroad. During the entire trip to Vienna Bandi read the papers, and before boarding the airplane in Vienna Airport, he gave them back to Krumey.

In Joel's opinion, Bandi was entrusted with the mission of liaising between British and American institutes and certain German institutes regarding terms of peace. If this assumption was correct, it meant that the Jewish matter was merely used by Bandi as a pretext to begin the negotiation. It was also possible that the Jewish matter was meant to prove to the Allies that certain German circles were willing to change their ways.

Should Bandi not return, no one would believe Joel, in which case his life would be in danger. But if Joel could bring some sort of an answer, also regarding Bandi's mission, this answer could serve as proof that Joel's words should be taken seriously, and Eichmann's group might cling to it. In Joel's opinion, Bandi would have been in a hurry to return had he brought a positive answer regarding his mission. However, since he realized that there was no chance of that, he decided not to go back. Bandi's wife was already in Istanbul and joined him on his trip to Aleppo.

Later on, Joel pointed out that one of the things that proved to him how serious the Nazis were was the way he was driven. He and Bandi were taken from Budapest to Vienna in Krumey's car, who drove with them. In Vienna, Joel stayed at the SD headquarters, and the following day Krumey drove him and Bandi to the airport and ordered the captain to take them to Istanbul. He shook Joel's hands and told him he hoped that after they hear abroad that he, Krumey, was involved, they would take Joel seriously.

The current situation of the Jews

Joel related, at the request of M.S., the situation of the Jews in Hungary at the time of his departure.

The anti-Jewish laws, which in other countries were introduced over years, were executed in Hungary in a matter of days. Economically, as previously explained, there were some conflicts between the Germans and the Hungarians, but this did not change the fact that immediately after the Germans' invasion, Jews were expelled from all economic positions and their property was confiscated. The immediate concentration of Jews in ghettos also began. As aforesaid, right after Joel had found out about the concentration in ghettos, he approached Eichmann, who answered: "Right—I gave an order to immediately concentrate in ghettos and camps 310,000 Jews." Joel did not receive an explanation for this number. Perhaps, according to the statistics Eichmann had, this was the entire number of Jews in the vicinity of Transilvania, Karpatorus, and Bačka (Bačka was the region that was annexed from Yugoslavia by Hungary). The towns and villages were suddenly surrounded by the Hungarian gendarmerie (this was on Monday, April 10) and the Jews were ordered to leave the place. They were sometimes allowed to take some jewelry and money, but there were cases that the gendarmes made death threats should even a twenty-heller coin be found on a Jew. The Jews were brought from the villages to county towns. In some towns, ghettos were arranged by allocating blocks of buildings and streets, and declaring them as ghettos. In other places, factories and warehouses outside the city became concentration camps. There were cases where the Jews were concentrated in open fields surrounded by fences.

For example, in Cluj (Klausenburg), the Jews were concentrated in the Iris brickyard. 20,000 people were about to be concentrated in an area of 17,000 square meters. In fact, 15,000 were concentrated because about 5,000 managed to escape. This area was equipped with only twenty water faucets. This camp housed Martin Erne (who edited the Zionist newspaper in Cluj) and Hillel Danzig (an active member of Iḥud who did a lot for the refugees from Poland and Slovakia).

In Bistriţa, the Jews were assembled near the city, in an open field. Officially they were permitted to take with them food for fourteen days, but in reallity they were informed of the order of deportation from the city at 6 am, and the order was to be carried out by 8 am. Those who had not prepared food could not buy anything. The concentration place was equipped with no water at all. The thirst brought the detainees to madness. They shouted for water like animals. There was much commotion among the non-Jews in Bistriţa and many hurried to the concentration place trying to throw bottles of water into the camp. To prevent that, the camp was separated with a "neutral" area from the city and no one was allowed to get close to the fence. The authorities supplied a single bowl of soup for seven people per day.

In Oradea Mare, all the Jews were taken out of the city and were ordered to dig holes as accommodation. After intervention from Budapest this edict was cancelled and a permit was obtained to create a ghetto inside the city. After the cruelty involved in some concentration camps was found out, the Jewish institutes considered the permits for organizing ghettos inside the cities as great relief, as such ghettos meant existing houses, water, light, and other facilities.

In Munkács the Jews were concentrated inside the city. An order was given that seven people must share a room. Even a small corridor, a bathing room, and a restroom were considered a room. Crowdedness was horrible. There was a case of a woman who was about to give birth and there was no place to let her lie down or even sit during the childbirth. Munkács saw the first case of mass shooting: two people were sent outside the ghetto to run an errand and they did not come back instantly. As retaliation, the SS people started shooting the crowd. The number of victims was unknown. However, it was known that one of the active Zionists, Spiegel, was among the victims.

In Košice, all the Jews were concentrated near the airport. From Bačka, most of the Jews were taken out. Some were brought to Košice and some were spread across various places. Some Jews were left in Nagykanizsa. In Budapest, many Jews were concentrated near parts of the city that were raided. About 150 young women were caught on the streets and were taken to unknown places. There was a concern that they were taken to military brothels. They made sure to catch pretty girls. As of April 5, the yellow badge in the shape of a yellow Star of David became mandatory and every Jew had to wear it.

In some cases, local Hungarian municipalities objected to the evacuation and concentration of Jews in ghettos. This happened in Pécs and in Sagasfélvár.[13] Their reason was that if the Jews were removed or concentrated in certain areas, the Allies would bomb the other areas.

The Jews of Subotica were transported to Poland. It seemed that a few families were left there.

Until Joel's departure, about 8,000 Jews had been deported from Hungary. In all cities and towns, many Jews were arrested—rich, activists, and half-breeds. Deportation began on Monday and Joel left on Wednesday. He still had the time to complain to Eichmann about the deportation and claimed that this was inconsistent with the agreement. As stated above, Eichmann answered that the deportation would continue and 12,000 people would be sent daily. Others said that people would be deported but not killed.

Nonetheless, Joel had the impression that the deportation ceased. He received a telegram from his wife. According to the arrangement they made prior to his departure, it could be interpreted as if the deportation was stopped (the content of the telegram is attached).[14] Joel also heard from another source, albeit not authorized, Bandi's friend, that the deportations had stopped.

Underground activities

During the past two years, a circle of Zionist activists, to which Joel belonged, has helped to smuggle the Jews of Poland and Slovakia into Hungary as this was the only country in Europe where Jews felt secure. To that end, a committee was founded named the *Tiyul*

---

[13] The spelling is unclear and the place is not identified.

[14] However, the content of the telegram is not attached and the deportations were not halted at that time.

Committee. The composition of the committee was as follows: Rezső Kasztner, Moshe Rosenberg, Zvi Szilágyi, Moshe Schweiger, Hillel Danzig, and Joel. The chairman of the World Zionist Organization, Ottó Komoly, provided all the required support to the activists. The committee distributed its work to several subcommittees: there was a sub-committee for obtaining documents. For a year, two printing houses had been providing documents to refugees all over Hungary. In some cases, help was also given to persecuted Democrat and Social-Democrat Christians. After the occupation, this activity was increased, and with the help of this organization, 20–30 percents of the deportees have evaded the concentration. Some were equipped with papers allowing them to stay in Hungary and some crossed the border to Romania. The best way to Romania was through Cluj, on the Hungarian side, to Turda on the Romanian side. The activists in this area were Hillel Danzig and Erne Hartzvi of Cluj.

In regards to the question of M.S. about an option to liaise with Tito, Joel answered that the option to escape to the partisans' area in Yugoslavia was brought up in the comrades' discussion. Yitzhak Knoll was entrusted with the task of checking the roads. The conclusion was that no attempts were to be made for the escape of individuals because organizing escape to this area was considered so important that it must not be endangered by uncalculated actions. There was a case of two comrades who tried to cross the Yugoslavian border, were caught and killed. No border was being guarded as much as the Yugoslavian border. There was great danger in liaising with the partisans as there had been many provocations, so this required extreme caution. The comrades in Budapest hoped that help in this aspect would be given from here. One of the tasks imposed on Joel on behalf of the Committee was to examine the possibility of help, in this aspect, by the comrades in Palestine. The comrades in Budapest also proposed that a comrade or several comrades would be sent to them via Yugoslavia and they were willing to lend their help to the success of such operation, if they were to be notified in advance. They also proposed several gathering places and several telephones through which contact could be made with the comrades. The person responsible for the *tiyul* activity was Joel. After he had left, Peretz Révész and Joel's wife took his place.

There is contact with Vienna. In Vienna there are currently two thousand Jews who arrived there from Poland and they are hiding in various places. Up until a short while ago there was contact with a (non-Jewish) woman, a resident of Vienna, whose name was Austern. She helped to transfer to Hungary Jews who arrived from Poland to Vienna and handled those who were hiding in Vienna. This woman was arrested and another woman, called "Batti," is now working instead of her. The contact with her was established by an officer named Imra on the Austrian border. While he received payment, he also had interest in the rescue issue itself. He would arrive at least once and sometimes twice a week from the Austrian border to Budapest and would always bring with him five or six refugees. The Committee appointed Leon Blatt from HeHalutz to be responsible to these *tiyuls*.

Right after the occupation, refugees from Slovakia, who first found refuge in Hungary, started flowing back to Slovakia. Recently, *tiyuls* of this kind stopped because most of the refugees were equipped with papers. The crossing points were near Košice and Nitra.

Haganah[15]

Before the Germans' invasion, the comrades in charge of the underground activities, started buying weapons. About one hundred and fifty guns were bought, third of which was unfit for use. About a hundred guns were in good condition. Two machine guns were also bought [Joel did not know of which model] as well as seven or eight small rifles [carbines]—a kind of short rifle used by the Hungarian cavalry. There was not enough ammunition for the existing weapons. There were guns equipped with five to seven bullets each and some with up to sixty. On average, there were about twenty bullets per gun. Rifles were equipped with

---

15 "Defense" in Hebrew.

twenty to thirty bullets per rifle. The machine guns had two belts per machine gun. If the weapons were brought together, they would suffice to arm a large group, but a mistake was made and the weapons were distributed by organizations and regions, and as a result, there was no group that could seriously defend itself using the existing weapons. A group of comrades started training in obtaining weapons. Plans have been discussed. There was a proposal to organize a group that would be in charge of stealing guns in barber shops and restaurants (German officers tended to remove their gun belts upon entering such places). They also thought about buying weapons from the Germans who retreated from the Russian front. The Haganah had about 2,000 people, including women. There were several commanders who previously served in the Hungarian or Yugoslavian army. In particular, Joel mentioned Widrich who served in the Yugoslavian army and was in charge of medical supplies at pharmacies. When his commander intended to hand over the supplies to the Germans, Widrich shot and killed him; and for that he was awarded a decoration by the Yugoslavian government in exile. There was also a plan to obtain weapons from Tito but it was unclear how to get there. At the question of M.S. whether there were radio transmitters, Joel answered that it might be possible to obtain parts to build radio transmitters, should they receive instructions how to do that.

The Hungarian Jewry currently understands the implications of deportation. They know it means extermination. In Joel's opinion, a group of Haganah people could gather many Jews who would be willing to defend themselves.

Bunkers had been prepared in Budapest, Satmar, and the Karpatorus. In Budapest there was a large number of bunkers. In the Karpatorus, the bunker was connected by means of a tunnel with an exit in the forest. The action plans included the gathering of groups in the forests, attacking trains that transported deportees, and releasing them. Joel emphasized the shortage of weapons and ammunition. He believed that there was no shortage of commanders.

Many Christians from the Social-Democratic party, from the Agrarian National Union, and from the Democratic party had disappeared and were hiding in bunkers. However, there was still no contact between the Jewish and non-Jewish undergrounds, except in several cases where the Jewish underground helped Christians with forged papers. Joel had no knowledge of the existence of partisans who had contact with the Czechs or communists in the Karpatorus. The Communists were active in Budapest and collected money for red help.[16]

Among the Christian population, there were many who sympathized with the Jews, were willing to help and even willing to hide Jews. Joel received multiple offers, on behalf of all sorts of circles, to hide him and his family. He mentioned that among those were a policeman, an important bank officer, a textile merchant, an old woman, and so forth. Joel believed that it was important to gather those hiding around the Karpatorus and Yugoslavian border, hoping that the Karpatorus would be liberated soon by the Russians, and those who would arrive in Yugoslavia would be able to reach Tito's territories.

————————

To the question of M.S. what, in Joel's opinion, the Germans' reaction would be, if the Allies approached Germany requesting to evacuate the Jews, Joel answered that the Germans would first ask: "what do we get for it?" Nevertheless, he believed that such approach may be beneficial.

Joel emphasized once again that it would be a catastrophe for the Hungarian Jewry if he was not allowed to return and if his trip was only used for his interrogation by Jewish and Allied institutes. He asked that every time a telegram is sent to his wife, it would indicate that the negotiations continue, in order to buy time.

[16]   Probably, for the Red Army.

Appendix 2: The Jewish Agency Rescue Policy[1]

1. The objective of the Rescue Committee of the Jewish Agency for the Jews of Occupied Europe

The territories of Europe in which war erupted, Germany, the occupied countries, and the Axis powers countries contain more than 7,000,000 Jews who face extermination, most of whom constitute the most vivacious part of Judaism—in national terms. The experience we have gained from the work of the committee thus far shows that rescuing these Jews or a significant part of them is not an option. Not only do the Jews not have sufficient means to that end, but all of the Allies together, had they wished to save so many Jews, have neither the practical capability nor ample material means to do that. Therefore, for lack of any other option, the work of the Rescue Committee is narrowed down to small-scale actions, namely to save [individual] Jews and small groups only. Despite the huge amounts this action requires, its results would at best be meager, as we know today that we cannot dream about saving more than twelve thousand or a few tens of thousands of Jews. Does this have any value in light of the danger facing 7,000,000 Jews? We must not delude ourselves but rather say that the Rescue Committee's action is in fact philanthropic and not public or political. Except for these special twelve or few tens of thousands, seven million Jews will have to save themselves and use their own powers and wits to flee danger. What the Rescue Committee can do in this sense is like a drop in the ocean; it is just self-illusion or putting one's conscience at ease rather than real action. We must hope that despite of all the horrors, thanks to their survival instinct, a substantial part of the European Jewry would be saved, in any event a much larger part than that the Rescue Committee is able to save.

If, then, the efforts of the Rescue Committee may lead to only extremely modest results, we should at least produce political benefits out of them. From a Zionist perspective, such benefit would

---

[1] Porat and Weitz, 2002, pp. 385–393, Central Zionist Archive S26/1236.

be produced, if: a) the whole world would know that the only country that wants to receive the surviving Jews is Palestine and the Jewish public who truly wants to absorb these Jews is the Jewish community in Palestine; b) the whole world would know that the initiative to rescue the European Jewry comes from the Zionist movement; c) this recognition will also be seared in the hearts of the Jews, who are facing extermination, those who will save themselves will know, during or after the war, that the Zionist movement and the Jewish community in Palestine made efforts to rescue them. If such recognition prevails in political circles, in non-Jewish public opinion, in Jewish public opinion in all the free countries, and in the hearts of surviving European Jews, this would improve the image of Zionist Palestine as having solved the question of the Jews, and as the only country to direct to the masses of Jews who have been deported from Europe. It would increase the help of the Jewish world towards building this country, and would direct to Palestine the immigration of Jews who have been saved from the global slaughter.

2. Practical accomplishments achievable through the Committee's work

We must be honest with ourselves in advance and say upfront that if these achievements cannot result in saving a considerable part of the Polish, Lithuanian, West-Russian, or Balkan Jewry, then in terms of the national revival and building of the working, agricultural Palestine, the work of the Rescue Committee is of very little value. From the experience we have gained so far, it transpires that we are unable to smuggle Jews out of Poland. A small number of Jews can surely be smuggled through the Hungarian border and brought to safety. While such smuggling is entailed with huge expenses and with holding many of our people in Hungary, and will at best result in the rescue of only a few hundreds of people and not necessarily those we are interested in, but especially the Jews who live in proximity to the border, we should nevertheless carry out this work, in order to save those who can be saved. This, however, will not be the rescue of the Polish Jewry, but rather the rescue of a few hundred Polish Jews. It may be that we can smuggle some Polish Jews using visas to the neutral countries in America. This path, too, entails large expenses and may only lead to the rescue of a few hundreds of people, but it is easier to use it to save those we are interested in, if we are only to learn of their whereabouts by means of our expensive, exhausting searches. We must, however, take into consideration that these searches, which are conducted, for the lack of any other choice, by suspected people who have contacts with the Gestapo, may inflict danger on the very people we are looking for who may have hidden away from the Germans. At the time of smuggling people to Hungary too these people might fall into the hands of the Gestapo, directly or through smugglers.

There are likewise no chances to rescue the other part of the Polish Jewry, which has been dwindling in Russia. In view of the relationship between Russia and Poland, new evacuation cannot be expected, and even if it can be, at the best-case scenario, it can be used to evacuate 5–6,000 Jews. Does this have any value comparing to 200,000–250,000 Jews who are still alive there? The condition of the Lithuanian and Latvian Jews in Russia is not better either. They are currently unable to leave Russia as they are considered Soviet citizens. The Lithuanian and Latvian Jews who stayed there and are still alive are under the same conditions as the Polish Jews. The only help we can extend to the Polish and Lithuanian-Latvian Jewry in Russia is by sending packages of clothes and food, but what amounts would be sufficient to provide consistent help in this way for more than 300,000 people? Would the governments permit to send materials and food to such a large number of people during war time? Indeed, in this area too we are merely doing philan-thropic work by sending help to a maximum of twelve thousand people.

The second largest group is the Romanian Jewry. The big plan of smuggling 70,000 Jews recently discussed and which only included 1% of the seven million Jews facing extermination was now reduced to the option of saving 5,000 orphans. Smuggling the Jews out of Romania should have cost huge amounts of money. This plan had been made public and this is why it was cancelled. On the other hand, no rescue plan of thousands of people can be carried out in secrecy as the required means cannot be secured if thousands of people do not know about it, and publicity destroys the chances of executing the rescue plan.

The plans to rescue the Slovakian Jews entail the risk of ordinary extortion. The Gestapo wants, probably by means of vein promises and threats, to extort large amounts of money in good foreign currency from the global Jewry. As long as the negotiation proceeds and concerns small advances only—the deportations are delayed. However, it is difficult to know whether at the end of the negotiation, the Gestapo will not steal substantial amounts of money, stop the extortion, and exterminate the Jews of Slovakia.[2]

The figures that reflect the options of smuggling some Jews from Hungary and Bulgaria are, in reality, very small, but this action also faces transportation difficulties on the part of Turkey. Perhaps a few thousand Jews can be smuggled from the Netherlands and some out of Italy, but we have no transportation means to that end. The statement of Lord Cranborne[3] at the House of Commons in Britanie, the discretion that lasted for a few weeks, where to convene the conference, the proposal to convene several delegates of the Allies in Bermuda, a small corner distanced from the center of the world and public opinion influence—all that shows that the important forces do not or cannot really help. They do not wish to accept the refugees, provide transportation etc.

The reluctance of the Allies, the impossibility to carry out the rescue operation in secrecy without their consent, the risk of counter-action on the part of these countries should we act openly – all that dictates that the rescue operation must be carried out as a conspiracy or nearly conspiracy and be reduced to the rescue of twelve thousand people only. This is not a public action but rather philanthropy. This should be coupled with the help we will provide by sending packages which in reality may benefit twelve thousand

---

[2]   In reality, this fear did not materialize, but the difficulty of the Slovaks in raising 25,000 dollars cost the lives of 3,000 Jews.

[3]   About some possible leniency in the British policy of preventing Jewish immigration to Israel.

people—hence, philanthropy again. No more than about 30,000 people will benefit from both kinds of aid, namely half a percent of the seven million Jews facing extermination. That is all.

3. Who should be saved?

If the aid and rescue actions are reduced, against our will, to philanthropic work and only encompass a limited number of people and therefore we are faced again with the approach to this issue from a Zionist perspective to the solution of the Jewish problem, we are faced with the following question. Can these modest actions be one hundred percent philanthropic, namely without distinguishing between the nature of the people to whom help is given, namely providing them to anyone who needs them? Should this action not be given Zionist-national character and should we not try to first and foremost save those who can benefit the land of Israel and Judaism? I realize that posing this question in this manner has a sense of cruelty to it, but unfortunately we must say that if we are able to save only 10,000 people and we need to save 50,000 who would be beneficial in the building of the country and revival of the nation, and on the other hand we have one million Jews who would be a burden and in the best case would be an indifferent element, we must control ourselves and save the ten thousands who can be saved out of the 50,000—despite the complaints and implorations of the one million. I find solace in that this principle cannot be one hundred percents implemented and that the one million will also receive something. Let it not receive too much!

Based on this assumption, children must be saved first because they make the best substance for the Jewish community in Palestine. Ḥaluṭz youth should be saved, but only that part who have training and who are spiritually capable of Zionist work. Zionist activists should be saved, as they are entitled to something for their work from the Zionist movement; they will be able to tolerate a lot of things in the Jewish community in Palestine, understand it, and possibly contribute more work.

Pure philanthropic work, such as rescuing the German Jewry, which was previously made without any distinction, can only cause damage from a Zionist perspective, in particular if the possibilities are so limited and the catastrophe is so big. We could apply this method to the German Jews as the survivors had one advantage— some sort of property that came with them; now the refugees are short of this advantage as they come to Palestine empty handed. They give nothing to Palestine and can only bring what many of the German Jews brought—total alienation from, and sometimes hostility to, Palestine, insolent attitude to everything Jewish and Hebrew, and prominent Germanized tendencies, which result in instilling the German spirit once again in children who have already received Hebrew education at school.

The immigration of adults from Teheran[4] also provides an example of what troubling results immigration without suitable distinction may lead to. Besides *halutzim* and Zionist activists, many people who have nothing to do with Zionism arrive, people who are tainted with total national demoralization. In the first days the youth goes to *kibbutzim* and agricultural settlements (this was the condition for receiving immigration certificates), but after several weeks they leave them and write complaints to the Polish Consulate and Delegatura [agency of the Polish government in exile] to the effect that the Jewish Agency forcefully manipulated them into *kibbutzim*. They privately chat that they have already worked in Russia and so why should they work in Palestine? Adults and mothers of children start complaining right after they arrive. They claim that the Jewish Agency does not give them ample care, that it should provide them with "rest" after their hardships in Russia, and provide them with money so that they can live the same life as before the war, without working. They also have complaints that the Jewish Agency is more interested in Zionist activists and *halutzim*. They inform on the Jewish Agency to the Delegatura and wish to educate their children in Polish and British schools. This is different with the Zionist activists who find themselves in the same circumstances. They are content with their lot, demonstrate

---

[4]   A group of about 1230 Polish Jews, 860 children and 370 adults, who legally arrived in Palestine through Russia and Teheran in February 1943.

tolerance to the many difficulties, and are grateful for all the help given to them.

Had we had the means to save both kinds, there is no doubt that we should have accepted things as they are, but unfortunately we do not have sufficient means to save the good elements, and therefore, for the lack of any other option, we are forced to relinquish saving the harmful element.

4. Aid to refugees after their arrival in Palestine

Saving the Jewish survivors does not end when they immigrate to Palestine. For the war survivors it is the same thing whether they die of hunger under the German occupation, in Russia, or in Palestine. In normal times, it was obvious that new immigrants only received "first-arrangement" help and afterwards took care of themselves on their own, since at the time the only people who could be taken into consideration were *halutzim* who went to *kibbutzim*, wealthy people, or professionals, and the latter could not claim better conditions than those in their countries of origin. The current refugees are different; naturally, except for the *halutz* youth. Most of them are old, broken people as a result of the war conditions, who immigrate to Palestine not only without money but often impoverished. They have no profession suitable to this country and they speak no Hebrew. These people—even the Zionists—need a period of time to rest and recover here after what they have been through, learn Hebrew and acquire a profession, and adjust to the new conditions. These people must find a roof over their heads and buy the most vital furniture and some clothes. The "first-arrangement" help will not suffice to this end. Larger-scale help is required here as well as a longer period of time, and larger amounts of money should be given at once since giving them in parts will not serve any purpose. The people will spend the money very quickly and not be able to buy anything substantial. Renting a flat requires at best payment of rent for one year in advance, and cash advances are also required for furniture, beddings, kitchen utensils, and so forth. If we do not provide the refugees with these items, we cannot derive any benefit from them and they will be demoralized. If we provide them with this help, they will become a positive element in the Jewish community. For this purpose we need bigger financial means, and the donations collected by the united committees will not suffice.

The maintenance and making arrangements for the Jews who have been rescued from the Nazi inferno are important elements in the rescue operation and, in fact, make the entire operation logical and purposeful. This is why some of the money intended for rescue should also be dedicated to making arrangements for the refugees in a manner which is suitable for the needs of this country, especially as the monies for rescue consist exclusively of funds received from Zionist institutions.

The war will end one day and some of the refugees, who are currently in Palestine, will go back to the Diaspora. A small part of the non-vital refugees will adjust to the life here and will stay in this country but most of them will go back to the Diaspora and will take with them bitterness regarding Palestine. We must not allow, then, that the disappointment and bitterness will spread out also among the unstable Zionist elements that will go back to the Diaspora and cause damage by making negative propaganda to our mutual cause. In order to aim for all these results after the war we must: a) refrain to the extent possible from bringing non-Zionist elements to Palestine; b) provide considerable help to Zionist refugees and integrate them in the social and financial life in Palestine.

5. No partners are needed

The entire aid and rescue operation can, thus, leads to small practical results and it involves huge expenses and great energies. From a Zionist point of view, Zionist benefits should be derived from this work, namely we must save everyone that can be saved for the sake of building the country and reviving the nation. We must not conceal, but rather emphasize, the fact that all the rescue efforts and initiatives originate in Palestine and in the Jewish Agency, that the Zionist Palestine is the only country that is willing to accept the survivors. Finally, we must conduct the rescue work such that no anti-Palestine and anti-Zionist propaganda would result from it on the part of the people who were saved and brought here.

If all the acts are to be conducted from a Zionist point of view, then the partnership with Agudat Yisrael[5] and also with the Revisionists[6] is not only unproductive, but also highly harmful. Huge amounts of money are required, and from our three-month experience it transpires that these partners have not given as much as a penny. That does not mean that they do not spend sufficiently substantial amounts of money to save their friends but they do it independently of the Rescue Committee while simultaneously also wishing to benefit from Zionist money within the Rescue Committee in order to save the same friends. This way they benefit twice thereby reducing the rescue fund required for the Zionists. Have we at least acquired their loyalty for this price? No. It is already now that they constantly and demagogically criticize, during the Rescue Committee meetings, the supposedly feeble action of the Jewish Agency. There is no doubt that when our work comes to an end and these bodies no longer benefit from this partnership, they will leave the Rescue Committee and make fuss about their disappointment with the Jewish Agency which not only did nothing by itself but also prevented them from taking any initiative, whereas the reality is that they have not made any practical proposal and so far have only made demagogic and sometimes indeed damaging proposals, only taking into consideration external effects. They have in fact done all that time the work that "Falcor"[7] is supposed to do, but at the same time, the public opinion is that everything that has been done in terms of rescue has not been done by the Jewish Agency but rather thanks to the inclusion of Agudat Yisrael and the Revisionists in the Rescue Committee. This will not improve the prestige of Zionism; on the contrary, it will weaken it. In addition, the presence of Agudat Yisrael and the Revisionists in the Rescue Committee meetings often prevents the Zionist representatives from making

5   Ultra religious, non-Zionist Jews party.

6   Non socialist, Zionist Jewish party.

7   Palestine news agency.

justified, constructive criticism of the Zionist institutions, fearing that these bodies would exploit the criticism for their own party-related purposes.

If there is no possibility for a large-scale rescue operation, we should at least use what we are doing in favor of Zionism, Palestine, and the revival of the nation. If our partners unknowingly disturb us in realizing this, what kind of value does this partnership have?

Nevertheless, despite of the pessimistic chances of the scope and results of the Rescue Committee's actions, we should make every effort but in our own name (and obviously in confidentiality, as required) and not together with partners who only wish to benefit from the profits.

Proposals

It is possible to move comrades from Slovakia to Hungary. This can only be arranged if we have the means. There is also a possibility to move people out from the southern parts of Poland.

The condition of the refugees in Hungary is extremely bad as they have no official papers. Money will go a long way. Help should also be given to the local movement people who are spread all over Hungary. Immediate help is required. It is also possible to smuggle from Budapest to Slovakia.

There is a Palestine Office in Budapest, which is headed by Mr. Krausz. This man treats halutz movements and those outside of Bnei Akiva[8] unfairly. In the two children groups, he discriminated against Dror members; HaShomer HaTza'ir; Maccabi youth movement; HaBonim, and HaNo'ar HaTzioni[9]; it is impossible that he should be the Jew who determines the order of immigration. There is no option to forward to him lists of exiles from here, and therefore it is vital that Joel Brand, member of the party, who greatly helps the members of HeHalutz in Hungary, should be given equal

---

[8]   Religious Zionist youth movement.

[9]   A list of Zionist youth movements.

rights to those of Krausz in immigration matters. So far Brand has only served as a consultant.

If future immigration is only of children, it is necessary that some of the refugees of HeHalutz and HaNo'ar [HaTzioni?] members, who due to their elderly age will be unable to immigrate, will be taken into consideration as escorts for the children. Our comrades have endured more difficult tests. The refugees will not be saved; they are faced with deportation on a daily basis.

It would be very helpful if the Jewish Agency sets the immigration key, namely the percent of organized HeHalutz and organized youth members which can be taken into account in every group of immigrants. An instruction to this effect should be given to the Palestine Office in Budapest.

The Polish Committee in Budapest treats the Jewish refugees in Hungary with hostility and open anti-Semitism. If the Jewish refugees receive [Polish refugee] documents from them, they will be free from deportation. The Polish Committee does not agree to provide such documents [to Polish Jewish refugees] whatsoever. Immediate intervention on the part of our institutes in this matter is vital.

Timetable

1867	Hungary was formed as a sovereign state within the framework of the Austro-Hungarian Dual Monarchy. The Emancipation Law gave equal rights to the Hungarian Jewry.
1895	Judaism was recognized as one of the state's religions, next to Catholicism and Protestant Christianity.
November 11, 1918	World War I ended for Austro-Hungary with a complete military defeat and the collapse of the Austro-Hungarian Empire.
March 23–August 1, 1919	The Hungarian Soviet Republic, led by the Communist Béla Kun, ruled over Hungary. This time is known as the period of the "Red Terror."
1919–1920	The period of the counterrevolutionary regime under Miklós Horthy. This time is known as the period of the "White Terror."
March 1 1920	Miklós Horthy is elected Regent as provisional head of state.
June 4, 1920	The Treaty of Trianon is signed.
September 21, 1920	The *Numerus Clausus* law (the first anti-Jewish law in post-World War I Europe) is enacted in Hungary.
1928	Hansi joins a Zionist youth movement in Hungary
1930–1932	Joel is active in Zionist and leftist organizations in Germany.
January 30, 1933	Hitler is appointed chancellor of Germany.
February 22, 1933	Joel Brand was sentenced to two years in prison in Nazi Germany.
September 6, 1934	Joel is released and flees to Romania from where he will move to Hungary after a few weeks.
October 30, 1935	Hansi and Joel are married.

May 28, 1938	The first major anti-Jewish law is enacted in Hungary.
July 6–15, 1938	The Évian Conference convened at Évian-les-Bains, France, to address the Jewish refugee problem and the plight of the increasing numbers of Jewish refugees fleeing persecution by Nazi Germany. The conference ended with very limited achievements.
November 2, 1938	The First Vienna Award and the beginning of the Hungarian annexation campaign.
March 11, 1939	The law for the establishment of the "Labor Service" in Hungary was enacted.
May 4, 1939	The second anti-Jewish law went into effect in Hungary.
May 17, 1939	The White Paper of 1939 on Palestine, which limited the Jewish emigration to Palestine, was adopted by the British Government.
September 1, 1939	Germany invaded Poland and World War II began
September 1939	Joel is drafted into the Hungarian army.
August 30, 1940	The Second Vienna Award, which that enabled the annexation of Northern Transylvania from Romania by Hungary, was signed.
June 22, 1941	"Operation Barbarossa," the German invasion into the Soviet Union, began and with it the Jewish Holocaust.
June 27, 1941	Hungary declares war on the Soviet Union and joins the war alongside Germany.
July–August 1941	The deportation of "alien" Jews from Hungary.
August 2, 1941	The third anti-Jewish law went into effect in Hungary.
August 27–28, 1941	The majority of "alien" Jews deported from Hungary are slaughtered by Germans near Kamenets-Podolsk, Ukraine.
December 13, 1941	Hungary declared war on the United States and the Joint representative in Hungary was forced to leave.

December 25, 1941	Kasztner (according to his own report) told the Jewish senior officials in Hungary that one million Jews have already been murdered.
January 1942	Hungarian military units massacred thousands of civilians in and around Ujvidek (Novi Sad—Bačka, Yugoslavia), many of them Jews.
January 20, 1042	The Vanessa Conference (der Wannsee Konferenz) took the decision to destroy all European Jews.
March 19, 1942	Reports were released from the Joint representative in Hungary and from the US Embassy in Moscow, confirming two hundred and forty thousand victims (by the end of 1941), with 100,000 Jews murdered in the Kiev region alone. These reports were published in Palestine but received no attention.
January–October 1942	The Jewish press in Palestine tries to undermine the credibility of reports received from Jewish, Russian, Polish, and English sources about the dimensions of the disaster. The climax comes in the publication on *Dabar* on March 17, 1942
March 27, 1942	The beginning of the extermination of the Slovak Jews.
March 1942	Slovak Jews began to flee to Hungary in significant numbers. Many of them found shelter in the Brand's home or were assisted by the Brands.
June 15, 1942	The extermination of Slovak Jewry was halted following (as it was perceived then) an agreement to pay ransom.
July 1942	A detailed report on the German extermination program was received by the Jewish Agency rescue delegation in Istanbul.
October–December 1942	Commencement of debates in Slovakia on the "Europe Plan."
November 7, 1942	Springman established contacts with the Jewish Agency's delegation in Istanbul (according to other sources—in the fall of 1942).

November 23, 1942	The Jewish Agency's management, for the first time, acknowledged and publicized the fact that there was reliable information on the systematic murder of hundreds of thousands of Jews in Europe.
January 1943	Kasztner informed the JA delegation in Istanbul that he has established the "Budapest Relief and Rescue committee." In reality, the committee began working many months earlier, before Kasztner joined it.
January 1943	The Second Hungarian Army is destroyed in the third battle of Voronezh.
April 19–30, 1943	The Bermuda Conference was convened to discuss the Jewish refugee problem. It ended with no results whatsoever.
May 11, 1943	Rabbi Weissmandl reported on Wisliceny's acceptance of the "Europe Plan."
March 16, 1944	A German agent warned Joel that Germany was going to conquer Hungary in the very near future.
March 19, 1944	Germany occupied Hungary.
March 21, 1944	A Jewish Council (Judenrat) was established in Budapest by German order.
April 4, 1944	Jews all over Hungary were ordered to wear the yellow star. The first meeting of Joel and Kasztner with Wisliceny took place.
April 6, 1944	The German-appointed Jewish Council appeals to Hungarian Jewry, encouraging obedience and calm behavior.
April 15, 1944	Eichmann summons Joel for the first time to discuss a vague "goods for blood" deal (other sources suggest April 25).
April 16, 1944	The beginning of the forced removal of Hungarian Jews from their homes and concentrating them in ghettos.

April 28, 1944	The Germans, Hungarians, and Slovaks agreed on a "transportation plan" to send 150 trains with Jews from Hungary through Slovakia to Auschwitz. The information was quickly leaked by the Slovaks to the Jewish leadership in Budapest, including to Kasztner (perhaps even before the final approval of the program).[1]
May 3, 1944	Kasztner's visit to Cluj.
May 4-6, 1944	The Germans, Hungarians, and Slovaks formulated the deportation plan.
May 12, 1944	The JA[2] delegation in Istanbul was informed about Joel's arrival (according to other sources—May 2)
May 15, 1944	The systematic deportation of the Jews of Hungary to extermination began.
May 17, 1944	Joel was sent to Istanbul to discuss the "Trucks for Blood" deal.
May 19, 1944	Joel arrived in Istanbul. No visa had been prepared for him. Bandi Gross arranges for them to leave the airport.
May 22, 1944	Kasztner's second meeting with Eichmann (the first likely took place on May 19 or 20).
May 27, 1944	Hansi, Kasztner, and other Committee members were arrested by the Hungarian police.
May 29, 1944	Joel and representatives of the Jewish Agency in Istanbul signed an "interim agreement."
May 31, 1944	Hansi was brutally interrogated by the Hungarian Gestapo.
June 1, 1944	The Hungarians released the members of the Rescue committee because of German intervention.
June 1, 1944	A telegram announcing the existence of an "interim agreement" reached Budapest but not the agreement itself.
June 7, 1944	Joel was arrested by the British in Aleppo.

June 8, 1944	Pehle (The director of the WRB) informed President Roosevelt about the basics of the Joel Brand offer.[3]
June 9, 1944	Eichmann threatened that if Joel did not return in three days he would "restart the operation of Auschwitz." In reality, he never stopped it.
June 9, 1944	Hannah Szenes crossed the border into Hungary and was caught immediately.
June 10, 1944	388 Jews from Cluj arrived in the Columbus camp in Budapest.
June 15, 1944	The "Jews on Ice" deal was formulated.
June 17, 1944	The "relocation" of Budapest Jews from their homes to the "Jewish Houses."
June 19, 1944	Peretz Goldstein and Yoel Palgi crossed the border into Hungary and immediately came under surveillance of the Hungarian police.
June 24, 1944	Hansi went with Yoel Palgi to the German Gestapo offices and presented him there as a messenger of the Jewish Agency who came to carry on talks instead of Joel. They both left safely.
June 26, 1944	Yoel Palgi was arrested by the Hungarians at the Brand family's home.
June 27, 1944	Secretary of State Cordell Hull issued a warning to the Hungarians concerning the treatment of the Jews.
June 30, 1944	Hansi and other members of the Rescue Committee were arrested by the Hungarians, while Kasztner, with the help of the Hungarian police, staged Goldstein's extradition.
July 1, 1944	The "train of the privileged" departed (at this point to Bergen Belsen).
July 2, 1944	Allied aircrafts made a massive daylight raid on Budapest.
July 6, 1944	Horthy ordered to stop the deportation of Jews from Hungary (before the beginning of the deportation from Budapest and after the deportation from the periphery was completed).

July 7, 1944	The "Interim Agreement" was received in Budapest more than a month after it was signed in Istanbul.
July 10, 1944	Hitler agrees to release 7,800 Jews from Hungary in exchange for the destruction of all other Jews by the Hungarians, including the 200,000 Jews of Budapest. This was actually Krauss's "rescue plan."
July 18, 1944	Kasztner was mysteriously arrested by the Hungarians. Apparently, he updated them on Joel's mission details. Kasztner was released unharmed after nine days.
August 10, 1944	Rabbi Freudiger, the head of Budapest's Orthodox community and member of the Judenrat, escaped from Hungary to Romania with about fifty of his associates with the help of Kraus and Wisliceny.
August 14, 1944	The Americans and the British (under the American pressure) accepted the so-called Horthy offer concerning the emigration of several thousand Hungarian Jews.
August 17, 1944	The first group of 318 Hungarian Jews from "the train of the privileged," which left from Bergen-Belsen, arrived in Switzerland.
August 21, 1944	The Hungarian Government accepted Eichmann's Proposal to rapidly destroy the Budapest Jewry starting on August 25.
August 25, 1944	Himmler's order to ban all further deportation of Jews from Hungary reached Budapest. This happened when Becher informed him on alleged progress in negotiations and asked to ban the deportations.
September 7, 1944	"Department A" of the International Red Cross headed by Ottó Komoly was established. Hansi managed the Economics Department, which is responsible, among other things, for providing food to the children's homes set up in Budapest.
October 15, 1944	Horthy announced his decision to withdraw from the alliance with Germany. Subsequently, Hungarian fascists (with German assistance) took over the country.

Octboer 25–31, 1944	The Commander of Auschwitz was ordered to stop the extermination (the exact day is unclear).
November 5, 1944	Contrary to instructions, Roswell McClelland (WRB representative) met Becher in Switzerland, thus helping to save Jews.
November 7, 1944	Hannah Szenes was executed in Budapest.
November 9, 1944	The beginning of the "death marches" of Jews from Budapest to Austria.
November 16, 1944	The commander of Auschwitz, Höss, arrived in Budapest to discover why he received orders to stop the extermination. Along with him came some senior German officers demanding to stop the death marches.
November 26, 1944	Kasztner claimed that Himmler ordered to stop the killing of Jews under Becher's recommendations.
December 2, 1944	Budapest Jews were concentrated in a ghetto.
December 7, 1944	1,368 Hungarian Jews from "the train of the privileged," which left from Bergen-Belsen, arrived in Switzerland. The members of Joel's family were left in Bergen Belsen.
January 1, 1945	Ottó Komoly was assassinated.
January 18, 1945	Pest was liberated.
February 13, 1945	Buda was liberated.
April 9, 1945	Kasztner visited Bergen Belsen and ignores the pleas of the starving Brand family members for help. The Brand family members were sent on a train to Theresienstadt, but were liberated in Tröbitz by the Russians at the end of the war.

December 9–24, 1946	The Twenty-Second Zionist Congress met in Basel, where Kasztner submitted his report. According to Joel, Kasztner sold his soul in this report.
December 24, 1946	For providing a desirable report to the leadership, Kasztner was acquitted of extradition of the paratroopers. In coordination with the leadership, he casts suspicion on Hansi.
June 10, 1947	Peretz Revesz (Révész) wrote to Joel from Budapest in response to Kasztner's report: "If we will now point to the lies of Kasztner, we will hurt the general matter. Only Kasztner himself can correct the distortion."
August 4, 1947	Kastzner gave an affidavit in favor of Becher in Nuremberg.
February 17, 1948	Kasztner was sent to Nuremberg with Jewish Agency funding to testify in favor of Nazis.
January–October, 1954	The Kasztner trial took place in Jerusalem. Kasztner denied testifying in favor of Nazis and lied about his handling of the paratrooper affair.
June 22, 1955	Judge Halevy announced the verdict in the Kasztner trial, declaring that Kasztner sold his soul to the devil.
1957	Joel's version of the events in Hungary is published In Germany under the title *Die Geschichte von Joel Brand* (*The Story of Joel Brand*). The formal author is Alex Weissberg. Next year, the book was translated and published in Israel, where the author was indicated as Joel Brand.
March 4, 1957	Kasztner was shot in Tel Aviv and died eleven days later.
1960	Hansi and Joel Brands' book *The Satan and the Soul* was published In Israel. The book includes most of the insights in this book, but without most of the documentation that establishes their position.
July 13, 1964	Joel passed away in Germany after testifying against two of Eichmann's closest aides in Budapest.
April 9, 2000	Hansi passed away in Tel Aviv.

January 11, 2015	Confidentiality was partially removed from the Cabinet meeting protocol on March 11, 1957. The Israeli daily *Ha'Aretz* published an article by Ofer Aderat entitled "The Assassination of Dr. Kasztner, a Study of the Protocol Only Deepens the Mystery Surrounding One of the Most Turbulent Events in the History of the Country."
February 15, 2020	The Supreme Court in Jerusalem considered a demand to remove confidentiality from secret service documents detailing the assassination of Kasztner. The secret service firmly objected, but was ordered to justify its position within 60 days.[4]

[1] Kasztner's report, 1946, p. 30. There is some uncertainty about the exact date.
[2] Jewish Agency.
[3] http://www.rebeccaerbelding.com/about-the-book/wrb-day-by-day/.
[4] As of May 2020, the decision has not yet been implemented because of the Coronavirus (COVID-19) crisis.

Bibliography

Avriel, Ehud, *Open the Gates!* London: Weidenfeld and Nicolson, 1975.

Barlas, Haim, *Rescue in Times of Holocaust*, Israel: GFH and HaKibbutz HaMeuḥad Publishing, 1975 (Heb).

Bar-Zohar, Michael, *Ben Gurion: The Man and the Legend, A Biography* (short edition), Tel Aviv: Ministry of Defence and Magal Publishing, 1986 (Heb).

Bauer, Yehuda, "Joel Brand's Mission," *Yalkut Moreshet* [*Heritage Files*], No. 26, November 1978 (Heb).

——, *Jews for Sale? Nazi-Jewish Negotiations, 1933–1945*, New Haven: Yale University Press, 1994 (Eng). Hebrew version: Jerusalem: Yad Vashem, 2001 (Heb).

Benshalom, Rafi, *We Struggled for Life: Underground Operations in Budapest in 1944*, Tel Aviv: Moreshet and Sifriat Po'alim, 1977 (Heb).

Beit Zvi, Shabtai, *Post-Ugandan Zionism in the Holocaust Crisis: A Study of reasons of the mistakes of the Zionist movement in 1938–1945*, Tel Aviv: Bronfman Publishing, 1977 (Heb).

Bin Nun, Hanna, *Back to that Place*, Kibbutz Dalia: Sifriat Po'alim, 1977 (Heb).

Biss, André, *A Million Jews to Save*, Cranbury, New Jersey: A.S. Barnes and Company, Inc., 1975.

Braham Randolph L., *The Politics of Genocide: The Holocaust in Hungary*, 1-2, New York: Columbia University Press, 1981; Revised and enlarged edition, 1994.

Braham, Randolph L., "The Kamenets-Podolsk and Delvidek Massacres: Prelude to the Holocaust in Hungary," *Yad Vashem Studies*, No. 9, 1973, pp. 133–156.

Brand, Joel and Hansi, *The Satan and the Soul*, Tel Aviv: Ledory Publishing, 1960 (Heb).

Brand, Joel, *Messenger on Behalf of the Condemned to Death*, Tel Aviv: Ayanot Publishing, 1957 (Heb). The official author of the same book in other languages is Alex Weissberg (see the entry under his name below). English versions: *Desperate Mission* and *Advocate for the Dead*; German version (original): *Die Geschichte von Joel Brand* 1956.

Brand, Joel, *Über die Jetzige Lage der Juden Ungarns sowie der Balkanländer deren Entwicklung und Vorschlaege zur Hatzala-Arbeit*, Report to the Jewish Agency, January 23, 1945.

Cohen, Asher, "The Outset of the Aid and Rescue Committee in Budapest," *Yalkut Moreshet* [*Heritage Files*], No. 29, May 1980 (Heb).

——, *The Halutz Resistance in Hungary 1942–1944*, Tel Aviv: HaKibbutz HaMeuhad publishing, 1994 (Heb).

Dafni, Reuven, "With Freedom Fighters," in: Zrubavel Gilad (ed.), *Secret Shield*, Jerusalem: The Jewish Agency Publishing, 2nd edition, 1949, pp. 345–405 (Heb).

——, *Kasztner: Leader or Villain*, Haifa: Gestelit Publishing, 1987 (Heb).

The Eichmann Trail Protocols, The State vs. Adolf Eichmann, 40/61, State of Israel Archive.

Eisen, George, and Tamás Stark, "The 1941 Galician Deportation and the Kamenets-Podolsk Massacre: A Prologue to the Hungarian Holocaust," *Genocide Studies*, No. 27(2), 2015, pp. 207–241.

Eckstein, Ze'ev, *Quilt*, Jerusalem: Carmel Publishing House, 2014 (Heb).

Elon, Amos, *Timetable*, New York: Doubleday & Company, 1980 (Eng). Hebrew version: Tel Aviv: Idanim, 1980.

Erbelding, Rebecca, *Rescue Board: The Untold Story of America's Efforts to Save the Jews of Europe*, New York: Doubleday, 2018 (Eng)

Ezuz, Yitzhak, *Understanding the Holocaust, Understanding the Potential of Nazism in Humans*, Tel Aviv: Resling Publishing, 2015 (Heb).

Friedländer, Saul, *The Years of Extermination, Nazi Germany and the Jews*, Tel Aviv: 'Am 'Oved and Yad Vashem, 2010 (Heb).

Friling, Tuvia, *Arrow in the Fog: David Ben Gurion, The Leadership of the Yishuv and Rescue Attempts In the Holocaust*, Beer Sheba: The Ben Gurion Heritage Institute, 1998 (Heb).

Goldfarb, Zvi, *On the Verge of the End*, Tel Aviv: GFH and HaKibbutz HaMeuhad Publishing, 1980 (Heb).

Gur, David, *Brothers for Resistance and Rescue, The Underground Zionist Youth Movement in Hungary during WW II*, Jerusalem: Association for the Study of Zionist Youth Movements in Hungary, 2004 (Heb).

Gutman, Israel, Béla Vágó, and Livia Rothkirchen (eds.), *Hungarian Jews Leadership in the Holocaust Crisis*, Jerusalem: Yad Vashem, 1976 (Heb).

Hadar, David, "The Superpowers' Attitude to Joel Brand's Mission: A Mystery only the Edges of which were Revealed," *Molad*, No. 4, 1971, pp.112–125 (Heb).

Hadari, Zeev-Venia, *Against All Odds, Istanbul 1942–1945*, Tel Aviv: Ministry of Defense Publishing, 1992 (Heb).

Hecht, Ben, *Perfidy*, Jerusalem: Gefen Publishing House, 1999.

Ishoni-Beri, Shoshana, "Kasztner Affair: The Question of Giving Testimony in Favor of Nazi Criminals — An Attempt to Explain Differently," *Yalkut Moreshet* [*Heritage Files*], No. 59, April 1995, pp. 86–87 (Heb).

Huban, David, *I Was Young and Wanted to Live*, Netley, SA, Australia: Griffin Press, 2004.

Irving, Arabella, and Harold Troper, *None is Too Many: Canada and the Jews of Europe 1933-1948*, Toronto: University of Toronto Press, 1983.

Kadosh, Avi, "Obstacle Race: The Youth Aliyah in Morocco, 1949-1961," in: Yitzhak Gershon (ed.), *Roots in the East: Studies of the Zionist and Pioneering Movement in the Communities of Spain and Islam*, vol. C, Ramat Gan: Yad Tabenkin, 1991, pp. 125–160 (Heb).

Kornianski, Josef, *On the Pioneers' Mission*, Tel Aviv: GFH and HaKibbutz HaMeuḥad Publising, 1979 (Heb).

Kashti, Yitzhak, *Rescue and Revolt: Jewish Children's Homes in Budapest 1944–1945*, Tel Aviv: Resling Publishing, 2014 (Heb).

The Kasztner Trail Protocols, The State vs. Malkiel Grunwald 124/53, State of Israel Archive.

Morgenstern, Aryeh, "The Methods of Organization and Work of the Jewish Relief Committee Attached to the Jewish Agency, During the Second World War," *Yalkut Moreshet* [*Heritage Files*], No. 13, June 1971 (Heb).

Nedivi, Ayala, *The Palestine Office in Budapest: Its Rescue Related Activities in the Years 1943–1944 and How They were Shaped in the Collective Memory*, Doctoral Thesis, Haifa University, 2009 (Heb). Later published as: *Between Krausz and Kasztner: The Struggle for the Rescue of the Hungarian Jews*, Jerusalem: Carmel Publishing, 2014 (Heb).

Netzer, Eli, *Above Their Fate*, Tel Aviv: Moreshet Publishing, 1995 (Heb).

Palgi, Yoel, "In the Hollow of a Sling," in: Zrubavel Gilad (ed.), *Secret Shield*, 2nd edition, Jerusalem: The Jewish Agency Publishing, 1949, pp. 409–428 (Heb).

——, *And behold, a Great Wind Came: The Story of a Jewish Paratrooper*, Tel Aviv: HaKibbutz HaMeuḥad Publishing, 1946, 2nd edition Tel Aviv: HaKibbutz HaMeuḥad Publishing, 1977 (Heb).

Picard, Avi, "The Beginning of Selective Immigration in the 1950s," *Thoughts about the Rebirth of Israel*, No. 9, 1999, pp. 338–394 (Heb),

Porat, Dina, and Yehiam Weitz, *Between the Star of David and the Yellow Patch: The Jewish Community in Eretz Israel and the Holocaust of European Jewry 1939-1945, A Collection of Documents*, Jerusalem: Yad Vashem, 2002 (Heb).

Porat, Dina (ed.), *When Disaster Comes from Afar: Leading Personalities in the Land of Israel Confront Nazism and the Holocaust, 1933–1948*, Jerusalem: Yad Ben-Tzvi Publishing, 2009 (Heb).

——, *An Entangled Leadership: The Yishuv and the Holocaust, 1942–1945*, Tel Aviv: 'Am 'Oved Publishing, 1986 (Heb).

Porter, Anna, *Kasztner's Train: The True Story of an Unknown Hero of the Holocaust*, New York: Walker & Company, 2008.

Reichenthal, Eli. *A Man Who Was Murdered Twice? Rudolf Kasztner and the Holocaust in Hungary, a Re-Examination*, Beer Sheba: Beer Sheba University Publishing, 2010 (Heb).

Reves, Peretz, *Against the Waves of Evil*, Kibbutz Dalia: Sifriat Po'alim, 2001 (Heb).

Ronen, Avihu, *The Fight for Life: HaShomer HaTsa'ir in Hungary, 1944*, Giv'at Haviva: Yad Ya'ari Publishing, 1994 (Heb).

——, *Condemned to Life: The Diaries and Life of Chajka Klinger*, Haifa: University of Haifa Publishing, 2011 (Heb).

Rosenfeld, Shalom, *Criminal Case 124, The Gruenwald Kasztner Trial*. Tel Aviv: Karni Publishers Ltd., 1955 (Heb).

Rotem, Judith, *A Man with a Soul: Zvi Goldfarb's Life*, Tel Aviv: The Association for the Study of Zionist Youth Movements in Hungary, 2002 (Heb).

Schmidt, Mária, "Mentés vagy árulás? magyar zsidó önmentési akciók a második világháború alatt," *Medvetánc: az elte kisz bizottság társadalomelméleti folyóirata*, Nos. 2–3 (1985), pp. 111–125 (Hun). *Yalkut Moreshet* [*Heritage Files*], No. 57, May 1994, pp. 61–77 (Heb. reprint).

Segev, Tom, *The Seventh Million*, Jerusalem: Keter Publishing, 1992 (Heb).

Vágó, Béla, "Intelligence Operations alongside the Mission of Joel Brand," *Yad Vashem Studies*, No. 10, 1975 (Heb).

Vági, Zoltán, László Csősz, and Gábor Kádár, *The Holocaust in Hungary: Evolution of a Genocide*, Lanham: AltaMira Press, 2013.

Weissberg, Alex, *Desperate Mission*, New York: Criterion Books, 1958.

Weitz, Yehiam, *The Man who was Murdered Twice*, Jerusalem: Keter Publishing, 1995 (Heb).

Wiesel, Elie, *Night*, New York: Hill and Wang, 1958.

Yisrael, Moshe (ed.), *Messengers, Implementers, Fighters and Rescuers: Pioneering Movements of Hakibbutz Hameuhad in Hungary*, book 2, part 1. Kibbutz Dalia: Sifriat Po'alim, 1999 (Heb).

Yisrael, Moshe, and Dov Lazar (eds.), *Dror, HaBonim, Ha'Oved: Pioneers Movements in Hungary*, Nahariya: Ronil, 1994 (Heb).

Joel Brand files in the British Intelligence, SIME/P.7769, Report No. 1, *Joel Jeno Brand, Hungarian Jew*, June 16–30, 1944.

Index

CPSIA information can be obtained
at www.ICGtesting.com
Printed in the USA
BVHW040730130821
613887BV00004B/65

9 781644 695005